D0406937

WITHDRAWN
UTSA LIBRARIES

ALSO BY ELIZABETH D. SAMET

Soldier's Heart: Reading Literature Through Peace and War at West Point

Willing Obedience: Citizens, Soldiers, and the Progress of Consent in America, 1776–1898

NO MAN'S LAND

NO MAN'S LAND

Preparing for
War and Peace in
Post-9/11 America

ELIZABETH D. SAMET

FARRAR, STRAUS AND GIROUX / NEW YORK

Farrar, Straus and Giroux
18 West 18th Street, New York 10011

Copyright © 2014 by Elizabeth D. Samet
All rights reserved
Printed in the United States of America
First edition, 2014

Portions of this book originally appeared, in different form, in
The New York Times Magazine (April 10, 2011), *The New Republic, Bloomberg View,*
The Wall Street Journal, Forum (a publication of the Association of
Literary Scholars, Critics, and Writers), and *West Point* magazine.

Library of Congress Cataloging-in-Publication Data
Samet, Elizabeth D.
  No man's land : preparing for war and peace in post-9/11 America /
Elizabeth D. Samet. — 1st edition.
      pages   cm
  ISBN 978-0-374-22277-2 (hardback) — ISBN 978-0-374-70901-3 (e-book)
  1. Veterans—United States—Psychology.   2. Homecoming—United
States.   3. War and literature—United States.   4. United States—History,
Military—Social aspects—21st century   I. Title.   II. Title: Preparing for
war and peace in post-9/11 America.

UB357 .S26 2014
305.9'06970973—dc23
                                                          2014008672

Designed by Abby Kagan

Farrar, Straus and Giroux books may be purchased for educational, business, or
promotional use. For information on bulk purchases, please contact the Macmillan
Corporate and Premium Sales Department at 1-800-221-7945, extension 5442,
or write to specialmarkets@macmillan.com.

www.fsgbooks.com
www.twitter.com/fsgbooks • www.facebook.com/fsgbooks

1   3   5   7   9   10   8   6   4   2
Library
University of Texas
at San Antonio

IN MEMORIAM

Captain Daniel P. Whitten
C Company, 1st Battalion, 508th Parachute Infantry Regiment,
4th Brigade Combat Team, 82nd Airborne Division
Killed, Zabul Province, Afghanistan
February 2, 2010

First Lieutenant Christopher S. Goeke
C Company, 1st Battalion, 508th Parachute Infantry Regiment,
4th Brigade Combat Team, 82nd Airborne Division
Killed, Kandahar City, Afghanistan
July 13, 2010

War is hell.   —attributed to Napoleon Bonaparte

There is many a boy here to-day who looks on war as all glory, but, boys, it is all hell.
—William Tecumseh Sherman, speech to reunion of veterans, Columbus, Ohio (1880)

War is hell. It's just not the same hell I thought it would be. The suffering and death I expected—the hell is how stupid it all is.
—U.S. Army captain, Afghanistan (September 2011)

CONTENTS

AUTHOR'S NOTE

Much of the motivation for, and many of the ideas within, this book were conceived during a period when in addition to maintaining a correspondence with former students deployed to Afghanistan and Iraq, I was directing West Point's freshman literature course, taken by more than a thousand plebes each spring. According to institutional lore, a plebe ranks in the hierarchy just above the superintendent's dog and the commandant's cat. But to my mind there's no one loftier.

Many of my best-spent hours have been in the company of plebes, finding their way in a new and seldom comfortable world. I like most the person I am with these young men and women. I see in them a vitality that battles against the destruction and death that have marked the century's beginning—an energy that helps me to navigate the perilous no man's land of readying them for whatever future awaits. To all those thousands of plebes, especially to that smaller set of cadets full of spirit and adventure who end up in my own seminar each spring, I owe the happiest of debts.

Long and robust conversations with associates, colleagues, and friends have enriched my response to the confusions of recent years. I am grateful to Nick, Max, Neil, Joey, Adam, Joel, Kevin, Renée, Grant, Emily, Sean, Whitney, Dan, Meghan, Kirsten, Liz, and many others for the correspondence we share. I thank Anne Taranto, Frank Rotondo, Daisy Miller, Seth Armus, Matt Boethin, and Jon Lewis for their long-standing loyalty and kindness. Scott Krawczyk, who now leads the literary way as head of West Point's Department of English and Philosophy, is indeed a "fit man for the constable of the watch." Damon Durall immeasurably enlivened the plebe course with his thoughtful perspective, unfailing honesty, and tireless labors. I am much the richer for Karin Roffman's conversation, unmatched dedication to our shared enterprise of teaching, and rare gift of tough-minded generosity; and for Suzanne Nielsen, wise and true friend. My parents, as always, have been patient listeners; they have also shared their own memories of life during wartime and peacetime since World War II.

I have greatly appreciated the encouragement and editorial sensibilities of Greg Veis and Frank Wilkinson over the last several years. My agent, David Kuhn, has been wonderfully energizing throughout this process. It has been a great pleasure to work with everyone at Kuhn Projects and FSG. And I am fortunate that my editor, Eric Chinski, is at once the most gracious and careful of readers.

I am grateful to the staff of the Fort George G. Meade Museum for helping me to discover more about the U.S. Army's theater history and to the Special Collections and Archives Division of the United States Military Academy Library.

In a few instances, a name or identifying detail has been changed.

The opinions expressed in this work are my own and do not necessarily reflect those of the United States Military Academy, the Department of the Army, or the Department of Defense.

NO MAN'S LAND

PROLOGUE
Earth's Melancholy Map

It is not so easy . . . to leave the front line for battalion headquarters; it has magnetized the mind; and for a moment one leans,
delaying, looking out over the scene of war, and feeling that "to
break the horrid silence" would be an act of creation.
—Edmund Blunden, *Undertones of War* (1928)

There is a lieutenant ever in my mind's eye. Sometimes this phan-
tom acquires the features of lieutenants I have known. At other
times it wears an anonymity at once reassuring and unsettling in
its promise of emotional distance. Yet no matter its form, my ghost
moves always through the same space, through a kind of no man's
land—that sinister, broken ground illuminated with such force by
the soldier-poets of World War I.

"No man's land" was associated with wilderness and death for
centuries before the phrase came to describe the shattered landscape of the western front. In the Middle Ages the term denoted
any stretch of waste or unclaimed land; the fourteenth-century
English chroniclers gave the name *Nonesmanneslond* to a particular piece of ground just beyond London's north wall where the
early Plantagenet kings executed enemies of the state. But the
expression acquired a new significance during World War I, when
the strip of land running more than 450 miles, from Belgium's
North Sea coast to the Franco-Swiss frontier, became a massive
killing field.

The imagery of no man's land, made familiar to us through literary, photographic, and cinematic accounts, endures despite the
new variations on destruction that technology has worked in the

years since. The belts of barbed wire, gaping shell holes, smoking hulks of wrecked airplanes, denuded trees, and rotting corpses rising through the mud have all lingered in the cultural imagination as emblems of a lost generation and a world plunged into disaffected, mechanized modernity. Representations of this world on film remained as full of fantastic terrors in 1957, in Stanley Kubrick's *Paths of Glory*, as they had been decades before in King Vidor's *Big Parade* (1925) or in James Whale's *Frankenstein* (1931), where the World War I veteran Whale found in the features of no man's land an ideal mise-en-scène for the horror genre.

Newly arrived at Passchendaele, in West Flanders, generally regarded as one of the front's most desolate stretches, Major C.E.L. Lyne of the British Royal Field Artillery declared in 1917, "Dante would never have condemned lost souls to wander in so terrible a purgatory . . . Even the birds and rats have forsaken so unnatural a spot . . . You see it at its best under a leaden sky with a chill drizzle falling, each hour an eternity, each dragging step a nightmare." The front had a dreamworld's characteristic exaggeration and distortion. In his novel *Under Fire*, Henri Barbusse described it as a "country peopled with ferocious, luminous apparitions . . . A tempest of hoarse, dull crashes, of furious yells, of the piercing cries of beasts rains down on the earth." Nothing in this landscape could be trusted, not even the senses. "Hearing and sight are strained to the utmost," reported Second Lieutenant H. E. Cooper of the Royal Warwickshire Regiment. "Tiny noises are magnified a hundredfold." Robert Graves recorded his first naive glimpse into the unknown beyond the first-line trench in his memoir *Good-Bye to All That*:

> The darkness seemed to move and shake about as I looked at it; the bushes started travelling, singly at first, then both together. The pickets did the same. I was glad of the sentry beside me; he gave his name as Beaumont. "They're quiet tonight, Sir," he said. "A relief going on; I think so, surely."

I said: "It's funny how those bushes seem to move."

"Aye, they do play queer tricks. Is this your first spell in trenches, Sir?" A German flare shot up, broke into bright flame, dropped slowly and went hissing into the grass just behind our trench, showing up the bushes and pickets. Instinctively I moved.

"It's bad to do that, Sir," he said, as a rifle bullet cracked and seemed to pass right between us. "Keep still, Sir, and they can't spot you. Not but what a flare is a bad thing to fall on you. I've seen them burn a hole in a man."

No man's land: the violent recrudescence of Freud's primal unconscious and the locus classicus for a twentieth-century understanding of the world's capacity for duplicity and destruction both together. Out of the western front emerged, as Ezra Pound affirmed in his 1920 poem *Hugh Selwyn Mauberley*, a combination of unprecedented candor and disillusionment. To Wilfred Owen, speaking for many of the war's participants, the experience of trench warfare exposed the ideal of a patriotic death— expressed in the old Latin tag *dulce et decorum est pro patria mori*—as an "old lie." Owen did not live to see the end of the war, but Pound suggests that those soldiers who did survive had been disabused of the "old lies" only to return home to "new infamy." The new world generated by the catastrophe of the western front was one in which, as Paul Fussell documents so forcefully in *The Great War and Modern Memory*, irony seemed to prevail and in which the novelist Erich Maria Remarque could imagine a combatant, Paul Bäumer (the protagonist of *All Quiet on the Western Front*), finding refuge from death only by burrowing in another man's coffin.

This is the earth into which my ghosts burrow, too. "Digging in" was the trope of the trenches, but it remains elemental to some soldiers' survival. "Cold mountain," a captain writes of his recent experience in Afghanistan: "Freezing rain that shudders your core. Your e-tool fights it out with the frozen earth. You dig deep because if you do not, it might not be enough." The captain lives in what I've come to think of as the no man's land of our new century. His peculiar world, full of hazard, doubt, and deceit, preoccupies me now. Some days I glimpse it from his foxhole; on other days I adopt the bird's-eye view of a pilot searching for a safe place to land his helicopter in the inhospitable Afghan mountains, which seem to him like the "surface of some alien planet."

The captain who has burrowed his way into the soil of Badghis Province, "Home of the Winds," northwest of Heart, moves at one point to a "mud cave," where he lives together with a small group of soldiers encircled by the stench of the fires in which they must burn their own waste. From the cave news comes to me that one of the soldiers is dead. The captain thinks of the words of Gilgamesh, grieving for his friend Enkidu, rendered here by Michael Ondaatje: "The joyful will stoop with sorrow, and when you have gone to the earth I will let my hair grow long for your sake, I will wander through the wilderness in the skin of a lion." From the cave come unanswerable questions, scattered on the wind like antique prophecies: "I wonder what will come of this generation when it's all said and done. Where do we go from here? How will our country remember the fallen and the broken? Will it ever be enough?"

The captain's message, sent from one no man's land, reaches me in another, which for all its physical safety and comfort nevertheless feels treacherous and bewildering. I reread his questions about the inadequacies of memory and the prospect of another lost generation on the eve of two events: 2014 marks the long-projected (if imperfect) end of major U.S. combat operations in Afghanistan and the centennial commemoration of World War I's beginning. This coincidence—this particular collision of war and memory—is just that, yet I can think of no better name than no man's land to describe the physical and emotional landscape in which so many of the soldiers I know dwell, and to capture my own state of mind.

The image of no man's land also reflects the national psyche itself, gripped alternately by paroxysms of sentimentality and by bouts of convenient amnesia for more than a decade of wartime.

Postwar America in the twenty-first century will be shaped by the way the country responds to a constellation of challenges. The decoupling in political discourse of the issues of war and economic austerity has helped to keep today's conflicts essentially at the edge of public consciousness, all the periodic indulgences in "support the troops" rhetoric notwithstanding. The difficulty of making sense of our military enterprises at the beginning of this century was also exacerbated by several late-twentieth-century cultural developments, chiefly the attention paid to popular culture representations of Vietnam and the fiftieth-anniversary celebrations of World War II. Vietnam came to seem at once an aberration and the definitive postmodern war, while the legacy of World War II was sanitized and simplified into an American parable about an earlier generation's superhuman mettle. The apotheosis of the Greatest Generation at the turn of the last century, coming on the heels of the lightning-quick and unequivocal display of U.S. military prowess in Operation Desert Storm in 1991, made it possible to reimagine, post-Vietnam, an outsize American hero: the twenty-first-century American soldier as comic-book figure complete with body armor that seems to have emerged from Batman's workshop.

To some, the soldier of the new American century was a liberator who would be welcomed with flowers and kisses, a righteous avenger doing battle with the forces of evil, the generous bearer of a democratic dream; to others, that soldier was the robotic emissary of imperial might. Either way, the American soldier has been reduced to little more than a caricature. While these narratives of the old school may provide some elusive comfort, they don't help us to understand the ways in which the last decade has transformed us as a nation and—what is perhaps more damning—the ways in which it has changed us not at all. Like the ongoing Civil War sesquicentennial, the hundredth anniversary of World War I presents fresh challenges to cultural memory by making it easier for the country to beat a nostalgic retreat to an earlier crisis instead of confronting the current one, to which we were enjoined from the first to pay as little attention as possible. Revisiting an earlier conflict in order to avoid a reckoning with the last decade's wars does little justice to anyone: to those who fought at Shiloh and Vicksburg, Vimy Ridge and Belleau Wood, Kandahar and the Korengal Valley.

In what now seems early days, I wove my own comforting narrative of the new century. I taught myself to interpret its story as a neat arc from peace to war. And it proved a most practical plot, at least for a time. I could lose myself in it as I might in any good yarn. Its sensational beginning and harrowing middle helped me for a time to ignore the fact that there was no satisfactory end in view. The plot reaffirmed my commitment to West Point, where I was charged with educating future army officers, by clarifying the enterprise in which I was ostensibly engaged: I was preparing the cadets in my classes to go to war. My students found a similar appeal in this narrative, particularly in its urgency. They thrilled to the idea that they were coming of age in a moment of crisis. "It is not in the still calm of life, or the repose of a pacific station, that great characters are formed," Abigail Adams wrote to her son John Quincy. "When a mind is raised, and animated by scenes that engage the Heart, then those qualities which would otherways lay dormant, wake into Life, and form the Character of the Hero and the Statesman."

Swept away by the momentum of their tale, cadets could keep at bay many of the doubts that typically dog college students even as they were forced to address other questions—concerning their courage, integrity, and capacity to endure—that usually vex us only much later in life. They would graduate from West Point, deploy to Iraq or Afghanistan, and lead a platoon into war in an army in which small-unit combat leadership remains the prevailing romance to which new lieutenants aspire and old generals cling. This was a future whose shape they could envision, whose promises they could believe.

In certain sensational aspects, twenty-first-century warfare seems like the stuff of science fiction. The rise of the drone, for example, along with other remote technologies, threatens to remake the battlescape as operators with joysticks hunt targets on another continent. But there is also an ancient strain in today's war story. The lack of an exit strategy and the apparent absence of a clear and consistent political vision guiding the war effort—What does victory look like?—forced many of the platoon leaders and company commanders I know to understand the dramas in which they found themselves as local and individual rather than national or communal. The ends they furnish for themselves—coming home without losing any soldiers or, if someone has to die, doing so heroically in battle—offer exclusively personal and particular consolations that make the mission itself effectively beside the point. At least in this respect, they seem to find themselves in an ancient narrative, a throwback to the world of Homeric epic, where there is no cause larger than that of personal honor and where mass battles are telescoped into individual contests over the armor-clad bodies of the slain. This focus perhaps comes naturally to an army, a land force that defines itself against the other services' comparative distance from the fight and heavy reliance on the machines of war and must therefore attribute a perverse, anachronistic glamour to being there—to having one's "boots on the ground," as the expression goes.

Stories grow ingrained by force of habit. We all rehearsed our war story until we became expert at telling it to ourselves and to others. War had become the normal state of things at West Point before I realized that its rhythms were not necessarily conforming to expectation and that the blueprint according to which we had been mapping our lives was not altogether sound. "We tell ourselves stories in order to live . . . Or at least we do for a while," Joan Didion proposes at the beginning of "The White Album," an essay that chronicles her recognition of the imperfect fictions we weave with such desperation. "I am talking here about a time when I began to doubt the premises of all the stories I had ever told myself," Didion explains of her time in California in the late 1960s. "I was meant to know the plot," she writes, "but all I knew was what I saw."

I, too, had arrived at a moment when the story I had been weaving so assiduously unraveled, leaving little but doubt as the campaigns in Iraq and Afghanistan rolled on. When I discovered that the stories I was telling myself no longer served, I started slowly to revise. I even began to congratulate myself on my prescience. Let my colleagues continue to think exclusively about the arduous voyage out, about the battlefield as ultimate destination. I would focus on the labor of coming home. Let generals try to impress on me a sense of my responsibility by showing me dramatic photographs of lieutenants perched on Afghan hilltops, youthful monarchs of all they surveyed. Let them tell me this was the "end state," or "outcome," I was always to keep in mind as I went about the business of teaching tomorrow's officers. No amount of bureaucratese could conceal the deep romance of the image, this heroic drama of "muddy boots." And I knew it was the wrong romance.

Others could go on imagining an *Iliad* if they liked: imagining that the end of the war—that victory—was the end of the story. I knew better. We were all of us—the ones who went to war and the ones who waited at home—inhabiting an *Odyssey* in which the hardest struggle comes after the battle has been won, the city sacked, the spoils taken, the dead buried, and the wounded there to remind us of a violent interlude we would sooner forget. Warlike Achilles on a hilltop wasn't the hero of the story I began to tell. My heroes became reluctant Odysseus, whose journey home to Ithaca proves more arduous than his war; Balzac's Colonel Chabert, resurrected from a mass grave at Eylau to arrive in Paris to everyone's surprise and inconvenience after ten years of travail; and the ambivalent

Captain Ivanov of Andrey Platonov's exquisite 1946 short story "The Return," who, after four years away at war, finds himself a shy intruder within his own family.

The new plot galvanized my teaching at West Point, where I found especial contentment in focusing on the institution's newest novitiates, the plebes, over a thousand each year, whose introductory core course in literature I directed. This second draft of my story was better, richer, and more complicated. It even had what looked like an end: coming home. This was something, yet not quite enough, for it didn't account for the fact that none of the soldiers I knew seemed to stay home for very long. Many of them felt a restlessness and an alienation they attempted to cure by means of a cross-country bicycle or motorcycle trip, a long vacation to South America, the ending of one romantic relationship or the beginning of another. Some kept moving by leaving the army and embarking on a new career or going back to school. Those who stayed in the service soon discovered that instead of simply going to war and coming home, they had become war commuters, shuttling back and forth on serial deployments. On his third Afghanistan tour in 2012, a helicopter pilot named Adam wrote to tell me, "This war has become more 'normal' to me than life at home." Soon after reaching the States, he mused,

> Well, I've been home for just over a week now. It's strange; I still don't quite feel as though I've arrived, if that makes any sense. Even on the flight home, I had the odd sensation that I was commuting—just making another transatlantic hop. I think the shortened dwell time between this deployment and the last may have contributed. [My wife] was remarking how great it is that we still feel like newlyweds after six years of marriage. I suppose that's one of the happier by-products of 2.5 deployments.

To the soldier who feels that he has become a war commuter, home is perhaps the strangest place there is. And it isn't quite the same strangeness we might associate with prolonged absence. The typical war commuter—tethered, like more conventional commuters, by e-mail, cell phone, social media, and Skype, even at the farthest geographical removes—has effectively punched a clock on a twelve-month (sometimes a fifteen-month) shift and then gone home to get ready for the next cycle. I don't mean to diminish the hazards of the job, merely to suggest the routinization of even the most extraordinary experiences. Writing on the *New York Times At War* blog on June 29, 2011, First Lieutenant Mark Larson explains, "As with anything that is done with enough repetition, deploying and training on a set schedule (one year deployed and one year at home) becomes a habit. Do it for ten years, and it becomes in-grained in the culture . . . It was just a given that you would spend a year overseas, regroup for a year at home and head back out again. The urgency was always there."

Adam's description of himself as a commuter put me in mind of Donald Hall's "The Man in the Dead Machine," a poem about the alternate flights of a World War II fighter pilot. Hall presents us first with the image of a sun-bleached, helmeted skeleton still strapped decades later to his seat in the cockpit of a Grumman Hellcat that crashed into an uncharted mountain in New Guinea in 1943. The second half of the poem sets the image of the dead pilot in relief against that of a pilot turned commuter who has exchanged the fatal entrapment of the cockpit for the figura-tive imprisonment of a seat on the train, gripping his briefcase and the postwar life that chance has permitted him. The quotid-ian replaces the extraordinary: the speaker has escaped one grim fate only to find himself enmeshed in another at once secure and ordinary. Adam's commute is a bit different: it has made something seemingly unexceptional out of the elementally hazardous.

Commuting is a plot without romance, a tale without an end, or at least without a recognizably heroic end. Even in the ideal case (in the movies, that is), years of commuting conclude inadequately with a farewell dinner and perhaps the presentation of a gold watch. The story of today's war commuter, if it doesn't end abruptly and violently, refuses to end at all. Instead, it is a story with a series of false endings, each homecoming but a prelude to the next deployment until, at last, the job ends. The terms most often used to describe the current epoch—long war, era of persistent conflict, war without end—do not adequately suggest the effects of this ambiguous, indeterminate passage on a new generation of war commuters, combat veterans who have become the objects of a public's simultaneously overheated and fleeting regard, or on the public itself. Adrift between war and peace, we have been living in an era for which we still have no satisfactory name. And in an archaic term inherited from the war that was supposed to end them all, I have found what seems to me the most appropriate description for the space we have entered.

Part of the problem can be traced to the framing of the wars that followed September 11, 2001, as but the overture to an era of persistent conflict or, to use the phrase now in vogue, "persistent engagement." Congress officially retired the term "long war" in 2007, but the idea of perpetual conflict continues to seize the military imagination in particular by investing it with an enduring sense of purpose and by delaying the aimless drift associated with military life in peacetime. The prospect of preparing for an endless future of persistent threats works like a tonic against poisonous visions of a "peacetime" or "garrison" army. That's something many soldiers dread, something they have already experienced in between deployments; it is often characterized by the triumph of what Paul Fussell called "chickenshit." "What does that rude term signify?" Fussell asks in *Wartime: Understanding and Behavior in the Second World War*:

It does not imply complaint about the inevitable inconveniences of military life: overcrowding and lack of privacy, tedious institutional cookery, deprivation of personality, general bore-dom. Nothing much can be done about those things. Chickenshit refers rather to behavior that makes military life worse than it need be: petty harassment of the weak by the strong; open scrim-mage for power and authority and prestige; sadism thinly dis-guised as necessary discipline; a constant "paying off of old scores"; and insistence on the letter rather than the spirit of ordi-nances. Chickenshit is so called—instead of horse- or bull- or elephant shit—because it is small-minded and ignoble and takes the trivial seriously.

"Chickenshit," Fussell concludes, "can be recognized instantly because it never has anything to do with winning the war." In the absence of war, the realm of chickenshit tends to expand.

Paradoxically, the picture of the future as a persistent struggle has done nothing to curb a communal craving for ends—especially on the part of an exhausted military—and so the last decade has also been characterized by a series of falsely definitive punctuation marks: a braggadocio's triumphant declaration on the deck of the USS *Abraham Lincoln*; the assassination of Osama bin Laden and the mindless celebrations that followed in the streets and subse-quently at political conventions; the withdrawal of combat troops from Iraq; and now the transition of U.S. forces out of Afghani-stan and the so-called pivot to the Asia-Pacific region.

In a major foreign policy speech delivered at the National Defense University in May 2013, President Barack Obama explic-itly addressed the conceit of "perpetual" war that the post-9/11 Authorization for Use of Military Force ushered in: "America is at a crossroads. We must define the nature and scope of this struggle, or else it will define us." Citing James Madison's admonition that "no nation could preserve its freedom in the midst of continual warfare," Obama declared his determination to recast the "bound-less 'global war on terror'" as a "series of persistent, targeted efforts to dismantle specific networks of violent extremists that threaten America." In officially announcing this shift from war to "counterterrorism" operations, the president also took the opportunity to reaffirm the administration's plan for a complete transition out of Afghanistan in 2014: "Our systematic effort to dismantle terrorist organizations must continue. But this war, like all wars, must end. That's what history advises. That's what our democracy demands." The distinction the president draws here invites us to consider what's in a name. How, precisely, does a "series of persistent, targeted efforts" differ from "perpetual" war? What does a systematic dismantling look like? Will the violence it requires differ from that effected by war? Will it be a difference of means, scale, or duration?

Perhaps we have such trouble calling a halt to war these days because we don't even bother to declare it anymore. The United States last made an official declaration of war against another state on June 5, 1942, against Hungary, Romania, and Bulgaria. Simmering wars, often lacking definitive punctuation, have been the custom of the country ever since: false starts and stops, noisy escalations, and quiet withdrawals. The United States, especially since World War II, has had some difficulty reckoning honestly with its wars and situating them within a convincing national narrative. We refer to Korea as "the forgotten war." The subtitle of Tobias Wolff's undervalued Vietnam memoir, *In Pharaoh's Army: Memories of the Lost War*, aptly captures that war's place in the country's memory. I suspect the current war will prove no easier to understand, either in relation to those earlier conflicts or on its own terms. From the first, the public has been encouraged at once to accept and to ignore a national commitment normalized as a long-term military struggle yet fought by less than 1 percent of the population. Not too long ago, an acquaintance who is about thirty announced to me over lunch, "The country has been at war my entire adult life, and you're the only one I know with any personal connection to the military."

Various factors contributed to the tendency of Americans to

pay as little thoughtful attention as possible to the fact that we have been at war. Postwar—the very phase we should have been thinking about even before the war began—has been just as difficult to imagine as war itself. Armies, and not just armies but nations, have been notoriously reluctant to imagine worlds after war. As the military historian Matthew Moten writes in the introduction to *Between War and Peace: How America Ends Its Wars*, historians, military theorists, and political scientists alike "have largely neglected the course of events leading to a given war's conclusion and its consequences for the peace that followed." Even Carl von Clausewitz, "preeminent of war's philosophers, rarely followed war to its very end."

It will be easy to forget the aftermath of our destructive presence in Iraq and Afghanistan, but legacies on the home front may prove more difficult to ignore: memorializing war dead; caring for the wounded; assuaging the persistent difficulties of the soldier's repatriation; understanding the role of a professional military force that has been shaped by a particular kind of warfare and that continues to be downsized as its mission shifts; energizing a citizenry and political elite unwilling to grapple with the responsibilities to which making war obligates a nation; acknowledging the degree to which a global war on extremism has at once reinforced and debunked various national mythologies, including the ever-seductive narrative of American moral and political exceptionalism.

Veterans of Vietnam returned to a country at best indifferent, at worst explicitly hostile to them. We remember the hostility because it makes such a good story but forget the competing sense of willful ignorance that eventually eclipsed it. On a visit to the National Memorial Cemetery of the Pacific, on the Hawaiian island of Oahu, in 1970, Joan Didion observed:

> Vietnam seemed considerably less chimerical than it had seemed
> on the Mainland for some months, less last year's war, less suc-
> cessfully consigned to that limbo of benign neglect in which any

mention of continuing casualties was made to seem a little coun-
terproductive, a little démodé. There in the crater it seemed less
easy to believe that weekly killed-in-action figures under 100
might by some sleight-of-hand add up to zero, a nonexistent war.

The fate of soldiers is in some significant ways even more disorienting today than it was during Vietnam's numbers game. Characterized by a state of knowing and not knowing we are at war, we
seem largely unable to respond to returning soldiers with anything
more substantive than histrionic gestures of gratitude typified by
the now obligatory phrase "thank you for your service." Our im-
pressions of soldiers are just as distorted as they have always been—
our attention span just as fleeting—but they are now masked by
largely symbolic celebrations of a service about which we remain
insufficiently curious.

I've thought a great deal about what it means for my former
students, junior officers with multiple tours in Iraq and Afghanistan, and the soldiers with whom they serve, to be defined by such
dislocation, to find both opportunity and devastation in this conflict; to learn as they redeploy, assume or give up command, return
to teach at West Point, or decide to leave the army altogether how
to negotiate the divide this age has produced between soldier and
civilian, between "over here" and "over there." I have been forced
to think long and hard about the nature of the responsibility entrusted to me as their teacher: how best to equip them for their
futures and to help them find whatever it is they will need to carry
on in relative peace when they feel, as Adam baldly put it, "this
war has become more 'normal' to me than life at home." It has become more normal to me, too, and I wonder about my own postwar direction.

Not long ago I heard an officer quite senior to Adam declare
that with the mission probably set to wind down in Afghanistan,
things would be "getting back to normal" in the army. By "normal,"
I took this colonel to mean the resumption of all the predictable

peacetime routines, rhythms, and pathways that had been altered, disrupted, or accelerated because of the exigencies of wartime. Yet at the end of the last century it was easy to find the same kind of officer, with no prospect of anything but a peacekeeping or humanitarian mission in his sights, lamenting the state of the peacetime army, where in the absence of a fight, the business of preparing for one had become a numbingly mechanical exercise. Soldiers who grew up in that era had trouble imagining there would be another war. With Adam's message about commuting fresh in my mind, I pointed out that for a generation of officers who have spent their entire careers commuting to war, peacetime would feel anything but normal; it would instead seem as defiantly unnatural as the renewal of prolonged conflict had appeared before September 11. It's never easy to define normal for armies, which exist in a perdurable state of unease that no amount of discipline can ever truly disguise. They are, after all, designed for something civilization has since the eighteenth century at least officially regarded as abnormal and primitive.

I have had to grow accustomed to the cyclical redefinition of normal within military culture. In fact, in an exercise akin to Hall's exploration of the pilot's forking paths, I sometimes imagine a different trajectory for myself. What would my relationship to this war have been were I a reasonably thoughtful and responsible citizen with no connection to the military? Had so many of my former students not been doing the fighting? Had I not the great good fortune to become a correspondent and, I hope, a friend to a group of young officers who have moved with such dispatch from classroom to battlefield? Had I not felt so keenly the loss of two former students, Captain Daniel Whitten and Lieutenant Christopher Goeke, both killed in action in Afghanistan?

I would probably have been just like the people I sometimes encounter at parties forced unexpectedly by my presence to confront an event they have chosen to regard as a spectacle occurring at some remove: disturbing, yes, but examined the way one might calmly watch a feeding shark through the thick glass of an aquarium. Nor have I been immune to distraction. I haven't been keeping watch all these years because I am possessed of some superior political intelligence or superhuman attention span. No, my vigil has been self-interested, personal, and particular: I acquired the habit of taking stock every morning—reviewing the latest DOD press releases and the *Washington Post's* Faces of the Fallen—to make sure no one I know had died in the night.

It was in the immediate aftermath of Chris Goeke's death, in the summer of 2010, that I felt most powerfully my own dislocation and saw most clearly the inadequacy of the ways in which I had thus far been attempting to arrange the story of the last decade in my head. It was during this period that the lieutenant in my mind's eye sometimes awakened me in the night because he looked so much like Chris. Feeling myself to be in the middle of no man's land, I developed an extreme case of war vertigo, and it was, of all people, the novelist Edith Wharton who taught me how to understand my own confusion.

Wharton is not a writer most of us probably associate with war. With the frosty, treacherous, yet bloodless drawing-room battles of Gilded Age New York, yes. With the stink and smoking gore of a trench on the western front, no. Yet there she was in France for the duration of World War I: working vigorously on behalf of numerous charities and relief organizations, sending dispatches from the front back to American readers, publicly and privately making the case for the United States to join the fight. Having lived in Paris for long stretches since 1907, Wharton eventually divested herself entirely of the Mount—a Palladian-style country house she designed and had built in the Berkshires of western Massachusetts—along with her increasingly unpredictable husband, Teddy. She had made France her home by the time hostilities broke out in

1914, and in 1916 she was awarded the French Legion of Honor for her war work.

Toward the end of July, a few weeks after Chris's death, I participated in a literary festival at the Mount. Assigned to a panel called "Channeling Edith Wharton: Writers in Wartime," I was asked to discuss the imaginative opportunities for, and moral obligations of, writers during war. Our session took place in the Stable, a building used primarily to house Wharton's motorcars. On the wall there is a photograph of Wharton with Teddy, two dogs, her friend Henry James, and a goggled chauffeur in a 1904 Pope Hartford. Wharton was a great enthusiast for what she called "motorflights." "The motor-car," she noted before the war, "has restored the romance of travel." Wharton several times toured the western front in her Mercedes, and she described her second excursion there to Henry James with a jauntiness I mistrusted: "It *was* less high in colour than the first adventure, & resulted in several disappointments, as well as in some interesting moments—indeed, once within the military zone *every* moment is interesting."

War, both as a general idea and as a feature of our own historical moment, seemed very far from this secluded estate in Lenox, with its elegant house, meticulous gardens, and annual "coaching weekend" of horse-drawn carriages. The property's airy beauty had the effect of intensifying a disjunction to which I was having great difficulty growing accustomed: the one between the physical settings of my own life—Central Park, the New York Public Library, the Hudson River, even West Point (however ostensibly martial in tone)—and the imagined landscape I carried within, a volatile no man's land of geographically distant wars richly and variously described to me by those at work within them.

The disconnection between my external and my internal worlds has proved to be occasionally dizzying. I wouldn't call what I feel at such moments guilt exactly, or regret, for it isn't that I think I should be doing something else or that I wish myself (to paraphrase Shakespeare's Henry V) anywhere but where I am. Nor is it the case that I feel unsuited to the particular role I inhabit, as I surely would were I to find myself on a battlefield rather than in a classroom. Nevertheless, living so far behind the lines presented to my imagination requires a significant psychological adjustment.

During my visit to the Mount, the scene I was trying to piece together had only just taken place in Kandahar City, where Chris was killed when his base was attacked with small-arms, rifle, and rocket-propelled-grenade fire. Meandering through Wharton's house into Teddy's sun-splashed den, across the terrace, and upstairs to the Henry James Guest Suite, I eventually found, as if in direct response to my discomfort, an exhibit titled *Edith Wharton and the First World War*, which began somewhat unprepossessingly in what was once the guest bathroom. There I studied a series of placards and photographs detailing the story of Wharton's war. Wharton was disgusted by American neutrality, contemptuous of Woodrow Wilson and his pacifist "apologists," persuaded that the war was, in the words of her biographer Hermione Lee, "somehow an inevitability, a product of a decaying civilisation." Wharton shared a disturbing faith in war as a kind of purgative with her friend and contemporary Theodore Roosevelt, even if her tone never reaches quite the fever pitch of Roosevelt's writing on the subject.

"Wherever I go among these men of the front," she wrote in *Fighting France*, an account of her life in wartime Paris and her 1915 visits to the western front, "I have the same impression: . . . that the absorbing undivided thought of the Defense of France lives in the heart and brain of each soldier as intensely as in the heart and brain of their chief." As I made my way through the exhibit and later through *Fighting France*, I grew impatient with the earnest romantic strains in which Wharton writes of war. Here, she describes a column of troops viewed from her car: "Close as the men were, they seemed allegorically splendid: as if, under the arch of the sunset, we had been watching the whole French army ride straight into glory . . ." But she knew where they were really going.

Wharton's wartime experiences and attitudes seem in so many ways the reverse of my own. She was physically close to war yet somehow fundamentally aloof from its combatants: she refers to the wounded as "poor bandaged creatures" in her letter to James. I have watched the recent wars unfold at a great geographical distance, but the soldiers I know form the core of my emotional life. The harder I tried to channel Wharton, the more frustrated I became. Her war writing is undeniably exuberant, imbued with a sense of exhilaration that would seem to preclude unvarnished reflection on the chaos and destruction all around her. Wharton was seduced by the "fabulous and epic" movements of an army on the march and by the "concentrated energy" of modern warfare. She was susceptible to jingoism and to overheated paeans to sacrifice.

Yet there are moments in *Fighting France* when her novelist's eye for the unexpected and oblique exposes the incompleteness of that robust, bellicose narrative. When she takes advantage not of her eyewitness proximity to the trenches but rather of the distance and off-kilter perspective that her noncombatant status and relative safety made possible, she seems able to report authentically the terror of the war. As I read, I discovered that Wharton was on some level attempting to reproduce the disorientation she had felt: leaving the front, she explains in *Fighting France*, "is like coming down from the mountains." Toward the end of the book I encountered a description of a picnic lunch arranged on the side of a ridge protected from an opposing German artillery battery. The passage feels frivolous until one realizes the depth of its self-awareness:

> As we sat there in the grass, swept by a great mountain breeze full of the scent of thyme and myrtle, while the flutter of birds, the hum of insects, the still and busy life of the hills went on all about us in the sunshine, the pressure of the encircling line of death grew more intolerably real. It is not in the mud and jokes and

every-day activities of the trenches that one most feels the dam-
nable insanity of war; it is where it lurks like a mythical monster
in scenes to which the mind has always turned for rest.

Wharton, it turns out, was not blind to the faces of the wounded,
those "poor bandaged creatures" whose experiences had had the
effect of "burning them down to the bare bones of character." Nor
was she oblivious, while driving through landscapes in the spring's
"first sweet leafiness," to "the choking air of present horror" that
seemed to wait always just around the next bend. She, too, sensed
the sinister presence of the "mythical monster": she felt its fiery
breath when she least expected it and where it seemed least to
belong.

In Wharton's attempts to articulate the sensation produced by
the collision of tranquil scenes with war's annihilating force, I discovered a version of my own war vertigo. The state of mind Wharton describes is akin to the one I experienced as a visitor to her
house—one of those settings to which a mind might ordinarily
turn for rest—coming face-to-face with what she called "the whole
huge and oppressive and unescapable fact of the war." As I drove
home early the next morning, my route took me over gently curv-
ing back roads through farm country and quaint New York villages. Admiring the view, accelerating occasionally to pass a poky
horse trailer, I thought of what an officer had just written to me
after climbing up to an isolated Afghan outpost at nine thousand
feet. "It is pretty country here," he noted, "if it weren't for the war."

Few World War I combatants responded to the sensory confusion
Wharton illuminates more shrewdly than did Edmund Blunden,
later the Oxford Professor of Poetry, who served on the western
front with Britain's Royal Sussex Regiment. Blunden makes frequent appearances in the no man's land of my imagination, which
owes as much to his depiction of that peculiar world as to any

other. As a battalion fieldworks officer and later intelligence officer in Belgium and France, he confronted all of the landscape's obligatory horrors firsthand. Working in the perpetual night of the sappers' tunnels or aboveground scouting no man's land in the moonless dark before an assault, Blunden learned the arts of physical and psychological survival and subsequently wrote of them in *Undertones of War*, a much quieter memoir than those of his contemporaries Robert Graves and Siegfried Sassoon and therefore perhaps less often read.

Blunden first tried to write the book even before the war had ended, but he didn't like what he came up with at the time and realized that some greater distance was needed. Repeatedly—ritually—in both poetry and prose, he returned to the scene of war. "I must go over the ground again," he declared in his preliminary essay to *Undertones of War*. It was "impossible not to look again, and to descry the ground, how thickly and innumerably yet it was strewn with the facts or notions of war experience." Indeed, Blunden wondered whether he might be compelled serially to revisit the war's "front-line meaning" until the day he died. "You will be going over the ground again," a voice within him predicts, "until the hour when agony's clawed face softens into the smilingness of a young spring day."

Without the electro-optical and thermal night vision devices or the Global Positioning Systems with which soldiers are equipped today—without proper maps, in fact—Blunden, whose nighttime missions sometimes took him dangerously close to the German lines, had literally to count his steps and memorize their direction in order to find his way out of no man's land. Nighttime proved "a perpetual tangle" full of unseen dangers, a world in which the very trees appeared to be enemy soldiers, every shadow a potential threat. On first arriving at the front, Blunden could make no sense of the complex network of British trenches. "Probably nobody else could," he suggests. Tom Allen, a lieutenant in the 1st Irish Guards, made a similar report from near Loos, in northeast France, in 1915:

"In these mazes where we have fought each other so often and each side has held the ground in turn, you can never be quite sure whether a trench won't lead you straight to the German lines." Although maps proved inadequate, they somehow comforted a soldier about to advance into the unknown. Blunden's "absurd" standard-issue map made him "feel safer." Fallible maps appear everywhere in *Undertones of War*: underground and above-ground, even on the underside of a tablecloth at battalion head quarters. Such maps become, in all their imperfection, the soldier's way of asserting a measure of control, albeit symbolic, over the darkness.

Blunden made his share of mistakes in no man's land, but he became extremely adept at deciphering his nocturnal universe. He learned to interpret what he called the "magical but terrible map of the underworld" and to endure the "land of despair" it depicted. Blunden deprecates his abilities as a cartographer, yet it becomes increasingly clear that he owed his survival to an uncanny ability to navigate the landscape in which he found himself at once confined and adrift: they nicknamed him Rabbit. Not everyone was so nimble and adroit, as he reveals in his account of the disappearance on successive nights of two officers on patrol. The first, armed with a complete set of official "maps, panoramas, photographs and assault programmes," failed to return. The second, an experienced veteran, likewise disappeared. On the third night Blunden himself is sent out, as he writes, "with one or two old hands to see what I could see." Moving over the surface of a topography radically deformed, Blunden owed his survival to skill and instinct but also to a great deal of luck: to a right or left turn, to an ill-timed barrage, to the wildness of his own startled movements.

Blunden can also be considered a survivor in another sense—a long-term survivor able to impose at least some order on the disordered wasteland he was lucky enough to leave behind. He preserved himself by listening attentively to the human undertones—the hidden traces and quiet murmurs of the living, the constant hum under the officer's shrill whistle, even the moans of the dying—beneath the inhuman bombardment and then capturing what he heard in writing. And from such undertones he wove a war narrative in which the soldier appears in the guise of a builder rather than a destroyer. Blunden rescued the dignity of the individual, whom the conflict, with its diverse, insidious, indiscriminate modes of death, almost succeeded in blotting out, by largely ignoring the epic labor of killing.

The soldiers in Blunden's book preserve their humanity in the face of mass devastation by fighting back against chaos and by attempting to salvage life from a waste of death. Rather than revealing them engaged in the business of killing, Blunden elects to portray them in the act of creating: They pen maps, dispatches, and poems; they carry duckboards to line the bottoms of trenches; they dig, mine, and tunnel; they refit dugouts and shore up parapets; they string defensive wire across the front line; they arm themselves with frying pans and buckets rather than rifles. In this way Blunden turns his fellow soldiers into the hopeful architects of their own survival.

Blunden responded to no man's land in both literal and symbolic terms, each mode of understanding complementing and enriching the other. Perhaps his most powerful weapon against annihilation was his favorite poem, Edward Young's *Night Thoughts*, an eighteenth-century blank-verse meditation on death. The poem casts its shadow across Blunden's entire memoir and helps to shape its vision of the war as something to be endured not exclusively in the company of comrades, for they are too likely to betray one by dying, but also within the heavily fortified sanctuary of one's own imagination. *Night Thoughts*, which Blunden carried always in his head and often in his pocket, offered him another, more oblique way of imposing order on the battlefield:

> At every spare moment I read in Young's *Night Thoughts on Life, Death and Immortality,* and I felt the benefit of this grave and

intellectual voice, speaking out of a profound eighteenth-century calm, often in metaphor which came home to one even in a pill-box. The mere amusement of discovering lines applicable to our crisis kept me from despair.

The correspondences Blunden found between his own surround-ings and Young's "melancholy map" of an imaginary world—"The land of apparitions, empty shades! / All, all on earth, is shadow, all beyond / Is substance . . ."—sustained him even as the war's bloody maw threatened to swallow him and his comrades up. He repeated lines from Young like mantras whenever he passed certain land-marks in order to steady himself in the midst of the war's sublu-nary "ghost story." Like wiring, digging, and building, reciting *Night Thoughts* helped Blunden to impose order on the entropic forces of war, to cure him at least momentarily of his war vertigo.

For Blunden, it was the poetry of Edward Young. For a twenty-first-century helicopter pilot, it might be Antoine de Saint-Exupéry's meditations on the early days of aviation or Joseph Heller's *Catch-22*; for an infantry platoon leader, Plutarch's *Lives*; for a captain of engineers, the essays of Montaigne; for a lieutenant running a bat-talion aid station in Paktika Province, a collection of World War II poetry; for a company commander at a combat outpost in Afghan-istan, Kurt Vonnegut's *Slaughterhouse Five*. For General Wolfe, it was Thomas Gray's "Elegy Written in a Country Churchyard," which he recited to his staff on the eve of the Battle of Quebec, an-nouncing, "Gentlemen, I would rather have written those lines than take Quebec." And for Alexander the Great, it was Aristotle's annotated copy of the *Iliad*, kept together with a dagger under his pillow on campaign. Other soldiers will draw on other resources, but they must know how to tap them. Blunden's combat equipment was comparatively primitive, but his cognitive and psychological tools were superior, and he kept them honed even in the midst of combat. They are the same tools that will help today's lieutenant, a wanderer in a new no man's land, to find the way when cast into the unknown and to find a way home again.

And so the meditations of a lieutenant who fought his war a hundred years ago have become strangely apropos. Blunden dug in the same ground over and over again trying to remember how it once had been. He discovered the ways in which his experience was an echo of so many that had come before as well as the ways in which his war was different and particular. Listening, like Blunden, for the undertones, I try in what follows to offer a counterpoint to the standard-issue stories that tradition handed me and that I once so hungrily embraced, to break apart the smooth and formulaic arc from peace to war, and to accommodate myself to a terrain that seems as strange as it ever was: a no man's land peopled by ghosts yet by the living, too. War vertigo is the order of the day for a generation of soldiers who are coming home to a country as confused as they are about the violence in which they have been engaged, about the responsibilities citizens bear to soldiers and soldiers to citizens, about the fact that none of those alluring old stories seem to work very well in the long run. Perhaps, too, if I keep on revising—breaking off the old story and beginning a new one—I might, like Scheherazade postponing execution by just one more night with the promise of a tale even more wondrous than the last, ward off a fearful end.

1

BETWEEN SCYLLA AND CHARYBDIS
Coming Home

FIRST SERVICEMAN: What gives?

SECOND SERVICEMAN: Oh, my folks had a barbeque last night. Turned out to be a homecoming.

FIRST SERVICEMAN: I had one of those things. It turned out to be murder.

SECOND SERVICEMAN: Half of them were afraid if they said something they'd upset me, and the other half were afraid if I said something I'd upset them.

FIRST SERVICEMAN: Look, my friend, let's face it, nobody's going to listen to us. Why don't we take off an hour someday? You tell me about what you did, I'll tell you about what I did.

SECOND SERVICEMAN: You got it.

— *Till the End of Time* (RKO, 1946),
directed by Edward Dmytryk

DEEP IN THE CANYON OF HEROES

Has coming home from a war—even a "good war"—ever been easy? Certainly not for Homer's mistrustful Odysseus, who returns in disguise to Ithaca to slaughter the suitors who have commandeered his house and whose loyal yet equally wary wife subsequently refuses to believe he is her husband, and not some impostor, until he accurately describes the bed they long ago shared. Nor for the Chinese soldier whose lament is recorded in a Han dynasty folk song: Having gone to war at fifteen, he comes home at eighty to find everything unrecognizable. A stranger tells him he will find his old house out by the burial mounds, overgrown with trees.

Birds roost in the rafters, and forest animals scurry through what used to be the dog's door. The old soldier cooks his dinner from the grain and sunflowers growing wild in the yard, but once the meal is ready, he realizes there's no one left to serve it to him, no one with whom to share it. The soldier's homecoming is as freighted with ambivalent myths as is war itself: two different parties, each with carefully crafted stories that depend on the other's absence, suddenly collide in a no man's land that, if partly of their own making, is primarily the inevitable residue of making war.

It's easy to imagine that there's safety in numbers, that mass mobilization makes repatriation a whole lot more routine. This is not necessarily the case. After World War II, the generals and the admirals (Eisenhower, Wainwright, Nimitz, Halsey) had ticker-tape parades through New York City's Canyon of Heroes. Most of the rest of the conflict's more than fifteen million veterans just sort of drifted home. When, on the night before being demobilized at Fort Devens, Massachusetts, in January 1946, my dad was finally able to call home for the first time in a few years, his own father didn't recognize his voice: "This doesn't sound like Teddy." My dad took the train home to Boston the following day. A few days later, realizing that he had nothing to wear but his uniform, he went down to a shop in Kenmore Square to try on a suit. He didn't even recognize the guy in civilian clothes he caught sight of in the mirror.

Despite similar episodes of uncertainty and strangeness, my father's transition ended up being a reasonably smooth one. Probably the biggest factor in it was the World War II Servicemen's Readjustment Act of 1944—the GI Bill—which sent him to college, something he otherwise could not have afforded. The naturalness with which he resumed civilian life was by no means a universal experience, but our fierce nostalgia for those good old, "greatest" days tends to obscure the postwar period's complexities in a mist of patriotic confetti. As the historian Kathleen Frydl argues in *The GI Bill*, the substance and legacy of the bill itself, especially the ambivalence with which it and its veteran beneficiaries were initially regarded by a range of constituencies, have been distorted by politics and the passage of time. We are justly outraged today, for example, by news of for-profit colleges preying on veterans in order to tap into the benefits they are receiving from the modern GI Bill, but Frydl reminds us that this particular swindle was born in the late 1940s, when there were so many more potential victims to exploit. One of the fantasies contributing to the present era's confused and overwrought civil-military relationship is that every World War II service member was warmly appreciated by a grateful nation and that every veteran felt a reciprocal gratitude. It takes a contemporary observation such as this one made by the poet Wallace Stevens in a 1945 letter to recall that even that war, all encompassing as it was, could still feel somewhat abstract to a civilian at home:

> All during the war there have been very few visible signs of it here in Hartford. Occasionally, on the street, one would see a long string of young men on the way to the draft board, but that was all. We were intent on the war, yet it was far away. At first, when someone that we had known was lost, there was an extraordinary shock; later, this became something in the ordinary course of events, terrifying but inevitable.

Three years earlier, in an account of a bond rally featuring the actress Dorothy Lamour in Bangor, Maine, E. B. White noted a similar indifference to those long strings of young men: "Dorothy . . . drove off through the cheering crowd in the blood-red car, up Exchange Street, where that morning I had seen a motley little contingent of inductees shuffling off, almost unnoticed, to the blood-red war." Today, the comparatively small number of those serving makes the average citizen's relationship to war even more attenuated.

Coincidentally, the Bangor International Airport, a frequent stopover for military flights, is now home to a nonprofit organization called the Maine Troop Greeters, whose mission "is to express the Nation's gratitude and appreciation to the troops, for those going overseas for a safe return and for those returning for a joyful homecoming and to make their . . . stay in Bangor as comfortable and pleasant as possible." An army major told me that one of the greeters is known as "the hug lady" and that every soldier who has passed through Bangor knows her. Even the hardest and most jaded can't help but smile on seeing the hug lady, this officer explained: maybe it feels a bit silly and awkward to be embraced by this grandmotherly stranger, he reflected, yet no one seems immune to the effect of a hug and a homemade cookie. How grateful, I wonder, is the nation on behalf of which the Maine Troop Greeters claim to speak? In what ways should it be expressing its gratitude? Is gratitude even the proper sentiment?

THE SEA OF VARIABILITY

The soldier's readjustment has always been a difficult art. "It'll take time, I guess," an uneasy veteran tells his father in the 1946 film *Till the End of Time*. "Sure. You didn't make yourself a soldier overnight," the father responds. "You can't make yourself a civilian again overnight." I've recently been struck by the number of films that depict World War II servicemen coming home to empty houses or, even more troubling, to houses full of strangers. Hollywood could be a sublime wartime propaganda machine; nevertheless, it refused to mute the ambiguities of the veteran's homecoming. Physical and psychological obstacles to readjustment crop up in various films of the period, most notably William Wyler's *The Best Years of Our Lives*, released the same year as *Till the End of Time*. Their scenarios expose all of the uneasiness on both sides that accompanied the influx of nearly sixteen million ex-service members (or ex-heroes, as they are sometimes rather bitterly referred to on the screen) into civilian society. The simple fact that there were so many veterans—the comparatively small totals of the 4.7 million veterans of the World War I American Expeditionary Force and the 8.7 million who served in Vietnam still exceed the approximately 2.5 million veterans of the wars in Iraq and Afghanistan—made their readjustment a pervasive societal feature rather than, as it is today, a somewhat unusual spectacle.

In *Pride of the Marines* (1945) a blinded veteran played by John Garfield sits awkwardly in the living room of the house in which he used to live repeating variations on a refrain as true as it is false: "Things pretty much the same, huh?" Garfield's mantra—a mantra he wants desperately to believe—makes me think anew about a visit I made a few years ago to Walter Reed, before the facility moved to Bethesda as part of Base Realignment and Closure. I was in Washington for a series of meetings at the Pentagon, where I had never been, with various people I had never met, but the hospital was the one item on the agenda that intimidated me. If you can't sing or tell jokes or sign baseballs or heal wounds, can you ever be something other than a war tourist on a military hospital ward? Shawn, the officer responsible for coordinating my trip, assured me that we would see only those patients who had signed up to receive visitors. Shawn and I had met only the day before, but because of the way he had arranged everything over the weeks of e-mails and telephone calls preceding my visit, I already trusted him implicitly: I would go to Walter Reed.

We met three patients that day: two soldiers and a marine. One soldier's mother sat in a chair, her face the exact and exacting mirror of a son's bewilderment and pain, more difficult to look at than the injured figure lying on the bed. The marine was a lieutenant, a stranger to me yet in some ways not so different from the many lieutenants I know. He was so happy and eager to please when we walked into the room, wheeled his chair over to us with such alacrity, that I was disarmed. It felt almost as if he had been expecting us, like a figure from a Greek myth, a host doomed perpetually to await the uninvited guests who alight on his doorstep.

The lieutenant had lost his leg, and he periodically returned to the hospital for weeks and months at a time for a series of operations. The same nurse, John, had been assigned to him on each occasion, and it was clear that this relationship sustained the marine. John helped him to remember things he no longer could. "John's my guy," he said after the nurse gave him a particular word for which he had been searching. Staring at what was left of his leg, the lieutenant told me that John had also given a name to the place in which he found himself. He called it "a sea of variability."

Sitting in the car after the visit, Shawn asked me whether we had made the right decision. "I didn't say anything before, because you had a job to do," he added, and then he told me his story. In Kuwait he had been in a tent into which a fellow soldier had thrown a grenade. The blast from the grenade sent fragments all around him, even through the family photographs he had hung up by his bunk. Shawn and the soldiers near him were wounded; the air force officer who had been next to him later died from his injuries. "I had to deal with the fact that everything wasn't the same, that it never would be, and that that's okay." This is the "heavy reckoning" of which Shakespeare wrote: the chaos of "all those legs and arms and heads, chopped off in a battle"—the unassimilable, ungovernable aftermath of war. For Shawn, accepting irrevocable change as a consequence of war was the necessary prelude to learning how to adjust to the sea of variability and to achieving some kind of new equilibrium in such an elastic state.

Violence works deep transformations in even the most self-aware soldier. Combat ages a veteran prematurely: sometimes the evidence is physical, while often it manifests itself in less tangible ways, in a certain gravity and presence, perhaps. After a year and a half fighting in Mexico under what he called the "Tropicle Sun," Ulysses S. Grant looked around to find too many of his friends wounded or dead. "At this rate," he wrote to his future wife, Julia Dent, "I will soon be old." "So you see," he observed later in the same letter, "it is not so easy to get out of the wars as it is to get into them." Navigating the volatile world of war, the soldier finds a powerful fantasy in the idea that somewhere else time stands still. Rich with narrative and dramatic potential, this fantasy has provided fodder for countless books and films. Of course things don't stay quite the same at home.

The 1946 Paramount noir *The Blue Dahlia* offers an especially painful version of the veteran's welcome home. Johnny Morrison, a navy lieutenant commander played by Alan Ladd, returns to Los Angeles from flying Liberators in the South Pacific knowing that his young son has died in his absence. He finds his wife, Helen (Doris Dowling), not grieving but hosting a party in her swanky bungalow. After being greeted at the door by a drunken woman who announces to the crowd with some amazement, "Helen's got a husband," Johnny has to break up an embrace between his wife and another man. "You've got the wrong lipstick on, Mister," Morrison tells the man (Howard Da Silva) before socking him in the jaw. It is only when Johnny sarcastically asks Helen whether he ought to apologize for his behavior that the real venom emerges: "Apologize, darling, but you don't have to. You're a hero. A hero can get away with anything." And when he subsequently tries to wrest a drink away from her, Helen snarls, "Take your paws off me. Maybe you've learned to like hurting people."

Helen's attack typifies one of the suspicions frequently voiced in these films: that the veteran has grown accustomed to violence and may even enjoy it. Sterling war records often provoke ambiguity in postwar cinema: routinely investigated by law enforcement officials and others, they are subsequently invoked as evidence of good character, competence, or trustworthiness even as they raise concerns that the erstwhile serviceman has developed a habitual reliance on violence to solve his problems. By proving a veteran's ability to kill, a service record sometimes makes him a likely suspect in violent crimes at home. Drifting through Anytown, U.S.A., in search of work or a new start, the mysterious veteran easily becomes a prime suspect in crimes otherwise attributable to uncomfortably familiar (and frequently upstanding) members of the community.

In the case of *The Blue Dahlia*, Helen's unfounded resentment leads her to project onto Johnny an attitude that might be called the presumption of heroes: namely, that everything at home will be just as they left it—maybe even better than they left it—no matter how much they dread otherwise and no matter how much war might have changed them in the interim. The *New Yorker* correspondent A. J. Liebling reveals the defensive urgency of this desire in his discussion of "a favorite army fantasy: what civilian life will be like after the war." He provides an example of the game as played by some airmen in North Africa who were being moved to a new field in 1943:

> Somebody said, "I hear they're going to start us here and let us hack our way through to South Africa."
>
> Somebody else began a descant on a favorite army fantasy: what civilian life will be like after the war. "I bet if my wife gives me a piece of steak," he said, "I'll say to her, 'What the hell is this? Give me stew.'"
>
> Another one said, "I bet she'll be surprised when you jump into bed with all your clothes on."
>
> The delicacy of their speculations diminished from there on.

The humor here is based on a profound conviction that war permanently alters the combatant. In the face of that radical change, home-front stability becomes an essential part of the fiction that sustains a soldier amid the disintegration of war and helps to allay what is in some, but not all, instances an unwarranted anxiety about the impermanence of relationships left behind. This aspect of homecoming finds one of its earliest incarnations in Homer's *Odyssey*, where it is manifested in the opportunistic suitors who use Odysseus's household—and its staff of serving women—as their own and compete with one another to take the absent king's place in Penelope's bed. Odysseus's response—slaughtering them all—is only the most extreme expression of the rage of the betrayed, while Penelope's absolute fidelity over so many years embodies the not-quite-believable dream of every absent soldier. Odysseus's story illuminates the ways in which home itself can come to seem an unfamiliar no man's land for the returning veteran.

CHAOS COME AGAIN

When confronted by Homer with the duration of Odysseus's absence—a decade at war and a second struggling against the petulant gods to reach home—we know that we are being asked to contemplate an outsize epic time. Yet in its stretching of the hero's journey to the limits of plausibility, the *Odyssey* neatly captures the distortion characteristic of wartime. Time moves slowly for the soldier, who comes home to find that normal processes—the growth of children, for example—seem to have accelerated in his or her absence. One father deployed for long stretches during the last decade confessed to me that he returned to teenagers he no longer felt he knew or fully understood. Sometimes, of course, wartime's distortion has a positive result, as in the case of Adam and his wife, who "still feel like newlyweds after six years of marriage."

War exaggerates the feeling that military time is being either distended or compressed, but even in peace military life tends to reconstitute time, a phenomenon encapsulated in the phrase "hurry up and wait." New soldiers must learn afresh how to measure their lives. One idiosyncratic officer I know used to calibrate his active-duty days according to something he called "time out of the greens," those hours he spent in civilian clothes. The army uses the term "BOG:Dwell ratio" to describe the way it apportions soldiers' time. BOG, an abbreviation for "boots on the ground," refers to deployments, while "dwell" signifies "dwell time," or the period spent at home station. The latter has become something of a fixation in the army. Officers with especially long dwell times tended to attract the attention of the army's personnel representatives, and this single factor has effectively become a shortcut to judging the value of an officer's contributions to the force. The concept of dwell time remains an organizational preoccupation even as opportunities for deploying dwindle.

This isn't the way the army alone measures time; it's the way I've come to measure it, too. The military chart used to project deployment cycles is called a patch chart or a horse blanket. For years now I have been weaving my own horse blanket of the mind, onto which I map the comings and goings of the officers I know. Their pre- or post-deployment leave often brings them to New York City, and it is not unusual for me to find myself in a midtown bar or a downtown restaurant listening to stories of combat tours just ended, learning about plans for the unit "train-ups" to which they will shortly return, or responding to a range of hopes, fears, and questions about life after the army.

I didn't become fully conscious of the degree to which I had been transformed by this system of timekeeping until I reread *Othello* in 2011, a decade after 9/11, in a Shakespeare course full of juniors and seniors. This particular tragedy has never been one of my touchstones. I've always found unpersuasive the ease with which Iago warps Othello, who is no insubstantial man, to his purposes. But when, on the first day of class, I showed the cadets a preliminary reading list and solicited additions, *Othello* was one of the first suggestions. Given their chosen profession, one student insisted, this was a play they "ought to read." So we did, and *Othello* became another of those texts altered for me by the experience of reading it in wartime.

In a very particular sense, Othello lives the life that my students, schooled so well by the last decade, have grown used to imagining for themselves and that I have imagined for them. The withdrawal from Iraq and gradual diminution of our commitment in Afghanistan notwithstanding, the rhythm of this particular calendar has been so deeply ingrained in military culture that it has become only gradually possible for its novitiates—to say nothing of many of its fully vested members—to envision a different kind of postwar existence even as they long for it. The deceleration of what soldiers call OPTEMPO, the pace at which operations move, is simultaneously craved and feared. Not so long ago I heard a senior officer tell a group of new lieutenants, "Make no mistake, you will lead soldiers in combat." Maybe. But there's no guarantee. And as I told a new class of freshmen at the beginning of the spring semester in 2014, they will need to consider a whole range of possible futures, paths denied to all those war commuters who came before them over the last dozen years. Nevertheless, the prospect of an army in which they might find it more difficult than their predecessors did to gain war experience is especially daunting to prospective lieutenants indoctrinated by an army still invested in the idea of combat experience as the paramount validation, a force that tends to devalue other types of military endeavors that nevertheless serve the national interest.

An anxiety occasioned by an acknowledgment that the wars of the last dozen years are essentially over and a need to believe in the enduring possibility of meaningful service can be seen in many cadets and officers. The content and significance of a contribution that doesn't look like fighting are difficult for them to envision. Where will today's soldiers, conditioned since the inception of their careers by war, derive identity and find fulfilling work in a future without war or one perhaps characterized by a very different mode of fighting?

The sixteenth-century Venetian Republic didn't have a very sophisticated force-generation model; Othello's BOG:Dwell ratio was not especially kind. At the beginning of the play, Shakespeare's general has been in Venice only nine months when the Turkish naval threat to the Italian city-state's interests forces him to sail for Cyprus with his new wife. Since the age of seven, Othello's life has been a relentless series of "battles, sieges," "most disastrous chances," and "hair-breadth scapes." In a speech to which no soldier who imagines one day finding love can fail to respond, Othello disputes the charge that he has somehow bewitched Desdemona: "She loved me for the dangers I had passed, / And I loved her that she did pity them. / This only is the witchcraft I have used." Desdemona, like Virgil's Dido before her, falls in love with a man after listening to him tell the story of his wars.

Othello's emotional volatility and capacity for violence, tragically realized in his eventual killing of Desdemona, prompted the class to consider the ways in which war might shape the individual. One thoughtful cadet speculated about his own attraction to military life in ways that reminded me of all those suspicions voiced in the films of the 1940s about the violent ways of GIs: Would being a soldier irrevocably alter his nature? Or was his choice of vocation an unconscious response to impulses buried deep within? This time through the text I was struck by Othello's recognition of Desdemona's importance to him as a bulwark against the disorder in which his life has been forged: "Perdition catch my soul, / But I do love thee, and when I love thee not, / Chaos is come again." While the play is not, I continue to think, primarily an exploration of the traumas of war, I now hear in Othello's "again" a reference to the simultaneous force and fragility of domestic bonds under the strain of repeated combat tours.

To my complaint about Othello's gullibility with respect to "honest Iago," several of my students had a ready response. For them, the answer was obvious: Iago and Othello had fought together. The trust welded by that battlefield history trumped all else, even the bond between husband and wife. I'm not sure this explanation is sufficient, but the vehemence with which the cadets endorsed it seemed a key to understanding their own attitudes toward loyalty, service, and hardship. Even though Shakespeare's tragedy reveals the badge of shared experience to be a guarantor of nothing, the cadets' trust in it seemed largely undiminished by the end.

The betrayal of assumed solidarity among veterans dramatized in *Othello* likewise colors an exchange from *The Best Years of Our Lives*: Coming home to find a man he doesn't know having drinks with his wife, Dana Andrews, a former B-17 bombardier plagued by nightmares and other sources of uneasiness, spots the Honorable Service Lapel Pin—also known as the Ruptured Duck—on the other man's suit jacket and scoffs, "Another ex-serviceman, huh? Greetings, Brother. Have you had any trouble getting readjusted?" "Not in particular," replies the other man. "It's easy if you just take everything in your stride." *Othello* now seems to me a tragedy at least in part about the extreme case of a life geared to serial deployments and homecomings. This is the life—that of the war commuter—for which the future lieutenants with whom I read it conceived themselves to be preparing, the life I had grown accustomed to picturing for them, the life to which so many remain psychologically committed even if the actual map of their careers may in the end look radically different. What we all underestimated was the degree to which commuting differs from coming home.

A ROOM OF ONE'S OWN

Healing, be it physical, emotional, or both together, is among the chief labors of homecoming. It demands the capacity to reconcile past and present and to navigate a future of yet invisible contours; the ability to weave new stories when the old ones no longer hold; the ability to discover a home in no man's land. The future officers with whom I've read Homer's epics might recognize the process as that of moving from the world of the *Iliad* to that of the *Odyssey*. The war at Troy only seems endless; the clearly defined lines of battle established there disintegrate into a postwar world of unknown

enemies and uncertain limits. It is a world in which the most pedestrian and the most fantastic monsters present equally dire
threats to the assumptions by which Odysseus has defined himself
at home and abroad. In following Odysseus home to Ithaca or Aeneas from the burning city of Troy to Italy, a soldier learns essential skills: how to differentiate false anchorages from true and how
to navigate disordered space and measure disobedient time.

It is this imaginative capacity that might help to counteract
what one lieutenant I know experienced as a sense of post-deployment
disintegration. "I went to a few weddings," Sean wrote when I asked
him how he had used his leave on returning home after a year in
Afghanistan commanding a detachment of troops who handle
military working dogs trained in mine detection. But these reassuring rituals were not enough: "I was so fragmented I found it hard
to get into the swing of things. This has happened from time to
time in my life, but it was especially strong when I returned home."
Sean's "solution" over the years for the problem of fragmentation
has been to return to the Benedictine monks who educated him at
the St. Louis Priory School. Sean's description of his retreat to the
monastery reminded me of Pico Iyer's essay "Chapels." Iyer, who
also goes on periodic retreats to a Benedictine hermitage, defines a
chapel as any place "where we hear something and nothing, ourselves and everyone else, a silence that is not the absence of noise
but the presence of something much deeper: the depth beneath
our thoughts." That's not a kind of silence easy to find in a war
zone, but it is also increasingly difficult to find it at home, in an
environment defined by connectivity, where, in Iyer's words, "Times
Square is with us everywhere." Arguing for our ever-present need
of chapels, Iyer explains, "We've always had to have quietness and
stillness to undertake our journeys into battle, or just the tumult
of the world. How can we act in the world, if we haven't had the
time and chance to find out who we are and what the world and
action might be?" Circumstances have led me to read Iyer's reference to battle in literal-minded fashion. Indeed, I don't know why

it should still sometimes surprise me that my own chapel has become Grant's Tomb, located on Morningside Heights, in uptown Manhattan. It is there that a silent solitude born of widespread indifference to an old soldier helps me to understand the significance of my commitments to new soldiers.

Sean has tried to relax on tropical vacations, but they don't provide what he needs: "the same sort of rest and centered reflection that I get in the stark, earwax-yellow walls of the monastery." Of his latest sojourn, he writes, "I planned on staying just a few days and going home . . . for New Year's Eve, but I ended up staying a full week. Not the most exciting type of redeployment, but . . . the priory is one of the only safe places I know; it is the only place where I know how to remember who I am and what I want to become." Remembering who you are and what you want to become isn't easy under any conditions, but military life tends to make the project peculiarly difficult. What Sean wants to do is to write. He's harbored this dream for a long time, and we met for many hours during his senior year at West Point to review his notebooks and journals. Sustaining his goal and cultivating a creative life in the army remain constant challenges. The military celebrates the value of reflection, especially in the context of the resiliency training devised in response to the alarming incidence of PTSD, yet it is a culture that remains deeply uncomfortable with sustained bouts of meditation. Fundamentally biased toward action, it pays lip service to the value of reflection while remaining uncomfortable with such invisible, unpredictable activity.

The ancient Roman poet Horace, who was briefly and ingloriously a soldier, insisted on a fundamental incompatibility of military service and the deeply imaginative, deliberative life in an ode (2.7) dedicated to his old friend Pompey, with whom he had served in the defeated army of Brutus during Rome's civil wars. From the comfort of his Sabine farm, Horace recounts how, throwing down his shield at the battle, he was whisked away to safety in a cloud by Mercury, protector of poets. The ode parodies the traditional epic deus ex machina: "But swift Mercury bore me aloft in my panic into a dense cloud; you a returning wave carried back again into the seething straits of war." In Homer the cloud is usually only a temporary stay of execution for the warrior; in Horace it succeeds in permanently removing the poet from the battlefield to the safety of his rural retreat.

Thanks largely to Wilfred Owen, Horace has become synonymous in the minds of many readers with the phrase *dulce et decorum est*, an uncomplicated expression of the patriotic ideal that it is sweet and fitting to die for one's country: Owen calls this the "old lie." Yet in this ode to Pompey, Horace manifests no illusions about the unalloyed sweetness and propriety of a battlefield death. "With you," he tells his erstwhile comrade, "I experienced Philippi and swift flight, a shield ill-left behind, when virtue was broken and threatening armies shamefully bit the dust." There is no necessary connection articulated here between the warrior's exploits and the poet's lines. Horace severs the worlds of poetry and soldiering. Cowardice—literally running away—liberates him into poetry and all its imaginative energies, while fate sends Pompey back to the battle and subsequently into defeat and exile. Martial vice becomes poetic virtue, and Horace never regrets his choice. Only, it seems, by turning his back on war can Horace begin to make art, his poetry a vocation the other life would not permit. Meanwhile, Pompey has been cheated altogether out of some other life, his steadfastness on the battlefield having been recompensed with exile in that second no man's land into which war so often deposits its survivors.

Some soldiers may find solace in retreat, be it a brief visit to a monastery or a permanent idyll as a gentleman-farmer drinking good wine and reminiscing. Others may attempt to "come home" in a psychological sense by returning to the actual field of battle: the great Gettysburg reunion of 1913, for example, in which Union and

Confederate veterans participated; the Normandy excursions undertaken by so many World War II veterans; or the more recent phenomenon of "peace" or "friendship" tours to Vietnam made by Americans who fought there. These pilgrimages are the modern echoes of an ancient trope that crosses cultures. The T'ang dynasty poet Wang Changling, for example, imagines one such return in "Song from the Borders." The scene is Lintao, near the Great Wall, where the poem's speaker recalls a battle that took place years before. Now, as his horse drinks in the river, all is quiet: dust obscures past as well as present while a thicket of bleached bones marks the landscape. Going over the battleground again allows a veteran to reprise the original experience at a remove and thereby to exert some kind of imaginative control over it. In this sense returning to the field of battle produces a reaction akin to the one Wordsworth associated with the process of composing poetry about scenes of nature: the voluntary recollection of emotions once involuntarily felt. In revisiting Tintern Abbey with his sister, Dorothy, the poet was able to "catch / The language of [his] former heart" in her purely sensory response to the thrilling scene. The soldier who willingly returns to the scene of battle, perhaps with siblings or children, might likewise find a way to wrest experience from fate or chance and to refashion it into a kind of story whose end she now knows.

Returning to the field of battle as a noncombatant is an option as yet unavailable to Sean and other veterans of the wars in Iraq and Afghanistan. Sometimes monuments at home can serve a similar healing purpose, as I was reminded on Memorial Day 2013, when I ended up at the Vietnam Veterans Memorial on the Mall in Washington, D.C. Many of the tributes and tokens left there asserted a kinship across wars. Perhaps the POW/MIA symbol so much in evidence that day on flags, placards, and motorcycle-club patches has endured long after the end of Vietnam in part because it expresses the fact that some of those who survived the conflict found themselves adrift in no man's land when they returned. It was clear from the messages deposited at the base of the wall that

Vietnam veterans see themselves, and the same potential for alienation, in the veterans of Iraq and Afghanistan.

The Vietnam Veterans Memorial was dedicated in 1982. Several years earlier, in March 1974, as the war was winding down, William Greider reported in *The Washington Post* on a banquet that was intended "to be a straightforward, if belated, tribute to all the millions of Vietnam veterans, but somehow the event evoked, not so much glory, but the grief that still lingers in some sectors of American life." The banquet, sponsored by the National Honor Vietnam Veterans Committee at the Washington Hilton, was "half-empty," while an acrimonious Senate hearing was full of veterans "choking on their bitterness," full of questions for the congressmen and VA representatives on hand. Greider's discussion of the real significance of that day for the bereft veterans of 1974 is instructive today, as the country enters another postwar period in which so many distractions inhibit the impulse to remember: "The old anger, the old pain came back briefly to haunt the nation's capital yesterday, a melancholy reminder of Vietnam, the war everyone wants to forget." Everyone would like to forget the wars with which our century opened, too, all those commemorations, tributes, and public service announcements notwithstanding. The power of the memorial, known informally as the Wall, owes at least in part to its bold acknowledgment of that war's deep ambiguities and betrayals: the names say everything that need be said. Visiting the wall, I was reminded of those questions that came to me from the mud cave in Afghanistan: "I wonder what will come of this generation when it's all said and done. Where do we go from here? How will our country remember the fallen and the broken? Will it ever be enough?"

In his book *English Villages*, Edmund Blunden describes the war memorials built on England's village greens after World War I, on which "are inscribed the names of those who died, in His Majesty's service, during the war of 1914–1918."

They are remembered not as soldiers or sailors, but as some of our parishioners, this one clever at figures, that one given to practical jokes at the bakery, another who was to have married the beautiful Alice C. They have all come back to us. They left their rifles and bayonets, their belts and bandoliers (which they took much pride in) at the place appointed, and are always somewhere about our houses or farms, getting on with the things that in the end mattered to them and us.

Divested of the weapons of war, the dead soldiers of Blunden's imagination return to the mundane arts of peace that characterized their lives: farming, baking, brewing, and bookkeeping. The wartime alienation of the soldier from civil life is here overcome through a ghostly return to everyday occupations and relationships. As the historian Jay Winter suggests in *Sites of Memory, Sites of Mourning: The Great War in European Cultural History*, the solidity of memorials like those that Blunden describes, anchored as they were in tradition and convention, helped to "heal" the sense of loss dominating Europe after World War I in ways that modernity's "multi-faceted sense of dislocation, paradox, and the ironic" never could. Where in an age of dislocation can one find a similar salve?

It was for a place of healing and consolation that my friend Joel was searching when we visited the 9/11 Memorial in New York City soon after its opening in the fall of 2011. During almost seven years of living in New York City, I had managed not to visit Ground Zero. My ambivalence about memorials owes to their tendency to oversimplify historical complexity, to filter the past through contemporary prejudices. And the unfinished Freedom Tower, looming over the memorial as it ascended toward its monstrously symbolic height of 1,776 feet, the airport-like security checkpoint, and the giant flags that ring the construction site, each one bigger than the next, in many ways confirmed my worst fears. But the cavernous subterranean fountains, dug into the footprints of the fallen towers, tell a rather different story, and the rush of water drowns out all other distractions, including that of war itself.

"I went carrying the two unit patches I wore on each deployment, planning to leave them behind," Joel, who served in Iraq, explained. "Seeing the names of these men and women arranged alongside their friends and coworkers prompted me to take the patches with me when we left. This was not some memorial for Iraq or Afghanistan. There will be a time and place for war memorials. That morning, walking around those names was the first time I really appreciated how distinct the events of September 11 were." Joel realized that the country doesn't yet have a place to memorialize his experience. Hoping to find in the 9/11 Memorial a kind of chapel, Joel had conflated the World Trade Center site with his own battlefields. Once there, he could not help but recognize the difference and his own continuing lack. Carrying his patches, he continues to search for the right place to lay them to rest.

EASY RIDERS

This visit was only the latest expression of Joel's search. Having left the army, anticipating his first year of law school, Joel found no space that satisfactorily bridged the realms of war and home. Without a narrative linking past, present, and future, he had spent the previous summer on an odyssey across the country in whose name he had been sent to fight. My connection to this journey began in the summer of 2010, with a text message instructing me to report to a sports bar in midtown Manhattan, where I would find the three members of Joel's expedition recharging before the next day's stage. Although I was meeting two of them for the first time, conversation was natural and easy even over the roar of the bar. Dan, lean and earnest, spoke of his last assignment in the army and added, with a distant, intense gaze I've now seen many times, that his old unit had recently deployed again. "But," he said, looking right at me, with the odd combination of determination and wistfulness veterans often bring to postwar life, "I'm doing this."

"This" was an almost four-thousand-mile bicycle ride from Maine to Southern California that would take the trio most of the summer. The cyclists—Dan, Pete, and Joel—graduated from West Point in 2005. Among them, they have five combat tours in Iraq or Afghanistan; at the time of the ride all three had just left the army. Dan went on to attend business school, Joel law school, while Pete, undecided at the time about what he would do next, subsequently took a job in the pharmaceutical industry. When we met up in New York City, they had just finished day five of their transcontinental ride. In the weeks after our meeting, I kept up with their progress through intermittent texting and by reading their blog, where they posted pictures of each stage: stymied in midtown Manhattan traffic; in front of Walter Reed in Washington, D.C.; looking a little road weary under a historic marker announcing that the state of Ohio has been, among other things, home to eight U.S. presidents; sunbaked and smiling in the high altitude beside a sign marked "Continental Divide."

They were riding to raise money for wounded soldiers attempting to make the transition back to civilian life. The importance of this cause in the eyes of combat veterans with friends and classmates among the wars' casualties was obvious. But the trip had other, less explicit, motivations. It marked their passage from a highly regimented mode of living to one whose outlines were not quite clear. After almost a decade in uniform (cadet gray followed by army green), the three men found themselves on the cusp of new lives, even as they were still trying to make sense of the old ones. This restlessness owed in part to their release from the structures of army life, but it also suggested the degree to which they needed to carve out some space in which to recollect (borrowing

Wordsworth's formulation) the previous overflow of powerful feelings as well as to mark with something solid and enduring the losses they had suffered.

I've known Joel since he studied English at West Point, and we have kept up a steady correspondence ever since. On his second tour in Iraq, he had been struck anew by the energizing sense of "focus" and the "no-nonsense feeling of purpose that takes over" in a combat theater. Meditating on the narratives of travelers in the Middle East such as T. E. Lawrence and Wilfred Thesiger, Joel confessed that he had once envied "their proximity to 'real life' and . . . 'real experiences' . . . Now," he reported from Iraq, "I feel I get to live the life of meaningful decisions again." To the untrained ear, this might sound like naive boyish enthusiasm: war as the ultimate adventure. But it isn't. With its clearly delineated units and chains of command, the army cultivates a deep sense of responsibility in those who are paying attention. Joel, like so many of his peers, discovered authentic experience in making "meaningful decisions" on which others rely. That is what so appeals to him about the sensibilities of a desert explorer like Thesiger, who valued some of the same things about a life of extremity. "Men trusted me and obeyed my orders," Thesiger writes near the beginning of *Arabian Sands*, his account of several treks in the 1940s across what was then known as the Arabian Desert's Empty Quarter in charge of an expedition party. "I was responsible for their safety. I was often tired and thirsty, sometimes frightened and lonely, but I had tasted freedom and a way of life from which there could be no recall."

Desert travel compelled "a life unhampered by possessions" for Thesiger, "since everything that was not a necessity was an encumbrance." There is hardship to such an existence but also immense clarity. I think it is a mistake to assume that the intensity of wartime service derives purely from proximity to danger and death. It seems more properly to owe to the paradoxical comfort and freedom—"a freedom," according to Thesiger, "unattainable in civilization"—of being able to distinguish between necessity and encumbrance as well as to the fact that relationships forged in the context of such heightened stimulation, connections first established in training through a shared imagining of suffering, have a force and simplicity more difficult to realize in everyday life. As had been the case on Thesiger's desert crossing, there was "a comradeship inherent in the circumstances" for Joel, Dan, and Pete.

Once they rejoin the ranks of civilian society, soldiers can find themselves forever searching for that same intensity of experience elsewhere, attracted to a life of risk, perhaps, or prey to nostalgic longings, unless they figure out a way to meet the world without the armor to which they have grown accustomed. "I don't want to be one of those guys," Pete insisted at the bar, as we contemplated his past and whatever lay ahead; he knew that he didn't want to live a life of perpetual questing in a postwar no man's land rehashing old war stories. As he was preparing to leave the army, Joel had shared with me a similar urge to make his next career as meaningful as his first: "Friday marks my last day in the army, and I hope I can someday find a career grounded as closely to purpose and duty as the military."

But the rules of engagement back home are different. Soon after his return, Joel had to figure out how to live the "temporary life" that would be his until he began law school the following fall. He found himself in Abilene, Texas, his "home of record," occupying his old room, leafing through his English course books, and staring at his autobiography on the wall: diploma, commissioning certificate, proclamations, and photographs from his Army football games. "I sit," he wrote to me, "in a museum of myself in another life—THAT other life." The realization that he had left the army "hit" Joel twice: once when he got his final farewell gift and a handshake from the sergeant with whom he had worked most closely; and again, weeks later, at a reception for prospective students at his law school. Having spent an inordinate amount of time figuring out what to wear, accustomed to being in rooms where, in important ways, everyone looked the same, he arrived to discover his difference: "all at once I was decidedly an individual . . . I could have shown up with a beard. I could have long hair and put my hands in my pockets. All the little things . . . added to a larger whole: you're on your own now . . . It was a very lonely morning."

And so to me anyway, it seemed entirely natural that before embracing his new life, Joel needed to bicycle across the country with some friends who would intuit his mood. Given the strangeness that attends even the warmest welcomes, is it any wonder that coming home can make a soldier want to hit the road all over again? Sometimes the goal is to return to war, but more often it is simply to keep moving, to embark on another journey. Popular culture tends to pathologize this instinct. Witness Martin Sheen's demoralized captain Willard in the opening minutes of *Apocalypse Now*, holed up in a Saigon hotel room, kissing with the end of a lit cigarette a photograph of his wife and pondering the emptiness of home as the snapshot sizzles: "When I was here, I wanted to be there. When I was there, all I could think of was getting back into the jungle." Lieutenant Larson expressed a similar feeling in his blog in response to the question of how it felt to be back home: "Yes, it's great to be around all the things that you are deprived of in Afghanistan . . . But the truth is that after six months of recuperation and rest, I'm ready to go back. Needless to say, my friends have quite the look of incredulity on their faces when I say that."

Joel's attitude is emphatically different from Larson's or Willard's even if it shares the same underlying recognition of enduring dislocation. "I now understand that bicycle trip as my need to not slow down—to see more, do more," he wrote just as he was about to embark on his final year of law school. "Somewhere along the way from civilian to cadet to officer, I acquired this persistent desire to accomplish the next task or tackle the next obstacle." Although he is "very happy" with both his chosen career, which has a different kind of structure and demands different kinds of "results," and his return home to Texas, Joel recognizes his susceptibility to nostalgia: "On the one hand, it is what I asked for. On the other, it is what

I got without appreciating what it would mean. Do not read this as a deep, enduring sadness. Quite the opposite. It is not a bad thing, it is just different." He is still learning how to pace himself, to re-wire his energies, yet he doesn't anticipate that the ungovernable open-throttle approach inculcated by military training will ever fully release its hold on him: "So, the bike ride was a way for me to subconsciously avoid the inevitable, to give it my all in a unique, demanding, and measurable way one last time. Or, at least, until the next time." I'm grateful for Joel's self-awareness. It is a decid-edly toxic romance that leaves its protagonist unable to find suste-nance in the very way of life he has been sent to defend.

THE ROAD TO ITHACA

The mood of impermanence Joel identifies also lurks at the heart of Odysseus's homecoming. Odysseus's war, like the one Joel, Sean, and millions of others have been fighting over the last decade, was a "long war." Having endured ten years of it, Odysseus returns to the island of Ithaca only after another lost decade. His family reunion is violent and mistrustful, while his ultimate hap-piness is clouded by a prophecy of further wandering. To get back to Ithaca, Odysseus and his crew must endure a series of trials, which he alone survives. The arduousness of coming home is perhaps no-where more clearly emblematized than in the monstrous figures of Scylla and Charybdis, the rocky crag and the yawning whirlpool between which their ship must pass. The enchantress Circe warns Odysseus that it will be impossible to weather this passage without losing some of his men; by the time he reaches Ithaca, Odysseus has lost all of them. In this respect his story also touches on one of the fundamental anxieties preoccupying today's military culture, that of leaving someone behind.

In the end, Odysseus's concern for his men is eclipsed by the epic's emphasis on the individual hero's struggle: the loss of his companions becomes yet another item in the leader's catalog of misfortunes. How many lieutenants and captains have told me that in the absence of transparent measures of victory, nothing matters more than bringing everyone home? Because this is an impossible standard to maintain in combat, the inability to keep everyone alive can sometimes derail a young leader. Craig Mullaney's memoir, *The Unforgiving Minute*, hinges on the loss of a soldier in a firefight, a loss Mullaney regarded as a personal failure: "I had failed to bring every man in my platoon home safely . . . Was that failure redeemable?" A group of Vietnam veterans once asked me to help them understand Craig's attitude and the fact that the loss of one soldier seemed to destroy him. They had lost soldiers on patrol every night and carried on regardless. What expectations, they demanded from the perspective of having served in a war with an altogether different tolerance for loss, have been created for today's young officers?

Their questions forced me to think about the ways in which our attitudes regarding casualties have changed over the last forty years. Have technological advances or the methods by which these wars have been fought (with an emphasis on force protection) made possible our fixation on the individual life? And if soldiers today are less accepting of loss, might it also be the case that society at large is somehow more accepting, despite our exclamations of dismay, because we employ an all-volunteer force and calculate that soldiers have, after all, signed up for whatever it is they get? The warrior's impulse to leave no one behind, almost certainly as old as war itself, transcends epochs, cultures, and nations. But it was in fact the war in Vietnam, with its indeterminacy and deception, its obsession with body counts on both sides, that seems to have turned a battlefield impulse into a national preoccupation. Those veterans who did not understand Craig could never have allowed the loss of one soldier to distract them at the time, even if everyone at home could count the bodies, which the wall tallies for our ongoing inspection. Today we identify the fallen individually and compile statistics to reveal, for example, "the deadliest month" of the war in Iraq or Afghanistan in part because those numbers, too large though they may be, are low enough to comprehend.

Odysseus lives in a world rife with loss; the deaths of his comrades seem almost a matter of course. When Homer's hero returns to Ithaca, things are not, of course, exactly how he left them. Although normally characterized by a restraint born of cunning, Odysseus's career is punctuated by occasional explosions of violence that seem to have an almost compensatory character: his bloodthirsty nighttime raid with Diomedes in the *Iliad*; his grisly, boastful blinding of the Cyclops in the *Odyssey*; but most of all the grotesque bloodletting in his own palace. When he learns of the suitors who feast there and the servingwomen who have become their concubines, he drenches his own house with their blood. His loyal old nurse, Eurycleia, discovers him surrounded by the "pooling blood" of "slaughtered corpses." He seems to her more beast than man (in Robert Fagles's translation):

> splattered with bloody filth like a lion that's devoured
> some ox of the field and lopes home, covered with blood,
> his chest streaked, both jaws glistening, dripping red—
> a sight to strike terror. So Odysseus looked now,
> splattered with gore, his thighs, his fighting hands.

The suitors having been dispatched, Odysseus initiates his son in the rites of killing by ordering him to execute the disloyal women: Telemachus strings them up from the rafters. Then, only after the ritual purification of the palace, can Odysseus resume his old domestic relations.

Penelope, it should be remembered, maintains her reserve with Odysseus, unsure after so long whether this man who has returned to her house is in fact her husband. A byword for fidelity, Penelope evinces a love ostensibly unquestioned and unquestioning; nevertheless, she also reveals deep unease at his return: "her heart / in

turmoil, torn . . . should she keep her distance, / probe her husband? Or rush up to the man at once / and kiss his head and cling
to both his hands?" Penelope chooses the former course and suffers
condemnation by the callow Telemachus for her seeming coldness.
Not before certain "secret signs" are exchanged between his parents, Penelope tells her son, will she know for certain that it is
Odysseus who has returned to her. When Odysseus passes the test
she gives him about moving the rooted olive-tree bed he built so
long ago, Penelope at last accepts that this stranger is in fact her
husband. She then admits to him that she has always feared the arrival of some man claiming to be Odysseus—the same plot of im-
posture fuels *The Return of Martin Guerre* and *Sommersby*—and
it is only after their physical reunion and a night spent reveling
"in each other's stories" that they can be said to be truly reunited.

That it is the exchange of stories, even more than their shared
sexual enjoyment, that effects their reunion is significant. Homer
depicts as well as anyone the role of the war story in the soldier's
successful repatriation: Odysseus hears his own story several times
on the way home, just as Virgil's Aeneas beholds his history, the
destruction of Troy, engraved on the walls at Carthage. When he
tells his story to Penelope, Odysseus can finally be said to have left
no man's land and come home. Their seemingly endless wander-
ings allow both Odysseus and Aeneas time to tell their stories, but
part of the challenge faced by today's war commuter is that there
is too little opportunity to weave a narrative. Jason, the young marine officer who goes missing in action in Lea Carpenter's 2013
novel, *Eleven Days*, contrasts his own experience with that of the
veterans who returned from World War II by boat. "Those crossings," Jason explains, "allowed the soldiers time to connect to
others who had fought. They had time to talk about what they had
been through, where they had been, what they had seen. I bet they
sat on those boats and they told stories. And then they came home,
and most of them didn't say a thing . . . After Vietnam, we airlifted
our guys out; they came home on planes. A few hours, and they

went from a jungle to a Dairy Queen. They didn't have the chance to talk. They didn't have a chance to share their stories." Jason wonders whether he will be able to catch what he calls "the slow boat home to civilian life."

Of course there remains a shadow over the reunion on Ithaca, a shadow that owes in part to Odysseus's brutalizing intimacy with violence and death. This is a history that must be expiated by a sacrifice to the vengeful Poseidon, whom Odysseus has offended. If he wants to die peacefully one day, an old man in his bed, Odysseus must leave home again. He must make a pilgrimage to a nation ignorant of the sea, where the inhabitants mistake the oar he carries for a farming implement. And there he must bury the oar in tribute to Poseidon. Skeptical, perhaps, of such an ending, Dante added another chapter to the Ithacan's story in canto 26 of the *Inferno*. There Odysseus (called Ulysses by Dante) reports setting sail once again from his island with "only those few souls / who stayed true when the rest deserted me." Together they will "experience the far-flung world / and the failings and felicities of mankind." In Dante's medieval coda we encounter the final irony of the warrior's repeated betrayal by the homecoming that is supposed to bring him peace but instead launches him into a second no man's land. Odysseus once feigned madness in order to avoid having to join the Greek army embarking for Troy; Ulysses has become so inured to the condition of travel that he cannot resist the urge—the "lust," in John Ciardi's translation—to leave everything behind all over again. They roamed the world's oceans, Ulysses reports, "till the sea closed over us and the light was gone."

Recalling Ulysses's late-life departure, another soldier I know explained, "Home is like finding a pair of shoes from your childhood. Even returning from a deployment to your own house can feel that way. It's too tight, too constricting." It was Dante's embellishment that Tennyson, unwilling to believe that the warrior-wanderer could endure the "still hearth" of home, seized upon in "Ulysses," which likewise discards the ideal of an enduring domestic peace in favor of a scenario of perpetual adventure, in which the hero's journey seems entirely voluntary. "I am a part of all that I have met," Tennyson's Ulysses explains, "Yet all experience is an arch wherethro' / Gleams that untravell'd world whose margin fades / For ever and forever when I move." After Homer, the story of Odysseus changes in a subtle and an important way. In Dante and Tennyson, Ulysses and his comrades set sail again because they cannot bear to stay home. The uncertainty of no man's land forever eclipses the stability of home.

The subsequent emphasis on the epilogue to Ulysses's story suggests a cultural shift toward an understanding of the warrior as permanently alienated from society, as much by his own proclivities as by any specific response from the home front. Joel, Dan, and Pete displayed a restlessness I've seen in many returning combat veterans, but they don't seem to be resigned to it as a habitual condition. Ultimately, they strike me as voyagers of a different kind.

In the sports bar, as the national anthem blared from one of the televisions broadcasting the NBA Finals, they looked at one another and smiled at their instinct, even here, to come to attention, as they had done automatically for so many years. When the singer concluded with a rousing pregame "Come on!" we all shrugged our shoulders. Pete smiled and said, "Yeah, that's the way I always remember it." The three men's epic journey, bridging as it did the community of warriors they had left behind and the civilian society they were poised to rejoin, seemed not a commitment to a peripatetic existence but a way of learning how to come home on terms they can sustain. This neglected, underemphasized art requires stamina and patience. It may even require periodic pilgrimages. History suggests that the warriors most skilled in the arts of war might well be the least adept at the very different art of coming home. "I know that it is socially acceptable to write about war as an unmitigated horror," A. J. Liebling mused after World War II, "but subjectively at least, it was not true, and you can feel its pull on men's memories at the maudlin reunions of war divisions. They mourn for their dead, but also for war."

TO THE BANKS OF THE GANGES

There are perhaps few more sensational cases of a real-world soldier incapable of coming home than that of Alexander the Great. When your ambition is to conquer the world, I suppose turning around can only ever feel like a colossal failure. On arriving in India, the farthest reach of his long eastward march, Alexander had an exchange with a philosopher who essentially told him to go home and rule his empire from there. But it was the unfolding map, life on the perpetual edge, that intoxicated Alexander, not the survey of a vast web of conquest from the comfort of its silken center. For Alexander there could be no real end, no tangible object of his quest: when he reached one border, there was always another to cross. He so thoroughly and persuasively imagined the world that he never gave any thought to how to come home. After his journey ended in India, there was no triumph, only the desultory march back to Macedonia. That's Alexander's tragedy and the tragedy of any soldier who can find no meaning in a life without war. In part, Alexander was a victim of circumstance. He lived in a "post-Homeric world" where, in the words of the historian Robin Lane Fox, "there was no question of ruling by being peaceful." But Alexander, transported by Homeric images of glory, also imagined himself engaged in a kind of competition across the centuries with Achilles. Rivalry with a legend committed him to a life of perpetual motion. His became a campaign of chronic dissatisfaction and compulsive restlessness, for there were always lands unvisited and nemeses unvanquished.

It was Alexander's mentor Cleitus, having watched the ways in which years of campaigning had changed the king, who had the temerity to suggest at a banquet that Alexander had begun behaving less like the heroic Achilles than like the tyrannical Agamemnon, whereupon Alexander killed him in a rage. The murder of Cleitus marked a turning point in Alexander's career. In the following year, 327 B.C.E., Alexander launched his invasion of India amid the increasing discontent of his followers, especially the Macedonians, who had felt for some time that he was abandoning them and their customs for the more despotic practices of those peoples he had conquered along the way. Alexander's dreams got larger and stranger; ambition began to overrule his normally shrewd military judgment. By the end, at least in Plutarch's version of the story, Alexander seems to have existed to a significant degree in a state of delusion. When his men proved reluctant to follow him across the Ganges, he "shut himself up in his tent and threw himself upon the ground, declaring, if they would not pass the Ganges, he owed them no thanks for anything they had hitherto done, and that to retreat now was plainly to confess himself vanquished."

The subsequent retreat, marked by Alexander's sad dissipation, also signals the end of his hopes for an *Iliad*. In Plutarch's biography of Alexander, the march back has the occasionally surreal feel of an *Odyssey*, yet it is aimless rather than deliberately digressive. Returning permanently to Macedonia was never really an option, and Alexander died in Persia. By the time he reached Gedrosia (in the Baluchistan Province of present-day Pakistan), all military discipline seems to have evaporated. The journey degenerated into a "disorderly, wandering march, [which,] besides the drinking part of it, was accompanied with all the sportiveness and insolence of bacchanals." Plutarch's Alexander becomes a creature of pathetic excess, someone ruled by superstition and surrounded by a "court thronged with diviners and priests." In some sense, perhaps, this is the only conceivable end for a warrior committed to the impossible project of attempting to live a myth.

Like everything else about Alexander, his constant motion is larger than life, but the disconcerting sense that "here," no matter the delights that homecoming brings, is not "there" is something I've noticed even in the most well-adjusted soldiers. Writing from Afghanistan, where he spent his share of nights in a foxhole, Joey captured the paradox of no man's land this way: "I can't decide if I want to live here and do this forever or leave and never come back." A veteran general told me that joyful as it is, coming home, which he has now done several times on his own war commute, nevertheless carries with it an enduring "sadness . . . in knowing that this was the most significant time of your life. And that's not to denigrate marriage, or babies, or grandbabies, or events . . . but it is to say that one knows that you might never contribute fully like this again."

GONE RAMBLING

Hitting the road—as an epic wanderer or a picaresque adventurer—is an elemental part not merely of the veteran's tale but also of the American myth of pioneering and westward motion. Romanticized by Walt Whitman and Mark Twain, the American road trip was subsequently reimagined by Jack Kerouac, Hunter S. Thompson, Robert M. Pirsig, and, more recently, Christopher McCandless, whose fatal journey to Alaska Jon Krakauer chronicled in *Into the Wild* (a book that has precipitated energetic debates among my students about the proper limits of personal responsibility). Whitman's "Song of the Open Road" establishes the fundamental tenets of what for at least some American travelers has amounted to a life's philosophy:

O highway I travel, do you say to me Do not leave me?
Do you say Venture not—if you leave me you are lost?
Do you say I am already prepared, I am well-beaten and
    undenied, adhere to me?

O public road, I say back I am not afraid to leave you, yet I
    love you,

You express me better than I can express myself,
You shall be more to me than my poem.

I think heroic deeds were all conceiv'd in the open air, and all
    free poems also,
I think I could stop here myself and do miracles . . .
. . . .
From this hour I ordain myself loos'd of limits and imaginary
    lines,
Going where I list, my own master total and absolute,
. . . .
Gently, but with undeniable will, divesting myself of the holds
    that would hold me.

For Whitman, taking to the road meant liberation from both practical and psychological constraints. The open highway offers fellowship yet also solitude. Most important, it is the lone remaining path that can give birth to heroic deeds in the modern age: knight-errantry once flowered in the forest, but the modern quest launches on the two-lane blacktop. Vital to subsequent incarnations of the myth is Whitman's notion that the road expresses the traveler better than the traveler could express himself.

These two archetypes—the wandering soldier and the road-tripping American—converged in the latter half of the twentieth century in the figure of the veteran motorcyclist. The ships borne on the seaways of ancient Greece or the whale road of Anglo-Saxon poetry gave way in the United States to the motorcycle on the open road: a Harley on the Pacific Coast Highway, U.S. 212 (the "Beartooth") from Montana into Yellowstone, Route 66 (the "Mother Road"), or some comparable asphalt ribbon unspooling its promise into the horizon. Hunter S. Thompson, who made his contribution to the national literature of the road in *Fear and Loathing in Las Vegas*, explores the origins of the legend of the veteran biker in *Hell's Angels: A Strange and Terrible Saga,* his 1966 book about the world's most mythologized motorcycle club:

> The whole thing was born, they say, in the late 1940s, when most ex-GIs wanted to get back to an orderly pattern: college, marriage, a job, children—all the peaceful extras that come with a sense of security. But not everybody felt that way. Like the drifters who rode west after Appomattox, there were thousands of veterans in 1945 who flatly rejected the idea of going back to their prewar pattern. They didn't want order, but privacy—and time to figure things out. It was a nervous, downhill feeling, a mean kind of *Angst* that always comes out of wars . . . a compressed sense of time on the outer limits of fatalism. They wanted more action, and one of the ways to look for it was on a big motorcycle.

One of the key moments in Thompson's "whole thing" was a 1947 Fourth of July motorcycle rally in Hollister, California, organized by the American Motorcyclist Association (AMA). Several "rebel," or "outlaw," clubs—clubs not sanctioned by the AMA—also showed up. Exaggerated reports of the drunkenness and brawling that ensued were enshrined in a staged *Life* magazine photograph of a man guzzling beer on a bike surrounded by scores of empties. One of the better-known non-AMA clubs, the Boozefighters, was founded by a veteran named "Wino" Willie Forkner, a waist gunner and engineer with the 7th Army Air Force, and evidently the model for Marlon Brando's character in *The Wild One,* the 1953 cult film about rival motorcycle gangs terrorizing a small California town. Not all of these clubs comprised veterans, of course, and of the outlaw clubs that still exist today, few perhaps have been engaged in the kinds of enterprises that have earned the Hells Angels a place on FBI watch lists.

Nevertheless, the ranks of motorcycle clubs swelled after World

War II and again in the wake of Vietnam. Despite what Daniel Wolf, in his ethnography of the Canadian Rebels Motorcycle Club, calls bikers' self-image as freedom-loving "frontier heroes," aspects of military culture exert a powerful attraction for these rebels. As my friend Max reminds me, motorcyclists—not just members of formal clubs—are often keenly aware of the role of the machine in warfare: they know all about its first military use against Pancho Villa on the Mexican border and its subsequent employment as a scout vehicle in both world wars. (Harley-Davidson has adroitly capitalized on these connections in its marketing in the years since.) Then there are the Patriot Guard Riders, an unchartered club that appears at military funerals today as a kind of voluntary honor guard.

Biking and military subcultures share an opposition to the conventionality, softness, or drudgery of "civilian" life. But there's a deeper affinity with military culture on the part of bikers. To survive as a subculture, Wolf explains, outlaw clubs must "operate with the internal discipline and precision of a paramilitary organization." There is a rigid hierarchy—complete with an enforcer called a sergeant at arms—and a set of rules. Club rides, or "runs," are done in formations commanded by a road captain, who also leads an advance party responsible for itineraries, logistics, supply, support, and security along the route. The irony of all this organization and regimentation on the part of a group of self-identified rebels isn't lost on an anthropologist like Wolf.

A further symbolic connection between bikers and the military is presented in the use of the patches and rockers sewn onto "cuts," a term (used interchangeably with "kuttes" and "battle jackets") to refer to the vests that signify club membership and rank. Such insignia often recall military unit patches, with a preference for skulls, death's-heads, or the wings common to air squadrons. The Hells Angels' adoption of a World War II army air forces symbol is only the most obvious example. The Angels, keen to dispel as apocryphal stories of the postwar motorcycle clubs being founded by drunken, undisciplined former fliers, take great pains on their website to assert the heroism of the various World War II units to which the club's name and symbol link it:

> Arvid Olsen, "Flying Tigers" Hell's Angels squadron[,] gave the idea of the name to the actual founders of the Hells Angels Motorcycle Club, in Fontana, California. The selection of our colors, red on white, is a result of the association of Olsen with the HAMC founders . . . The insignia of the HAMC, our copyrighted Deathshead[,] can also be traced to two variant insignia designs, the 85th Fighter Squadron and the 552nd Medium Bomber Squadron.

Pop culture's most recent reinforcing of the link between veterans and motorcycle clubs is the FX network series *Sons of Anarchy*, to which my friend Sean lured me with the promise that it was "Hamlet on Hogs," which in some measure it is.

As it happens, Sean had seen only part of one season when he recommended it to me so enthusiastically, an imperfect devotion I exposed once I took to it with the alacrity of an addict and started asking him questions about the plot for which he had no satisfactory answers. Having now watched every episode extant, we exist in a state of perpetual mechanized anxiety for the next installment in this brutal saga. The gang has a rigid hierarchy and code of conduct: the members follow Robert's Rules of Order at their meetings, and only once do I recall the gavel being used as a weapon. Most significant, the charter members of the Sons' Redwood Original chapter were Vietnam veterans, and at different stages in the series we learn a bit more about them through photographs and allusions to the experience of war and the bonds forged there. Those bonds end up being a great deal more fragile than the rhetoric might suggest, but Clay, the club president at the start of the series, wears his "jump wings" on his cut, their glint serving, along with the recurring shot of another member's standard government headstone, inscribed with his rank, division, and the word "Vietnam," as a constant reminder of the club's roots in a military association and of the magnitude of the betrayals that ensue.

Of course the allure of the motorcycle extends well beyond the demimonde of biker gangs. There seems to be something especially appealing to soldiers and former soldiers about the physical experience of riding, alone or with others. My friend Max insists he would "sell his organs" before his Fat Boy. Max did "some serious riding" when he returned from his Iraq tour, and he has been to several rallies and ridden cross-country twice since leaving the army in 2006. When I asked him what he thought about the relationship between veterans and bikes—whether it was myth or reality or a little of both—he replied,

> Had you asked me this question when I just returned home from Iraq, I'm not sure what my answer would have been. I've always loved motorcycles. For me, it was easy. I'm a third-generation Harley-Davidson rider . . . But asked this question now . . . and given some distance from the war, and some much-needed perspective, my answer would have to be that it's a support network without the appearance of being a support network . . .
>
> When veterans return home, they need time to think, time to come to terms with quite arguably the most intense situation and experience they'll ever find themselves in. They need to learn to accept who they are now, and let go of who they were. 'Cause no matter how hard you fight it, you're forever changed. You can never go back to who you were. Your only choice is to accept and come to terms with the version of you that's returned . . . Not necessarily changed for better or worse. But different . . . And being on the back of a motorcycle does just that. It allows the rider time to think . . . to make peace with everything . . . It's detox. Rehab. Till this day, I still do my best thinking on the back of a motorcycle.

In addition to the bonds cultivated or preserved by riding in the midst of a group of like-minded bikers, there is for Max and others with whom I've discussed this subject an elemental freedom to the motorcycle: riding creates a space in which the mind can wander along with the body—in which a veteran can afford, as Max puts it, to think about "all of the shit you either didn't have time to think about over there . . . or you obsessed about . . . only to return home and find out it didn't matter." For Max, the road is the place where he can be understood without having to explain himself.

One memorable trip Max took to the Outer Banks with two fellow veterans was distinguished for its stoic silence: "I swear all of three or four sentences' worth of talk was uttered the entire trip. We just rode, sat, ate, smoked cigars, slept, rode." To Max this is a kind of reconciliation: "Perhaps it's truly the closest a lot of us veterans will ever come to that ideal, the idea that we're fighting for a freedom, for a better world . . . only to realize that nothing is ever that simple. So we return home, and we find that nugget of an idea or an expression of an idea (no matter how small) that proves that ideal true if only from point A to point B. But it exists. It's not a total lie. So maybe whatever was done or lost overseas was not in vain." Sometimes Max is less sanguine and admits that maybe a motorcycle ride is not the best way to grind out one's problems, but even after many of his illusions have been shattered by real-world experience, he retains his romantic faith in the road: "I hear her calling now. Every time I look in my garage and see dust falling on my motorcycle. The road has all the answers . . . The road is a promise fulfilled."

In his desire to become "as much a part of the road" as he can, Max recalls Whitman's joyful articulation of taking to the open highway. Of course Whitman was a pedestrian; the use of the motorcycle as a means to the same self-actualization acquired the cultic aspect it has retained ever since through the work of Robert M. Pirsig. His book *Zen and the Art of Motorcycle Maintenance* establishes the philosophy, a central tenet of which posits the supe-riority of the motorcycle as a mode of transport:

> You see things vacationing on a motorcycle in a way that is com-pletely different from any other. In a car you're always in a com-partment, and because you're used to it you don't realize that through that car window everything you see is just more TV. You're a passive observer and it is all moving by you boringly in a frame.
>
> On a cycle the frame is gone. You're completely in contact with it all. You're *in* the scene, not just watching it anymore, and the sense of presence is overwhelming. That concrete whizzing by five inches below your foot is the real thing, the same stuff you walk on, it's right there, so blurred you can't focus on it, yet you can put your foot down and touch it anytime, and the whole thing, the whole experience, is never removed from immediate consciousness.

The bikers I know freely acknowledge the unpleasantness of being pounded by debris and soaked by the elements. They can't help but focus on the road surface, the wind and the smells it brings, the temperature drop at elevation; they are more attentive to things like state lines and the rotation of crops from one region to the next. Inconveniences are compensated for by the sense of proxim-ity to the earth that Pirsig articulates. "You're simply more aware of the world. You're more alert," Max writes. "As a result, I think you feel more alive. As close to a feeling of peace as most war vet-erans can get."

Kevin, a captain who recently returned home from a second tour in Afghanistan, also finds clarity on a bike. He spent his mid-tour R&R leave reading *War and Peace*—Tolstoy's book, he wrote to me from Afghanistan, "sees right through people like no writ-ing I've ever read before"—and riding motorcycles in Australia. For Kevin, reading and riding are part of a quest for simplicity and understanding. "I've done some thinking about what makes a good ride," he wrote to me recently. "Good views are obviously a must. Water is desirable. Winding roads are necessary—riding a road that makes you pay attention to it is like having an interesting conversation with someone." Riding engages him by penetrating to essentials, and bikes have the great virtue of being "uncomplicated." "You can see all the parts and can pretty much grasp what's going on in the person-sized apparatus beneath you. If something isn't working, you know right away and have a pretty good idea how to fix it." As soon as he got home, Kevin set off on his Suzuki Boulevard M50, an 800cc cruiser, along Highway 1, traveling light: "Seattle to Monterey and back with nothing but a sleeping bag and a toothbrush."

Kevin feels a kinship with rebels of many stripes and is attracted by the outlaw sensibility that attaches to bikers: "I wonder if the responsiveness of a bike is part of what gives it appeal to outlaws and vets alike. We've been outside society and seen that the whole thing is obviously a facade. Meanwhile, the simplicity and responsiveness of a motorcycle make it obviously real. And its maneuverability lets you tear all over the place scoffing at imaginary traffic laws and painted lines." Kevin told me the story of a friend who bought a bike after coming home from a deployment and was pulled over for doing less than ten miles over the speed limit on a highway. Trained to obedience, Kevin and his friend have nevertheless come into a new relation with law and convention. Their war experience opened up a chasm between them and the society they left behind:

> To him, as to me, as to most of us coming back, policemen are almost quaint and laws aren't real. We know we have to obey them, but all of a sudden this lifelong lawfulness isn't easy—it's rather a conscious effort. When the police officer told him how fast he was going, he ridiculed the cop. He might have been able to talk himself out of that ticket, especially if he played the

military card (though this guy would never), but instead he got the full fine. Maybe that's not Hells Angels tearing up [a town,] but the incident struck me as a good example of the clash between society and us.

Kevin and his friend aren't prepared to reject society for the outlaw's life, but they are clearly inclined to push limits and test boundaries. They grow frustrated quickly with the constraints under which life at home must be lived: to be a rover on a bike is to consign oneself to the very different code of no man's land.

In a November 2013 *New York Times* article on the evolving image of the Hells Angels, Serge F. Kovaleski called attention to the enduring appeal of the motorcycle club to war veterans. Kovaleski cites the example of Andres Ospina, a marine veteran of the war in Iraq who "has struggled with post-traumatic stress and depression" but "found solace in the camaraderie of the club, which he likened to 'going back to your platoon, your safe place.'" Ospina believes the club saved his life: "I had two choices: I could have become antisocial and locked myself in an apartment and cried about things that upset me, or I could be social with people who are like-minded." Kovaleski describes Ospina "clutching his Hells Angels vest" and saying, "This is my armor now. It keeps people away. I am literally fighting for my own right to be who I want to be, and to be left alone."

The chief boon of motorcycling for Kevin seems to be the measure of control it gives him—a sense he lacked in combat situations:

Motorcycling is all about self-assertion. Maybe you can find a better word for that, but hear me out. In Afghanistan, I was immersed in a world of violence and chaos. At the same time I was part of the huge army machine spread out all over the country trying to accomplish some vague objective of stability. There's so much uncertainty, so little control. I was strung up by some serious red tape on our end, and yet outside the wire I could immediately sense how impotent our bureaucracy was with the illiterate agricultural society we were trying to save. A bike, on the other hand, registers your slightest command. It will go wherever you want as fast as you want it to.

This theme of control is one to which the bikers I've talked to frequently return. Max calls it the sensation of "being in control and out of control simultaneously. On the very razor's edge. And maybe that's why motorcycles are so alluring to veterans. It's that same . . . feeling that follows you everywhere in a combat zone." Damon, who prefers BMWs to Harleys, has often talked to me about what he regards as the largely illusory relationship between riding and control. He classifies motorcycling and war together as examples of a Faustian bargain. Control and autonomy are simply delusions common to the experiences of riding a motorcycle and fighting a war:

> [Both] provide the "necessary" fiction of control at the risk of the eternal soul. Motorcycling clubs, like so many communal experiments, seek a type of masculine utopia—a Peter Pan Never-Never Land of physically obtained status and sexual promiscuity. Membership in the larger community, and its social rules, are traded for another. Although the myth of autonomy animates the rhetoric of such clubs, there seems to be much less of it. Similarities can be drawn to military service. In the place of the motorcycle as the fetishized item we can insert another machine, the machine gun. In the place of control over sex we can observe control over violence.

The knife-edge that Damon recognizes, and has himself navigated both on a bike and in Iraq, is shrouded in romance—the romance of living forever in no man's land. As he well knows, it is a romance that seduces even as it betrays. At its paradoxical heart lies the ultimate test of self-control together with the great temptation to total surrender—in a burst of speed, perhaps, or a burst of gunfire.

It's the same psychic space that at once attracted and repelled another desert warrior, T. E. Lawrence, whose legend has enjoyed something of a resurgence in recent years because of his guerrilla experience in the Middle East during World War I. Lawrence died in 1935, of injuries suffered in a crash while riding his 1932 custom Brough Superior SS100 motorcycle. Before the war, as a junior officer in Egypt, Lawrence evidently used to scandalize some of his superiors by racing around Cairo on a Triumph. Afterward, he defined his chief "post-war pleasure" as being "fit enough, and rich enough to have a motor-bike and ride it hard."

Postwar pleasure was rather difficult to come by for Lawrence, who was deeply ambivalent about his role in the Arab Revolt because the European powers ultimately betrayed many of the promises they had made to the Arabs in order to secure their participation in the Allied fight against the Turks. Believing himself a "trickster" and a "fraud," transformed (as both victim and perpetrator) by violence, half in love with the fame he hated, Lawrence found it excessively difficult ever truly to come home. His story, complete with its fatal coda on a motorcycle, offers a suggestive modern parallel to the ancient saga of the soldier's troubled repatriation.

Lawrence tried in vain to hide himself away after he came home from the war, but it was impossible for "Lawrence of Arabia" to remain under the radar for very long after the American newspaperman Lowell Thomas turned him into an international celebrity. The mythology that grew up around Lawrence exposes important aspects of what might be thought of as a post-heroic narrative of homecoming. It dramatizes the particular challenges faced by the modern soldier, a stranger in an alien culture, at war in a world that regards the enterprise with some mistrust: enthusiastically celebrating the endeavor in the abstract yet recoiling from its actual violent practice—and from its practitioners.

Owing to accidents of geography, Lawrence's experience of warfare was vastly different from that of his contemporaries fighting on the western front. Yet he shared with many peers who survived the trenches and subsequently wrote about the war an ineradicable wanderlust. In 1924, Lawrence wrote to Robert Graves, "What's the cause that you, and S.S. [Siegfried Sassoon] and I . . . can't get away from the War? Here are you riddled with thought like any old table-leg with worms: S.S. yawing about like a ship aback: me in the ranks, finding squalor and maltreatment the only permitted existence: what's the matter with us all? It's like the malarial bugs in the blood, coming out months and years after in recurrent attacks." Lawrence's autobiography, *Seven Pillars of Wisdom: A Triumph*, published in 1926, emerged from the expansiveness and desolation of the desert rather than the suffocating, entrenched destruction endured by Graves and Sassoon. Like the wars of today, Lawrence's had no fixed "front." In a sense, it was all a vast no man's land of violent unpredictability. In Arabia he was effectively isolated from that larger fraternity. A corresponding quality of Odyssean rootlessness informs his entire book. In fact, Lawrence was later to translate Homer's *Odyssey* at the request of the book designer Bruce Rogers, who had been commissioned to produce an art edition and was searching for a collaborator. The translation would eventually be distributed in the form of an Armed Services Edition to millions of American sailors, soldiers, airmen, and marines during World War II.

Finding his ideally ambiguous mirror in Odysseus, Lawrence allied himself as autobiographer, adventurer, and translator with Homer's postwar wanderer. The *Odyssey* was a text he carried with him "always, to every camp," he wrote, "for I love it." It seemed a natural choice for a man who proposed that "accident, with perverted humour," had cast him "as a man of action . . . in the Arab Revolt, a theme ready and epic to a direct eye and hand," yet not to his own indirect eye and hand. "The epic mode was alien to me, as to my generation," Lawrence insists in *Seven Pillars*. "Memory gave me no clue to the heroic." David Lean's 1962 film *Lawrence of Arabia*, with Peter O'Toole in the title role, elides many of the complexities of Lawrence's war. His epigrammatic response to a reporter's question about why he likes the desert—"It's clean"—is typical. The sojourn in the desert was in fact one of defiant uncleanness, of mind as much as body, as well as of the corrosive guilt that attended his relationship to violence. It was an experience Lawrence never succeeded in escaping, except ephemerally on the back of his motorcycle, as under a succession of pseudonyms he drifted in and out of military service after the war in the army and the Royal Air Force (RAF).

In the late 1920s, posted to central Asia with the RAF under the assumed name T. E. Shaw, Lawrence worked steadily on his translation of the *Odyssey*. He thought the locale perfectly suited to the poem on which he labored: "The work has been very difficult: though I'm in a Homeric sort of air; a mud-brick fort beset by the tribes of Waziristan, on a plain encircled by the hills of the Afghan border. It reeks of Alexander the Great, our European fore-runner; who also loved Homer." Perhaps because he spent so much of his adult life in locations of deep archaeological and military-historical significance, Lawrence felt that he lived a belated life. He carried *Le Morte d'Arthur*, Sir Thomas Malory's medieval romance, in his "saddle-bags" on campaign to help relieve his "disgust" with the whole enterprise. Writing in a similar vein from the front in 1917, Blunden also characterized war as less a matter of gallantry than a series of sordid financial transactions. The emphatically unromantic business aspect of war has perhaps never been more apparent than it is today: the contracting, the large sums of money paid out in Iraq and Afghanistan to win hearts and minds, the belated bill now due.

Lawrence's most effective therapy turned out to be the open road. "The extravagance in which my surplus emotion expressed itself lay on the road," he wrote in *The Mint*, an account of the years he spent hiding as an enlisted soldier under a series of aliases.

"So long as roads were tarred blue and straight . . . so long was I rich." Lawrence's "pleasure" in motorcycles owed something to the strenuousness of motorcycling and to the risks of riding at high speeds—he writes of the punishing wind, insects, bumpy roads, and crashes—but his letters also suggest the unalloyed joy of "flight," as he often called it, at the helm of a powerful machine. There, again, is that alluring sense of control that so intrigues Max, Kevin, and Damon. In a letter Lawrence explains that the bike was his mode of escape when army life in the ranks became overbearing: "My motor-bike is called into use when I find myself on parade facing an unconscious sergeant with my fists hard clenched. A hundred fast miles seem to make camp less confined afterwards." The rides, representing as they did "hours of voluntary danger," cooled "hot" moods and reanimated the spirit when he was feeling numb. Lawrence acknowledged the odd "craving for real risk" such motorcycle adventures entailed, but they were the only thing that saved him from his own "jaded" nerves. On those days when he was able to escape, Lawrence thought nothing of putting five hundred, sometimes as many as eight hundred, miles on the road, as he reported to George Brough, the designer of his bike, in a letter announcing that he had reached a hundred thousand miles in four years on a series of five different Brough Superiors. They were, he told Brough, "the jolliest things on wheels."

I can see a similar unfettered enthusiasm for the motorcycle in Kevin, who dreams of buying a BMW GS but just finished a cross-country trip on the bike he happens to own, a now-battered Suzuki Boulevard M50, which he told me was all wrong for this trip: it isn't a touring bike, and his gear, piled up under a tarp on the back, looked like a giant trash bag billowing in the wind. His fairing broke loose in Texas: he had to hold on to it with his hand to keep it from slamming him in the face. And he spent much of the trip without proper gloves. Yet all of this did nothing to diminish the experience. Kevin decided to leave the army in 2013. Before figuring out what to do next, he embarked on this seven-week adventure, which he chronicled on a blog called "Gone Rambling," on which he described himself as follows: "Ex-army, still wears boots, has lit-crushes on Thoreau, Emerson, Whitman. Shares a birthday with 13th century Persian poet Rumi, thinks that's significant." To the question "why?" he offered: "Because I can. Because I couldn't before and I might not be able to again. Because I can't think of a better use of my time than to marvel at the beauty of the world and the people in my life. Because some of us are just built to roam."

In March, Kevin let me know he was heading out and would see me in a few months. In early May, the eastward leg of his trip complete, we were catching up over beer and tacos in Greenwich Village. Although we have been regular correspondents over the years, this was the first time I had seen him since his graduation. He was working hard at a Walt Whitman beard but otherwise looked the same: lean and serious. He still has that bright eye and curious spirit I remember so well, and he has come away from his experiences, dispiriting as many of them have been, with, if anything, a more optimistic view of human nature than he had before. We revisited many of the themes that have preoccupied our e-mails over the last several years, but mostly we talked about his journey and the job search ahead of him when he returned to Seattle. During his trip Kevin's military service often came up naturally in conversation and served as a point of contact with fellow riders as well as with the many people he met along the way. His engagement with the homeland he was traversing depended in large measure on the fact that he was wearing the leather gear of the motorcyclist, not the uniform that marks service members out and sometimes complicates their communication with civilians. Kevin came away from the trip feeling as if his interactions with his fellow citizens, brief though they had been, constituted real and honest connections, animated by generosity, solidarity, and a healthy curiosity.

THANK YOU FOR YOUR SERVICE

Soldiers no longer have to wear their uniforms off duty or on leave, and if you don't live near an army post or in Washington, D.C., seeing someone in uniform—except through a television screen or at transportation hubs—is likely to be something of a rarity. It used to be the case that service members had to wear their uniforms during wartime. Watch a film from the 1940s or 1950s, for example, especially one set in a city like New York or San Francisco, and you are sure to spot him: straphanging on a crowded subway car, buying a newspaper at a kiosk, or sitting in a coffee shop. The anonymous man in uniform, on leave during World War II or the Korean War, is a stock extra in these films, as elemental to the urban landscape as the beat cop, the woman with the baby carriage, or the couple in love.

Today, a woman or man in military uniform dining in a restaurant, sitting on a bench in Central Park, or walking up Broadway constitutes a spectacle. I have witnessed this firsthand whenever one of my military colleagues and I have gone to the city on an official trip to attend a performance or to visit a library or museum. My civilian clothes provide camouflage as I watch my uniformed friends bombarded by gratitude. These meetings between soldier and civilian turn quickly into street theater. The soldier is recognized with a handshake. There's often a request for a photograph or the tracing of a six-degrees-of-separation genealogy: "My wife's second cousin is married to a guy in the 82nd Airborne." And each encounter concludes with a ritual utterance: "Thank you for your service."

One former captain proposed that "thank you for your service" has become "an obligatory salutation." Dutifully offered by strangers, "somewhere between an afterthought and heartfelt appreciation," it is gratifying but also embarrassing to a soldier with a strong sense of modesty and professionalism. "People thank me for my service," another officer noted, "but they don't really know what I've done." He's implying not that he is an underappreciated hero but rather that many Americans are ill informed (or willfully ignorant) about the broad range of actual duties a soldier might perform. For what, specifically, are they thanking him?

Sometimes, the drama between soldier and civilian turns downright weird. One officer reported that while shopping in uniform at the grocery store one evening, she was startled by a man across the aisle who gave her an earnest, Hollywood-style, chest-thumping Roman salute. My friend is unfailingly gracious, but she was entirely at a loss for a proper response. On another occasion, this same officer was greeted by a stranger in the commissary parking lot of a military post with an even more mysterious utterance: "I got out, but I'm glad that you stayed in. Thank you for your service." "I really wasn't sure what to do with that," she told me afterward, "though it seemed intended to be an appreciative gesture." Such transactions resemble celebrity sightings—with the same awkwardness, enthusiasm, and suspension of normal expectations about privacy and personal space. Yet while the celebrity is an individual recognized for a unique, highly publicized performance, the soldier is anonymous, a symbol of an aggregate. His or her performance remains largely unseen.

Whether anyone ever spat on an American soldier returning from Vietnam remains a matter of debate. Many veterans will argue fiercely that these incidents occurred, but the sociologist and veteran Jerry Lembcke disputed such tales in *The Spitting Image: Myth, Memory, and the Legacy of Vietnam*. One Vietnam veteran suggested to me that it was inconceivable to imagine scrawny hippies in tie-dye spitting on trained killers, while others have told me the exact date and location of spitting incidents. Apocryphal or not, this image has become emblematic of an era's shame and of the nation's failure to respond appropriately to the people it had sent to fight a bankrupt war. The specter of this guilt—this perdurable archetype of the hostile homecoming—animates today's encounters, which seem to have swung around to the other un-thinking extreme. "Thank you for your service" has become a mantra of atonement. No longer do we wish to cast veterans out into no man's land; in proclaiming our appreciation, we quickly satisfy an honest but largely inchoate desire to bring them home. As is all too often the case with gestures of atonement, however, substance has been eclipsed by mechanical ritual. After the engage-ment, both parties retreat to separate camps, without a significant exchange of ideas or perspectives having passed between them. The successful reincorporation of veterans into civil society entails something arguably messier and more painful. It is a complex, evolving process. Today, the soldier's homecoming has been fur-ther complicated by the absence of a draft, which removes sol-diers from the cultural mainstream, and by the fact that the wars in Iraq and Afghanistan have had little perceptible impact on the rhythms of daily life at home.

When I broached this subject with a major in whose company I had experienced the phenomenon as we walked through Central Park, he wrote a nuanced response. Although he's convinced that "the sentiments most people express appear to be genuinely FELT," he nonetheless distrusts the performance. "Does the act of thank-ing a soldier unconsciously hold some degree of absolution from the collective responsibility?" he asked. No reasonable person would argue that thanking soldiers for their service isn't preferable to spitting on them. Yet at least in the perfunctory, formulaic way many such meetings take place, it is an equally unnatural exchange. The ease with which "thank you for your service" has circumvented a more enduring human connection doesn't bode well for long-term mutual understanding between soldiers and civilians. The inner lives of soldiers remain opaque to most of us, while soldiers, for their part, have adopted an often defensive posture.

In his 2011 West Point commencement address, the then Chair-man of the Joint Chiefs, Admiral Mike Mullen, addressed this di-vide. "I'm going to ask you to remember that you are citizens first and foremost," he insisted. "We can never forget that we too are the people." Mullen elaborated on the uneasy dynamic between the citizenry and its military:

> We're also fairly insular, speaking our own language of sorts, living within our own unique culture, isolating ourselves either out of fear or from, perhaps, even our own pride. The American people can therefore be forgiven for not possessing an intimate knowledge of our needs or of our deeds. We haven't exactly made it easy for them. And we have been a little busy. But that doesn't excuse us from making the effort. That doesn't excuse us from our own constitutional responsibilities as citizens and soldiers to promote the general welfare, in addition to providing for the common defense.

Mullen's allusion to pride seems especially pertinent at a time when the military's identification of itself as a profession has largely eclipsed the ideal of the citizen-soldier inherited from George Washington. It was Washington who knew as well as anyone the need to preserve both components of his identity. "When we assumed the Soldier," he told the New York Provincial Congress in June 1775, "we did not lay aside the Citizen," and he looked forward to the day when he and his fellow soldiers could "return to our private Stations." That rhetoric is much more difficult to sustain in the age of an all-volunteer force that has so resolutely embraced a rhetoric of professionalism. Something vital—something instrumental to the art of coming home—has perhaps been lost in the process.

"Deep down," the major, who served in Iraq, acknowledged, "my ego wants to embrace the ritualized adoration, the sense of purpose, and the attendant mythology." The giving and receiving of thanks is a seductive transaction—much more seductive, perhaps, than imagining oneself a citizen-soldier not all that different from the rest of the citizenry—and no one knows that better than this officer: "I eagerly shake hands, engage in small talk, and pose for pictures with total strangers." Juxtaposed in his mind with scenes from Fallujah or Arlington National Cemetery, however, his sanitized encounters with civilians make him feel like Mickey Mouse: "Welcome to Disneyland." Thanking soldiers on their way to or from a war isn't the same as imaginatively following them there and back. Conscience-easing expressions of gratitude by politicians and citizens cloak with courtesy the often bloody, wounding nature of a soldier's service. Today's dominant narrative, one that favors sentimentality over scrutiny, embodies a fantasy that everything will be okay if only we display enough flag-waving enthusiasm. More than a hundred thousand homeless veterans, and more than forty thousand troops wounded in action in Iraq and Afghanistan, may have a different view.

If our theater of gratitude provoked introspection or led to a substantive dialogue between giver and recipient, I would celebrate it. But having witnessed these bizarre scenes firsthand, I have come to believe that they are a poor substitute for something more difficult and painful—a conversation about what war does to the people who serve and to the people who don't. Too many Americans fail to consider that waging war, or even being, as many claim to be, for the troops but against the war, entails responsibilities to veterans that will long outlive the conflict itself.

Few Americans have understood more clearly the seductions and inadequacies of professing gratitude than Abraham Lincoln. Offering to a mother who had lost two sons—originally thought to have been five—in the Civil War "the consolation that may be found in the thanks of the Republic," Lincoln nevertheless acknowledged "how weak and fruitless must be any word of mine which should attempt to beguile you from the grief of a loss so overwhelming." Expressions of thanks constitute the beginning, not the end, of obligation. Welcoming soldiers home is a much more time-consuming proposition than our current practices would suggest.

My Memorial Day visit to the Vietnam Veterans Memorial Wall in 2013 reinforced for me how very complicated and unfinished the work of coming home could be. The sights and sounds of that afternoon—the choppers roaring through D.C.; the booming business at the merchandise booth of the Rolling Thunder motorcycle club (a nonprofit organization devoted to publicizing POW/MIA and other veterans issues), which had sold out of much of the military insignia it normally stocks; the various patches adorning biker vests—"Gulf War Veteran," "Jane Fonda American Traitor Bitch" (worn upside down), "I wasn't there but I still care"—the cultic aspect to the mementos left at the base of the wall—all asserted a kinship across wars as well as an equation between a biker outlaw sensibility and the mindset cultivated by fighting wars beyond the pale. In the expression of this transhistorical solidarity among individuals who are never quite at home long after coming home, there was a promise—even a romance—of perpetual alienation. The idea that one has left behind something irreplaceable can prove just as seductive and destructive as those rousing, unreflective heroic narratives of the old school. Charting an endless course through no man's land is no easy ride.

2

"THE ONE THING NEEDFUL"
Paradoxes of Preparation

Looking back on the past six months, Margaret realized the chaotic nature of our daily life, and its difference from the orderly sequence that has been fabricated by historians. Actual life is full of false clues and sign-posts that lead nowhere. With infinite effort we nerve ourselves for a crisis that never comes. The most successful career must show a waste of strength that might have removed mountains, and the most unsuccessful is not that of the man who is taken unprepared, but of him who has prepared and is never taken. On a tragedy of that kind our national morality is duly silent. It assumes that preparation against danger is in itself a good, and that men, like nations, are the better for staggering through life fully armed. The tragedy of preparedness has scarcely been handled, save by the Greeks. Life is indeed dangerous, but not in the way morality would have us believe. It is indeed unmanageable, but the essence of it is not a battle. It is unmanageable because it is a romance, and its essence is romantic beauty.

—E. M. Forster, *Howards End* (1910)

LUCKY CHARM

In baseball, streaks are something to write home about: Cal Ripken Jr.'s 2,632 consecutive appearances; Joe DiMaggio's fifty-six straight games with a hit, and Ichiro Suzuki's ten seasons in a row with at least two hundred hits, a streak that ended in 2011, when Ichiro fell a bit short with 184. My father would never forgive me if

I failed to mention a couple of Ted Williams's streaks: reaching base safely in eighty-four consecutive games in 1949, and maintaining an on-base percentage of .400 or better for seventeen seasons in a row. These feats are all the more remarkable for the fact that Williams, a marine fighter pilot, missed three full seasons during World War II and most of two more in Korea, where he flew thirty-nine missions in an F9F Panther jet with the 223rd Squadron of the 3rd Marine Air Wing. My streak was, everyone agrees, a magical run. Of course I couldn't write about it until it was over; I couldn't write about it until I had lost. I say *I*, but it's as irrational to insist I had anything to do with the losing as it is to imagine I influenced the winning. Unless, that is, you're superstitious—which I'm not. At least I never used to be until I started spending afternoons in the dugout with the Army baseball team.

In 2009, I became one of the team's several faculty representatives. This assignment involves serving as an academic mentor to the cadets and providing moral support during the season, including taking a periodic turn in the dugout on game day. The streak started with my very first assignment, an early season contest in March. It wasn't yet baseball weather in the Hudson Valley: swaddled in a full-length parka, ski cap, and mittens, I kept warm by pacing the dugout, flapping my arms, stomping my feet, and trying to will a quick victory. My record at day's end: 1–0.

Spring eventually came to West Point and, with it, high-stakes league games and dreams of a postseason trip to the NCAA tournament. My next turn in the dugout was the first game of a Sunday afternoon doubleheader against Holy Cross, a Patriot League opponent. Army had dropped two to the purpled Crusaders the day before; the mood in the dugout was grim. When Army won in resounding fashion, 8–1, Coach pointed to me from the other end of the bench and said,

"You're staying for the second game."

"But, Coach," I said, "Major K. has the second game."

"He can stay, too," Coach replied, "but if we start to lose, he's got to go. Okay?"

How can you say no to such a request, slightly odd though it may be? And, frankly, why would you want to? If, as I do, you still remember the day your father brought home two brand-new Franklin gloves, stiff as stones, pockets yawning, and a hulking Hillerich & Bradsby Louisville Slugger; if you hear a siren song in the crack of a bat; if you enjoy the company of smart, funny, dedicated twenty-year-olds; if you derive an indescribable sensation from standing on the first-base line before the game while the national anthem plays, then there really is no finer way to spend an afternoon.

It is traditional for the faculty representative to bring a robust supply of sunflower seeds and bubble gum to the game. I started to secure tubs of Bazooka, which isn't as easy to come by as it used to be. I got mine from a guy in Queens. The old-school, groan-inducing comics—which Topps killed a few years ago—were still a universal hit with the team, but the assorted tropical flavors had edged out the traditional variety. In the dugout, I learned quickly to duck both the arc of spit seed shells and the occasional errant throw from second. I learned above all to relish the chatter, equal parts morale boosting, material assistance (to a runner, let's say, who's trying to avoid getting picked off at first), associative wordplay, nicknames, and chanted mantras: "Hey, kid . . . attaboy, Meatball . . . up . . . down . . . back . . . room . . . way to work it, Cheese Rat . . . good boy . . . good eye . . . not you . . . all you . . . way to battle . . . wait for yours . . . so what . . . OH yeah . . . oh YEAH . . . oHIo . . . no one better, baby!"

This poetry is a vital part of an elaborate set of rituals, both verbal and physical, that characterize a game in which chance can defy even the most meticulous training and discipline and leave the best prepared defeated. As the modernist poet and avid Brooklyn Dodger fan Marianne Moore wrote, in baseball you never know "how it will go" or what variable might "modify conditions." This phenomenon is, as Moore recognized, the source of the excitement common to poetry and baseball, but it is also the origin of an uncertainty for which it is impossible to control. In a 1968 article in *The New York Times*, Moore admiringly quoted the St. Louis Cardinal first baseman Orlando Cepeda's appreciation of the unexpected. "One of the things that makes baseball so fascinating to me," Cepeda explained, "is the number of non-standard plays—plays you're seeing for the first time—that occur in baseball. Stan Musial said that even after twenty years in the game you constantly keep seeing things you have never seen before, which makes baseball a lot different than so many other sports." Many ballplayers respond to the game's fundamental unpredictability— the bad hop, the bottom suddenly dropping out of a split-finger fastball, an umpire's arbitrarily shrinking or expanding strike zone, the carom, the wind and the rain—by embracing superstition. Watching a major leaguer on television skip over the white lines, maniacally unfasten and refasten his batting gloves, or scratch runic symbols in the dirt with the end of his bat before stepping into the box, I've often had the impression that it's all a performance. But the more time I spent in the dugout, the more clearly I saw that ballplayers aren't doing any of that stuff for us.

I noticed a Mr. Potato Head by the Gatorade bucket one day, a miniature Greek battle helmet the next. Someone hung a stuffed "victory" vulture from the netting on the first-base side. I watched an outfielder place his glove at the same angle in the same place at the end of every inning, a relief pitcher touch the bill of his cap a precise number of times. When things weren't going well, a fellow perched on the railing would jump down and move to the other end of the dugout, murmuring, "Gotta change spots." I had always thought I understood the difference between constructive habit and superstition, but I grew unsure when I became a talisman. There are countless superstitions at West Point, but most of them involve inanimate objects (or ghosts), not actual people.

Army won the second game of that doubleheader against Holy Cross, and the team's fortunes turned. People remembered. "You're undefeated," other faculty representatives noted to me in passing. (I wasn't keeping track of their records.) After another regular season game, I was still unbeaten, and Coach started calling me "a good-luck charm." After he mentioned my new role to a faculty job candidate when we happened to run into him on the day of her visit, the bewildered look in her eyes made me recognize the rich strangeness of the compact into which I had entered. I tried to duplicate all the things I could remember having done during that first game. I took the same path to the dugout from the parking lot, trotted along the sidewalk in front of the stadium, carried the Bazooka in the same bag, exited the field after the game by circling behind home plate and out the third-base gate. I even added a few rituals just in case. On a visit to the army's vaunted Ranger Regiment I had been given a ceremonial coin, which I kept in my pocket during the game. If things were looking bleak, I switched pockets. A few seasons later, when the commander of the 3rd Battalion, 187th Infantry Regiment, sent me one of his unit's "Iron Rakkasans" coins from Afghanistan, I started toting that one to the park, too. The longer the streak lasted, the more difficult it became. I started to brood: if I lost, I would become an outcast, a Jonah, a latter-day, landlocked incarnation of Coleridge's Ancient Mariner.

When Army drew Holy Cross in the opening round of the Patriot League conference tournament, I got the call for the first game of the best-of-three series. Army chalked up another win: 5–1. Clearly, I had the Crusaders' number, but I had to skip the second game of the afternoon to give a final exam—and Army lost. Now there seemed to be incontrovertible proof that I was a rabbit's foot. I slept fitfully that night, for the next day I was due back in the dugout for the decisive game, which Army won 11–0. The following week, I was there as the team swept Lafayette to clinch the Patriot League championship. I ended the season with an unblemished record. In the weeks that followed, I watched from home Army's plucky run in the NCAA Regionals in Texas. From that distance, I rid myself of my belief in magic powers I didn't quite know how to manage, and I was left to ponder what everything that had happened over the season really meant: the way in which coincidental patterns had begun to exert such a strong influence on my mind. I told myself I was performing all these rituals for the team, but maybe I had also started to do them for myself. More important, I wondered what roles luck and superstition would continue to play in the cadets' lives after they exchanged their baseball jerseys for combat uniforms. The idea that you might be able to prepare for—even shape—the future by adhering to ritual is a sharp spur.

Perhaps the only people more superstitious than ballplayers are soldiers. In war, of course, unpredictability acquires much deeper significance. Warding off misfortune becomes a sublime form of art: the art of survival. Ulysses S. Grant, who graduated from West Point in 1843, a year behind baseball's mythological founder, Abner Doubleday (for whom Army's field is named), wrote freely about superstition in his memoirs:

> One of my superstitions had always been when I started to go any where, or to do anything, not to turn back, or stop until the thing intended was accomplished. I have frequently started to go to places where I had never been and to which I did not know the way, depending upon making inquiries on the road, and if I got past the place without knowing it, instead of turning back, I would go on until a road was found turning in the right direction, take that, and come in by the other side.

Refusing to retrace one's steps in peace is one thing; in war, it is potentially quite another. Maybe Grant's superstitious fear of retracing his steps was the secret source of his tenacity in pursuit of the enemy as a commander. He was known for aggressively, relentlessly pushing ahead. That's how he won, sometimes at great cost.

Napoleon perceived inauspicious omens in bad weather and evidently refused to go to battle on Friday the thirteenth, while Julius Caesar might have been better off had he canceled his engagements on the ides of March. I asked a few officers I know about their own combat superstitions. One, who had also been an intercollegiate athlete as a cadet, told me about a stuffed dinosaur given to him by one of his children before he left for the first Gulf War. "Dino" has now redeployed after serving multiple tours in Iraq in two wars: first with this officer, then with each of his sons. Another told me that he always wore the same floppy, wide-brimmed hat in Vietnam. Sure, it shaded him from the sun, but that wasn't the point. He refused to go anywhere without it. He wore it on every helicopter ride—even wore it under his helmet—and he lovingly preserved it for years afterward.

Joel shared with me the ritual he followed before every mission in Iraq: "I always . . . did the same things . . . Grab a bottle of water and stow it in the same place by my seat, tap the forward assist on the rifle three times, grab the radio, check the FBCB2 (digital map), and always look at the same place outside the gate from inside the gate, the place where the conditions change. It helped me change my mind from 'here' to 'there,' where the stakes are a little higher." The routine served as a "mental checklist," Joel explained. It ensured that he never went out on a mission without taking every possible precaution. Yet, when the order in which he executed the sequence became nonnegotiable, the ritual took on a quality beyond responsible preparation: "Things were normal if I did it that way, and things were not if I didn't." Feeling that things are normal, no matter the irrational means by which one arrives at that conclusion, is no negligible achievement in a combat situation. If a given routine enhances an individual's mission focus, then it becomes difficult to begrudge certain idiosyncrasies. But where does one draw the line between a salubrious routine and an unjustified obsession? At what point does the sustaining faith in a particular pattern of actions become a liability or an obsessive distraction? And how does one ever finally disentangle the consequential from the irrational? Luck, good or bad, often comes to eclipse the role of individual agency in the stories we later tell.

My own luck had rolled over into a new spring. After a perfect regular season, I was summoned for the first game of the league playoffs against Bucknell on May 15, 2010. Plagued by injury all year long, Army had nevertheless reached the conference tournament once again. I can't tell you what I did differently that day—I know that I believed as fervently as ever in the team's ability to pull out a victory—but they fell behind early and had to play catch-up most of the way. Resilient, Army answered repeatedly but not quite loudly enough. They lost 11–9. My streak had finally snapped at ten games and with it a strange spell. The alchemical pinball machine of physiology, psychology, and chance that determines "how it will go" had produced, at last, a loss that had so very little to do with me but for which I nonetheless felt gravely responsible. No one banished me from the field or cast me adrift in a dinghy on the Hudson. I've been back in the dugout several times in the ensuing seasons, and I've started a new run of victories. My record is considerably enhanced, moreover, whenever the upperclassmen transmit it to the new players each spring, that sad, lonely *L* somehow eclipsed in the long string of *W*s.

The lasting force of this experience was not that it enslaved me to superstition—much of that original weirdness faded—but that it made me even more aware of the physiological weight and complexity of preparation during wartime. All those long hours at the baseball field, watching a game in which no one quite knows "how it will go," reinforced for me that I had not only to prepare my students for war—for battlefields where no one quite knows "how it will go"—but also to help them, in Joel's words, learn how to change their minds from "here" to "there" and back again as they embarked on the long war commute. It was a certain elasticity, rather than some myth of perfect preparation, that we all needed to embrace.

KEEP YOUR POWDER DRY

One need spend only a short stretch of time in military culture to realize how easily the endeavors of preparation and training can acquire a ritual, almost sacral dimension. The military is dominated by two apparently compatible impulses: moving forward and preparing to do so. Many U.S. Army unit mottoes express one idea or the other, usually in English, but sometimes in other tongues, and on occasion with a certain poetic quality. "Follow Me!" exhorts the infantry's motto, an exclamation sometimes accompanied by an authoritative wave of the arm. The 14th Cavalry Regiment urges the same in French: "Suivez Moi." The 151st Field Artillery declares, "En Avant!" Not to be outdone, the 160th Field Artillery boasts, "Toujours en Avant." The classically minded 45th Infantry Regiment declares, "Semper Anticus," while the folksy 102nd Cavalry Regiment rings in with "Show 'Em the Way."

Less dramatic and intoxicating perhaps than mottoes describing life at a place known colloquially as "the tip of the spear"—but resonant to someone, like me, working in a military academy classroom behind the lines—are those that celebrate the enterprise of preparation. Multiple units share the tag "Semper Paratus" (always prepared), and there are numerous variations on the theme: "Prepare the Way" (116th Engineer Battalion), "Prepared for All Things" (300th Support Group), "Never Unprepared" (25th Signal Battalion), "Paratus Semper et Ubique" (prepared always and everywhere; the 84th Tank Battalion), and the pithy "Prepared" (346th Field Artillery Battalion and several others). The 5th Army's "In Peace, Prepare for War" covers all the bases, but my favorite is the 181st Infantry Regiment's defiantly old-fashioned "Keep Your

Powder Dry," a vestige of the days when soldiers needed to safe-guard the gunpowder they carried. This maxim is said to have originated with Oliver Cromwell. According to Edward Hayes, whose nineteenth-century collection of Irish ballads includes one called "Oliver's Advice," "On a certain occasion, when his troops were about crossing a river to attack the enemy, he [Cromwell] concluded an address . . . with these words: 'put your trust in God; but mind to keep your powder dry.'" The line was subsequently popularized in the ballad's refrain:

> The night is gathering gloomily, the day is closing fast—
> The tempest flaps his raven wings in loud and angry blast;
> The thunder clouds are driving athwart the lurid sky—
> But, "put your trust in God, my boys, and keep your powder
>   dry."

Derived from legends such as this one or from historical incidents, military mottoes appear on wonderfully colorful coats of arms hung up in unit headquarters, emblazoned on flags, and worn in miniature on uniforms. Official insignia must be submitted for approval to the U.S. Institute of Heraldry, a New World government office with a defiantly Old World set of preoccupations: chevrons; finials and ferrules; griffins rampant. The institute characterizes heraldry as "a system for clear communication and identification on the battlefield . . . As important for the modern soldier's success as it was for that of the medieval knight, heraldry refuses to be just another relic of feudal or imperial times of old. Heraldry is alive and well, still helping to solve the timeless problem of making identification as effective as possible."

The institute's claims notwithstanding, considerable advances in communications have probably rendered the army's bellicose menagerie of elephants, dragons, serpents, and bears largely symbolic. Nonetheless, as emblems operating in a culture freighted with custom and tradition, the coat of arms and the motto do a serious kind of work, something I discovered recently, when I was asked to help devise a motto for a new brigade and to compose a narrative about its insignia. Heraldry signals to soldiers and civilians alike what armies are all about by offering graphic confirmation that they are either fighting or making ready to do so. During wartime they must do both together, and the question of the optimal balance between the two enterprises becomes contentious.

Peacetime theoretically provides an opportunity to prepare more thoughtfully and thoroughly, but it demands an extraordinarily supple imagination to envision how one might prepare for the unseen and the unknown. In the absence of the long view—the view that sees war and its inevitable aftermath as a no man's land of ungovernable, unpredictable space—peacetime training can become a rote end in and of itself. In wartime, by contrast, certain routines and procedures are jettisoned for the sake of expediency: training is curtailed, promotions accelerated. Emergencies have the power to summon extraordinary creativity in the field, while focus tends to sharpen on a particular kind of tactical preparation at home, even as the time to do it right seems to evaporate.

As a civilian professor at West Point, charged with particular aspects of the development of future military officers, I felt the uncomfortable, and sometimes illogical, pressures of wartime preparation quite keenly during the last twelve years. Moreover, I grew increasingly dissatisfied with received wisdom about what it means to prepare young men and women for military service and, more generally, for life in the twenty-first century. The great clarity of the mission, the all-encompassing transformation from peace to war, had dissolved into a murkiness that demanded a very different perspective. The further into no man's land I ventured, the easier it was to get stuck. "It sounds stupid," wrote Lieutenant G. Havard Thomas to his parents from the muddy Somme in 1916, "but it is absolutely true, the more one tried to move the faster one sticks and of course the weaker one gets." Charge ahead, and you won't get anywhere in such terrain. The only thing left to do, it seemed to me, was to wait and to work on a kind of patience and deep attention in myself and in my students that seemed entirely at odds with the urgency all around us. War teaches us that it is somehow unwise and irresponsible to look too far into the future. In combat there are undoubtedly many occasions when this makes sense, but it is impossible to sustain such a perspective if we hope to endure the no man's land that follows. "The times were full of certainties," Liebling writes in the foreword to *Mollie and Other War Pieces*. "It had attractive uncertainties, too; you never had to think about the future, because you didn't know if you would have one. Yet the risk was so disseminated over time that you seldom felt that *this* was the moment when the future might end."

Superficially, at any rate, preparation seems a rather straightforward concept: from the Latin meaning "to make ready," it involves fitting something or someone for a given "action or purpose." Where equipment is concerned, preparation might involve any number of tasks from bore sighting a weapon to inspecting the track-shoe wear on a tank. In the case of people, preparation entails education and training for a range of anticipated tasks and responsibilities. However, because not everything can be anticipated, there is always an element of guesswork involved in the act of preparation. And armies, for whom questions of life and death are paramount, don't ordinarily relish guesswork. As then secretary of defense Robert Gates suggested in a 2011 speech to West Point seniors, we aren't all that adept at forecasting the future for which we are preparing: "When it comes to predicting the nature and location of our next military engagements, since Vietnam, our record has been perfect. We have never once gotten it right."

Owing to the various pressures imposed on military organizations during wartime—shortened timelines, psychological and physical stressors, resource reallocation and constraints—robust conceptions of preparation tend to erode into more restrictive projects governed by that narrowest of standards: relevance. Relevance, of course, encompasses whatever is most directly related to the matter at hand. It doesn't usually extend, in the understandings of those who most zealously trumpet its virtues, even to the next battle. Standard-bearers for relevance—those who would seek to impose on us what I've taken to calling a tyranny of relevance—have little time for the exploration of risk and uncertainty. They often lack sufficient patience and trust to allow their charges to fail, and they usually refuse outright to confront the unsettling possibility that, all those inspirational mottoes notwithstanding, neither individuals nor armies can ever be comprehensively prepared for every contingency. War has far more "nonstandard" plays than baseball. "No other human activity is so continuously or universally bound up with chance," wrote Clausewitz. "And through the element of chance, guesswork and luck come to play a great part in war." Chance is one of the distinctive features of no man's land. In trying to deny it, armies risk ossifying, condemned, as the old adage goes, to fighting the last war rather than the present one.

War has defined us now for over a decade: it's the zeitgeist, at least for those of us who are by circumstance attuned to its rhythms. Only about a decade into war did we finally begin to allow ourselves to imagine something else. To look toward the future was no longer to be considered guilty of trivializing the present. We were already too late. With the exit from Afghanistan under way, with a series of force-wide budget and personnel cuts ongoing, reckoning with a new world has become a necessity. We can begin without an irrational sense of guilt to ponder the postwar issues we should have been thinking about all along. Cadets focused for so many years on the specific challenges of combat tours in Iraq or Afghanistan must imagine a scenario in which they end up fighting different wars in new places or in no place at all. Conditioned since their first day in uniform as new cadets—well before, for the many who define themselves primarily as a post-9/11 generation—to become veterans of particular wars, they will have to figure out how to redefine themselves and their service, to adapt to the possibility that they will not undergo the same experience that has shaped those they follow. One day, that very experience, which now frames the military's (especially the army's) view of the world and the nation's view of the military, will not be the clearest lens through which to make decisions about the future. Perhaps it never has been: tactical decisions made in response to imminent danger do not necessarily translate into long-term strategic plans. Skilled tacticians cannot be assumed automatically to possess capacious visions.

What seems most sorely lacking, at both the individual and the institutional levels, are imaginations bold enough to anticipate a future that may look nothing like the past or remarkably like some forgotten past. Critics in uniform and out—from the defense commentator Thomas Ricks to the army's own Colonel (Retired) Paul Yingling—have called attention to a deficiency of strategic thinking in the military's senior ranks, and over the last several years the military itself has begun to admit its own failure to produce leaders with this capacity. In 2012 the army launched an initiative called the Advanced Strategic Planning and Policy Program, designed to prepare officers "for service as strategic planners through a combination of practical experience, professional military education, and a doctorate from a civilian university." The largest annual cohort selected thus far, twelve officers, is tiny, and the challenges of managing those officers through a multiyear program that interrupts graduate study with a military assignment and reserves only one year for the writing of a doctoral dissertation have yet to play out. By taking these strategic thinkers out of the military mainstream yet not allowing them time to acquire the most robust academic credentials, the program could foreclose as many career possibilities as it opens. Such initiatives also have larger contexts, and at least for the army that context is the mythology that there can be no experience more important than leading a battalion, especially in combat. For their part, civilian policy makers also often make facile assumptions about war and military service, and a superficial relationship between most soldiers and civilians seems likely to dominate the postwar period just as it has characterized wartime.

A decade's fixation on a future of endlessly simmering conflicts has effectively forestalled a consideration of various issues. Only lately have military and civilian leaders begun in earnest to study what a postwar army, to say nothing of a postwar nation, ought to look like. Hours of planning have been devoted to numbers, organization, and force structure, but comparatively little attention has been paid to those less tangible elements of the culture that are harder both to measure and to change. War works transformation: the end of the combat-exclusion ban on women, the repeal of Don't Ask, Don't Tell, the concerted response to PTSD and traumatic brain injury. But the military continues to struggle with sexual assault, while the VA remains overwhelmed by its creaking bureaucracy and its backlog of claims.

As recent history suggests, discussions about the skills necessary for leaders to solve these problems are too often mired in sentimentality. A hypothetical scenario from the future may help to illustrate the point: The year is 2050. The president is making the case for the next secretary of defense. The nominee, a two-term senator from Maryland and member of the Senate Armed Services Committee, also happens to be a decorated combat veteran of the wars fought at the beginning of the century. Twice deployed to Afghanistan as a member of a Cultural Support Team supporting special-operations combat forces, she earned a Combat Action Badge and received a Silver Star for her actions during an ambush by insurgents in Kandahar Province. Leaving the army after five years, the nominee went on to acquire extensive policy experience in several government agencies before running for elected office.

Yet in any discussion of the nominee, the president leads with her combat experience rather than dwelling on the credentials earned in the intervening decades in graduate school or in the political arena. She is instead celebrated as a pioneer who by her courage under fire demonstrated to leaders the obsolescence of the combat-exclusion policy. This focus suits both an electorate willfully ignorant of a military populated exclusively by volunteers and a constituency of veterans clinging defensively and reflexively to the badge of service in a nation for whom the unpleasantness at the dawn of the century is but a vague memory. The hypothetical nominee's actions in uniform many years earlier were admirable, her contributions significant, but in precisely what sense are they germane to leading the government's largest department?

By the middle of this century, the generation that devoted its twenties to fighting the foreign wars of the last decade will have reached the age of those Vietnam veterans (John Kerry, Chuck Hagel, and John McCain most salient among them) who currently occupy the national stage. Erstwhile soldiers may indeed make fine political leaders but not as a result of military service alone. Endorsing some magic correlation between battlefield sacrifice and preparation for political office demonstrates our fundamental inattention to the nuances of the veteran experience. Does anyone imagine that Kerry and Hagel are qualified to be secretary of state and secretary of defense respectively because of their decades-old combat experience in Vietnam? Instead, their qualifications more logically derive from policy expertise acquired through subsequent careers in public service. Nevertheless, President Obama's speeches during the confirmation hearings as well as a raft of opinion columns repeatedly adduced both men's identities as decorated veterans as evidence of their suitability. There was particular emphasis on the relevance of Hagel's experience as an infantryman to the office of secretary of defense. "Chuck knows that war is not an abstraction," the president declared at the press conference announcing the nomination. "In Chuck Hagel our troops see a decorated combat veteran of character and strength. They see him as one of their own." Animating the claim that military personnel regard Hagel "as one of their own" is a belief that veterans, evincing what is perhaps a natural subcultural solidarity, are predisposed to trust one another. And while it is true that fellow veterans are capable of an almost automatic exchange of trust—recall my students' assumptions about Othello and Iago—this ready confidence tends just as speedily to evaporate in the wake of perceived betrayal.

Faced with prolonged senatorial resistance to Hagel's nomination, President Obama took the opportunity presented by his farewell remarks for the outgoing secretary of defense, Leon Panetta, to reiterate his theme: "Keeping us prepared will be the mission of my nominee to be the next secretary of defense, a combat veteran with the experience, judgment and vision that our troops deserve, Chuck Hagel." There are some largely unexplored assumptions here about the role of combat in shaping a veteran's character, insight, and perspective. There's also something a bit Shakespearean about repeated references to a nominee's day of battle. It calls to mind Coriolanus, the victorious general appointed consul by the Roman senate and then asked to follow custom in courting the people's vote by ceremonially showing off his wounds. "Let me o'erleap that custom," Coriolanus pleads, "for I cannot . . . / . . . entreat them / For my wounds' sake to give their suffrage." The appeal to combat experience might prove rhetorically expedient, especially for a president who represents a party reflexively charged since the Vietnam War with being soft on defense. But the sentimental currency of this argument seems far more substantive than its intellectual weight. Made during wartime, the allusion to concrete experience tends to carry a mythic force that wards off explanation or examination. Because this won't be the last time such a claim is made on behalf of a candidate or nominee for political office, it is worthwhile trying to figure out more precisely what the potential utility of military service as preparation for something else might mean.

Of course for most Americans today, war actually is, to borrow the president's word, an abstraction, or maybe a kind of video game. In a country in which few citizens enter uniformed service, actual experience of war, and military service more broadly, are rare commodities among public officeholders. And there is a powerful corresponding sense in which the veteran himself or herself has become an abstraction to many Americans: a hero, an object of sympathy, perhaps, yet still something of a mystery—and safer that way.

Combat experience itself is not a monolith: the pilot dropping bombs miles above a target has a profoundly different experience from that of the infantry soldier laying an ambush in a jungle. Even soldiers of the same unit fighting together in a battle have come away with radically different understandings generated by a variety of factors, many of which—emotional and rational intelligence, maturity, sensibility, life experience—are entirely independent of combat and predate initiations into war. Those who witness and deal death almost certainly know something particular, but it is facile to suggest that all veterans return from all wars knowing the same thing. There are soldiers for whom the crucible of combat is transformative, others for whom it is but one episode in a life filled with vivid and diverse engagements. Among war's survivors are some who fight only to prevent its reoccurrence and a few who can't survive without it—who find its rhythms more congenial than those of peace. "I hate war as only a soldier who has lived it can, only as one who has seen its brutality, its futility, its stupidity," Dwight David Eisenhower declared, while Theodore Roosevelt, a veteran of the Spanish-American War, felt a "power of joy" in combat and remembered to his death the Battle of San Juan Hill as "the great day of my life." The invocation of veteran status as shorthand for some particular quality or capacity we all think we can identify (but remain reluctant to define) seems, among other things, to be a symptom of the current civilian-military gap. The universalizing of wartime experience ignores differences in rank, branch, and service culture; in the nature of the conflict; in the duration of combat service; in the length of a military career.

A comparison of two World War II–era soldiers, George C.

Marshall and Audie L. Murphy, might help to illustrate the point. Both men solicit our admiration: they made extraordinary sacrifices, displayed remarkable strength and endurance, and proved themselves exceptionally resourceful soldiers. But Marshall and Murphy drew on entirely different skills and attributes to fight their wars. The scale of the endeavors of, on the one hand, managing a vast, complex organization of eight million people as the army chief of staff and, on the other, displaying audacity under fire as a private soldier and later in command of a company is wildly disproportionate. How much of what a secretary of state or a secretary of defense must know and do is developed by the experience of combat? How analogous is leading a small unit in a tactical environment, as Kerry and Hagel both did, to managing, and shaping strategy for, large government bureaucracies like the Department of State and the Department of Defense?

One of the most appealing, powerful, and practically significant assumptions about veterans who hold public office is that they will be more circumspect than peers without military service regarding decisions involving the use of force. But in a 2001 study of the declining number of veterans in the U.S. Congress, William T. Bianco and Jamie Markham found that "the impact of veteran status on how a representative voted" on "use-of-force questions . . . as well as votes on other military matters . . . is generally quite small" and "primarily indirect." "Whatever information or perspective military experience conveys," they add, "this effect will often be washed out by the impact of other factors on the vote decision." As a senator Hagel voted in favor of the 2002 resolution for the use of force in Iraq, as did Kerry, but by 2005 Hagel had become an outspoken critic of the Bush administration's war policy, earning in the process the enduring mistrust and resentment of some of his Republican colleagues. "Experience proves," Ulysses S. Grant once noted, "that the man who obstructs a war in which his nation is engaged, no matter whether right or wrong, occupies no enviable place in life or history." When he wrote these words, Grant was thinking of the Mexican-American War, in which he fought, even though he regarded it "as one of the most unjust ever waged by a stronger against a weaker nation." And neither that conviction nor the gruesome scenes he experienced as a young lieutenant on the battlefields of Mexico stopped him from rejoining the army to fight in the Civil War, which he judged a war of principle.

The argument in blood, as we might call it, has a double edge. In 1971, John Kerry told the Senate Committee on Foreign Relations, "The country doesn't know it yet, but it has created a monster, a monster in the form of millions of men who have been taught to deal and to trade in violence, and who are given the chance to die for the biggest nothing in history; men who have returned with a sense of anger and a sense of betrayal which no one has yet grasped." When a veteran is paraded before the nation as a potential cabinet member, we are meant to see not a monster or a broker in violence but a person of superior wisdom, restraint, and stability. Ironically, as a recent study by the Center for a New American Security reveals, some employers are quicker to see monsters in their veteran job applicants: negative stereotypes about PTSD and anger issues, the study found, may play a role in the significant unemployment rates among veterans. The lingering fear that war has irrevocably transformed soldiers, unfitting them through the practice of violence for resuming civilian lives, echoes all those ambivalent references to military service in the films of the post–World War II period. We may be more politic than the pilot's wife in *The Blue Dahlia*—we may not say that veterans have "learned to like hurting people"—yet there's a deep, perhaps unconscious suspicion that it's true just the same. It is easier to pathologize soldiers than it is to examine our own relationship to violence.

The hero of a tragedy, Coriolanus offers the ultimate case. His attitudes are defiantly out of the mainstream. Arrogant, unyielding, insufferably contemptuous of the civilian population for whom he fights, he is no thoughtful voter's idea of a successful political leader, and he is unlike most of the soldiers I know. But no one—least of all today's myriad out-of-work and homeless veterans—would likely quarrel with the wisdom of his demurral: "I had rather have my wounds to heal again / Than hear say how I got them."

DOUBLY ENVELOPED BY RELEVANCE

Balancing the short and long term; recognizing the value of the seemingly irrelevant to one's future; acknowledging the ways in which even the best preparation can blind us to certain truths about going to war and coming home—none of this is easy for cadets or their teachers. The fundamental paradox of military preparation is that the more exhaustively and exclusively one prepares for a particular event, the more one unfits oneself for any other. I don't wish to gainsay the value of military training and preparedness, but I have become increasingly concerned with identifying the point at which preparation induces paralysis. To imagine that any regimen can eliminate the unexpected is to embrace a dangerous fantasy. And how best to prepare soldiers for the inevitability of their own unpreparedness is a conundrum with which anyone responsible for their education must reckon.

Armies may not be the only organizations in perpetual "preparation mode," but they apply themselves to it with an intensity, urgency, and procedural exactitude absent from many institutional cultures. As John Keegan observes in *The First World War*, the military cult of preparation grew up in late-nineteenth-century Europe with the emergence of staff colleges, institutions devoted to the business of abstract planning. War plans were made with mathematical precision: the most promising graduates of staff colleges were put to work, Keegan explains, "arranging mobilisation schedules, writing railway deployment timetables and designing plans for every eventuality in national security." Alexander the Great, Hannibal, the Duke of Marlborough, Napoleon, Sherman—they all had plans. Nevertheless, as Keegan notes, these generals essentially made those plans "on the hoof, when war threatened or had actually begun."

Hannibal had a plan of sorts—to invade Italy—but he met surprise with equanimity, and he sometimes experimented on the march rather than executing a rigid plan. His expedition over the Alps, for example, was a miserable success. "Most of the climb," reports the Roman historian Livy, whose account makes up for in drama what it lacks in geographical precision, "had been taken over trackless mountain-sides; frequently a wrong route was taken—sometimes through the deliberate deception of the guides, or, again, when some likely-looking valley would be entered by guess-work, without knowledge of whither it led." Hannibal also had to contend with the fear of his soldiers, for whom alpine reality outstripped even the most fabulous report. "The dreadful vision was now before their eyes," Livy writes, "the towering peaks, the snow-clad pinnacles soaring to the sky, the rude huts clinging to the rocks, beasts and cattle shrivelled and parched with cold, the people with their wild and ragged hair, all nature, animate and inanimate, stiff with frost: all this, and other sights the horror of which words cannot express, gave a fresh edge to their apprehension." Although their general kept "his eyes open and alert for every contingency," he was occasionally outfoxed by the terrain as well as by the local tribes. Thousands of Carthaginians died along the way. Nevertheless, Hannibal adapted and advanced, accompanied all the while by those formidable elephants, who proved a burden on the narrow mountain defiles yet intimidated the region's hostile inhabitants, who had never before seen such fantastic creatures.

The army's descent, at once shorter and steeper, was even worse than the climb. Knowing the travail ahead, Hannibal reportedly attempted to inspire his men by telling them that in crossing the Alps, they were in effect "walking over the very walls of Rome." Then his army lurched its way down the mountainside. Amid the chaos of stumbling animals and men, encountering an impassable precipice on the way down, Hannibal figured out, after some exhausting trial and error in deep snow, that he would have to cut his way through the rock, a feat evidently accomplished by means of fire, sour wine, and picks. With these ingredients the Carthaginians carved a switchback along a cliff face over which the column could pass.

The alpine crossing was an adventure that might have ended just as easily in disaster as in triumph. But it was not this aspect of the Carthaginian's generalship—this peculiar hodgepodge of instinct and error, design and dumb luck, audacity and blundering—that obsessed future military theorists, notably Alfred von Schlieffen, chief of the Imperial German General Staff from 1891 to 1906. It wasn't the wonder of those thirty-seven elephants that engaged Schlieffen's military imagination: those terrifying engines of war, at once totem and astonishing impracticality, their provenance still a mystery to modern day archaeologists, crossing the Rhône on rafts, outrunning the Allobroges, sliding their way past Celtic enfilades, and surviving the alpine crossing only to draw nearer to an imminent extinction. Only one of them, "the Syrian," reportedly Hannibal's own, lived to see the end of the war.

No, Schlieffen was instead preoccupied with Hannibal's subsequent tactical tour de force at Cannae. The Carthaginian's successful double envelopment of the Romans in that battle remains one of the most celebrated maneuvers in military history, a subject of careful study by everyone from Schlieffen to Marshal Zhukov. Innovative battle order and superior cavalry enabled Hannibal to defeat eighty-seven thousand Romans with a much smaller force of fifty thousand troops. The defeat spurred the development of the vaunted Roman phalanx, a formation that would make the legions invincible for centuries. The significance of Hannibal's generalship in this engagement cannot be overstated. "The turning point in the history of ancient warfare was the battle of Cannae," observes the historian Gordon A. Craig in a representative encomium, "where the Carthaginians under Hannibal overwhelmed the Romans in the most perfect tactical battle ever fought." The appeal of Cannae owes to the enduring seduction of the decisive battle.

In the late nineteenth century Schlieffen looked to Cannae for inspiration in devising his own plan for encircling his potential enemy, France, with the German army's right wing. He started to think about his grand plan as early as 1891 and continued mono-maniacally to revise it, even after his retirement, until his death just before World War I. "He was a man without hobbies," Keegan reports. Schlieffen devised an aggressive but thoroughly inflexible plan marred by his refusal to consider political realities and by his obsession with victory by means of a decisive battle. Schlieffen subscribed to the fantasy that, as Gunther E. Rothenberg explains, "preplanning and centralized command" could effectively neutral-ize the role of chance and accident in the execution of a battle plan. It was this scientific approach to war that Leo Tolstoy satirized in *War and Peace* in his characterization of the German "military theorists" who fought with the Russians against Napoleon: men like Karl Ludwig von Phull (called Pfuel by Tolstoy), "who believed that there was a science of war and that in this science there were immutable laws—the laws of oblique movement, of outflanking, and so on." The decisions of such theorists were, according to Tol-stoy, motivated by a belief in "precise laws set down by the imagi-nary theory of war, and [they] saw in every departure from that theory only barbarism, ignorance, or ill will."

An intriguing exception to this rule was Schlieffen's predeces-sor Helmuth von Moltke (Moltke the Elder), who accepted the vicissitudes inherent in any plan's execution. "No foresight can guarantee . . . a final result," he wrote. "This depends, not merely on calculable factors, space and time, but also often on the out-come of previous minor battles, on the weather, on false news; in brief, on all that is called chance and luck in human life." Here it is again: that mysterious element of chance or luck, denied by some, courted by others, useful to those who wish to make some sense out of a sequence of not-altogether-explicable events. There was little allowance for such contingency even in the revised plan on which the German offensive of 1914 was ultimately based: no remedy for delay and no recourse to prevent the entrenched stalemate that ensued. There is a certain point at which inevitability becomes as seductive as chance; both narratives relieve the individual of agency and responsibility.

Hannibal is very much a purist's general, just as Cannae is a purist's battle. It was the centerpiece in a bold campaign that ultimately failed in the face of Rome's superior resources. Despite his brilliance in the field, Hannibal never took the capital, about three hundred miles northwest of Cannae. To divorce this one engagement from its larger context is to surrender to a blinding love of practice. The romance of practice, which concentrates on process over goals and on the discrete event rather than its larger contexts, satisfies the technician's obsession with detail and the trainer's fixation on routine. It might also offer consolation to the defeated or to those who wish to explain away their heroes' embrace of dubious outcomes. Finally, it is a sometimes necessary tonic to a soldier's ambivalence about the cause for which he or she fights. If all of your physical and psychic energy is devoted to pulling at the oars, you don't have to concern yourself with the possibility that the ship might be headed for a reef.

To celebrate Cannae is also to ignore the inordinate suffering of those who fought there: forty-eight thousand Roman soldiers died in the battle. "The rate of killing," notes Robin Lane Fox, "has been estimated at 500 lives a minute." More modest estimates put the number at a still-astonishing 100 lives a minute. The carnage stunned even the victors, who beheld the thousands of dead and wounded Romans heaped on the field at dawn the next morning after that mad press of men and horseflesh. According to Livy, some of the wounded "were found still alive with the sinews in their thighs and behind their knees sliced through, baring their throats and necks and begging who would to spill what little blood they had left. Some had their heads buried in the ground, having apparently dug themselves holes and by smothering their faces with earth had choked themselves to death." Decoupling tactical genius both from the slaughter it produced and from the ultimate futility of the campaign requires a certain clinical mind set.

There is yet another aspect to Hannibal's story that tends to be eclipsed by a focus on this one battle. The career of one of Hannibal's adversaries, Fabius Maximus, the Roman general who figured out how to defeat his country's terrifying enemy and whose dismissal from power was the prelude to Cannae, offers a parallel study in unorthodox, countercultural thinking and in the wisdom of delay. And it is this chapter in the story that has the greatest significance for anyone trying to understand the proper place of bold dissent and resistance to custom and tradition within military culture. Fabius offers an example of a general who refused to panic or to surrender absolutely to the fever of urgency that seized so many of Rome's military and political leaders when Hannibal threatened.

Plutarch, less interested as a historical biographer and moralist in the tactical aspects of war than in the ways in which its attendant extremities reveal human nature, devotes but a brief passage to Cannae in his life of Fabius Maximus. He is far more interested in the policy of delay that would come to be known, after its inventor, as Fabian strategy: because "the Carthaginians were but few, and in want of money and supplies, he [Fabius] deemed it best not to meet in the field a general whose army had been tried in many encounters, and whose object was a battle, but to . . . let the force and vigour of Hannibal waste away and expire, like a flame, for want of the aliment." Plutarch then follows Fabius through Italy as he harasses but refuses to engage Hannibal. There is far less said about the logistics of the campaign than about the stubborn determination of Fabius, who had to withstand abuse and accusations of cowardice from his fellow Romans. Fabius, unlike many of his contemporaries, was evidently not intimidated by the aura that surrounded Hannibal ever since his prodigious alpine crossing. Largely unperturbed by the "utterly strange portents" that reportedly attended the Carthaginian invasion, Fabius was much more interested in the fact that Hannibal's army was small and inadequately supplied. As a result of this intelligence, Fabius, who was possessed of "invincible patience," warned of the folly of attempting to defeat a tactically superior general by means of a decisive battle.

Nor was Fabius intimidated by the weight of Roman military tradition. Instead, he was willing to court disdain for his lack of convention. Apparently, the only one who understood Fabius's approach was Hannibal himself. Employing a type of irony to which he often has recourse, Plutarch assigns the most probing assessment of the situation to the enemy: "Hannibal was himself the only man who was not deceived, who discerned his skill and detected his tactics, and saw, unless he could by art or force bring him [Fabius] to battle, that the Carthaginians, unable to use the arms in which they were superior, and suffering the continual drain of lives and treasure in which they were inferior, would in the end come to nothing."

For his part, Fabius remained unencumbered by a fixation on decisive battle. Instead, he understood that he had to find a different and far less popular way to defeat Hannibal. His seeming reluctance and indecision were in fact the counterintuitive path to decision. Evincing superior patience, he proved able to deny himself the certainty of a definitive end. When all of Roman history and culture had prepared him to imagine his role one way, to fight like a Roman, Fabius retained the independence of mind and spirit that enabled him to play against type. Military culture, predicated as it is on uniformity and conformity, is essentially conservative and suspicious of change. In this respect it differs little from other bureaucracies and large organizations. But there is within the military the added burden of expectations about public displays of physical courage. Intellectual courage, the courage of a Fabius to buck tradition and endure condemnation as a result, is perhaps especially challenging to exercise in a culture that has historically prepared its members to risk their lives by too often insulating them against the ever-present "why." Prepared to be a model Roman, Fabius nevertheless retained the courage to prove an unconventional one. His example seems especially illuminating now in an age when at least a few farsighted leaders, like Robert Gates, have been urging young officers to "chart a different path."

MILITARY ARTS AND SCIENCES

Perhaps one's attitude toward military preparation hinges on whether one defines war as a science or an art. In the preface to a little gem of a book, *The 1865 Customs of Service for Officers of the Army*, August V. Kautz explains that a thorough knowledge of the "laws, rules, and regulations" of the service are essential to the officer. "To this extent," he asserts, war "is an exact science, and may be acquired by application and experience; anything beyond this," he goes on to say, "is the application of the art to extraordinary circumstances and difficult tasks, depending for success upon the capacity of the officer intrusted with the execution. The art of war, *a la Napoleon*, is but the same work by a superior artist." It is that capacity to which those who work within military culture might profitably pay more attention. A century before Kautz wrote his book, Major Robert Rogers, who founded the Rangers during the French and Indian Wars, celebrated two habits of mind in a soldier: "reason and judgment." Rogers's 1757 "Rules for the Ranging Service," still studied by the army's Ranger Regiment today, consists of twenty-eight rules. Like the list of rules for writers George Orwell includes in his essay "Politics and the English Language," Rogers's concludes with a rule that accounts for all those situations not covered by the rest. A "thousand occurrences and circumstances," he writes, require the Ranger "in some measure to depart from" the rules "and to put other arts and stratagems in practice; in which case every man's reason and judgment must be his guide, according to the particular situation and nature of things." Any of the rules might be ignored, but the one "maxim never to be departed from by a commander," Rogers insists, is the preservation of "a firmness and presence of mind on every occasion." When I talk about this quality with cadets, I usually call it plain common sense: that, plebes usually reply, is what they lose first on arriving at West Point. I had a running joke with one class of plebes that I had stolen their common sense back for them like Prometheus stealing fire, and that they were therefore obligated to use it to justify the risk I had run. Army doctrine is far more voluminous and detailed than it was in Rogers's day, but military careers remain full of situations not accounted for in any field manual, situations that require the presence of mind to which Rogers called attention.

Several years ago I gave a talk on the thorny subject of preparation to senior leaders at the army's Training and Doctrine Command, the very people responsible for guiding and shaping military preparation. Before I went, I sought some help from the seniors I was teaching at the time. I told them that this was their chance to speak truth to power. When I asked them what it meant to be prepared for military service, they offered nuanced responses. These soon-to-be lieutenants seemed eminently capable of adopting the long view. Indeed, they proposed that their ability to do so differentiated them from their predecessors. Suggesting that they were at once "softer and wiser than previous generations," one added that they were also "more aware of the side effects of war and the necessity for a postwar plan." I'm not sure this claim of superior prescience is entirely accurate, but it was interesting to me how emphatically they believed it because it revealed the way they wanted to see themselves: namely, as autonomous, strategic thinkers.

Several of the cadets spoke of the importance of knowing the purpose of the training exercises they are asked to complete, of the need to avoid acquiring "tunnel vision" and becoming imprisoned within "a mold of rigidity," of a desire to receive pre-combat training "on the mental/psychological level" and to have an overarching "understanding of army operations." One advocated the utility of an "interdisciplinary" approach to training. And a cadet named Colin, an English major who had spent his summer on an army-sponsored trip teaching orphans in Thailand about nutrition and physical fitness, suggested, "Preparation is about seeing and doing, not about memorizing . . . [field manuals] . . . Nothing makes me more excited than being given a task, given the pieces, and being told to go figure it out." Another reinforced the idea that figuring out "the one thing needful," to borrow a phrase from Charles Dickens's blistering attack on Victorian educational practice in *Hard Times*, is not so easy as the tyrants of relevance would like us to believe: "You never know what you'll need to know to understand something."

Of course, when you give a twenty-year-old, never mind a forty-year-old, the pieces, you have to accept the fact that sometimes you'll end up with a pile of those same pieces or with a configuration entirely different from the one you initially envisioned. That kind of risk is often incompatible with an army culture that tends to interpret all failures as "failures of leadership" because it invests itself so thoroughly in the idea of a commander's responsibility. When you make assignments or design training scenarios so open-ended that they provoke discomfort in those who have grown accustomed to regimentation, you must resign yourself to the fact that some of your pupils will fail.

If you regard that eventuality as somehow a failure of your leadership, then you will instead ensure that the twenty-year-old in question has a foolproof set of instructions, and you probably won't distract him with things like the purpose of the task you've assigned. Every leader feels this temptation at some point—it is the unhealthy, paternalistic flip side of the army's emphasis on taking care of people—but approaching the development of leaders without the willingness to take risks, and to allow subordinates to take risks, reveals a profound lack of faith in the potential leaders being developed. It requires a commander less interested in the mystic cords of authority than in a more democratic principle whereby a leader uses that authority to underwrite the initiative of others.

In today's army there seems to be a substantial divide between senior and junior officers. As a result of the last decade's wars, young officers have been promoted more quickly than their prede-cessors at the end of the last century and have had less time to learn and to practice some of the administrative procedures that dominate life in garrison. In the face of this, some senior officers—the same ones who wax lyrical about the hardships that lieuten-ants and captains have endured in combat—display considerable impatience with them. They like to talk, in tones that have more than a whiff of Paul Fussell's chickenshit, of their subordinates' ignorance of procedures, supply discipline, resource management, and standards. They praise their "sacrifices" yet simultaneously think of them as cowboys who have had too much autonomy in Iraq and Afghanistan. And they want to train these young officers in the routines of army life as if they were new lieutenants rather than captains and majors who have spent the majority of the past dozen years operating in a different universe altogether.

Junior officers, for their part, entrusted with significant re-sponsibility in combat, often in remote locations where decisions must be made quickly and independently, return frustrated and impatient to garrison life's cult of preparation, attendant inflexi-bility, and atmosphere of fear that innovation might open the door to disaster. Used to operating beyond the reach of routine, these officers return to find their lives scripted down to the last detail, mired in layers of bureaucracy. Insufficiently explained activities and requirements acquire in the absence of war's urgency what seems only the fiction of importance. But if it is true that some of these junior officers, promoted early and lacking certain kinds of conventional experiences, have not had the chance to grow up in the army and to learn its ways as their predecessors did, it is also the case that those years of difference can't be erased. The long-term health of the force depends on retaining the smartest, most ambitious of these young leaders, who seem to be leaving the army in droves not, as more than one has suggested to me, because they have wearied of the war commute but rather because they cannot endure the chickenshit of life in garrison.

I'm not sure Napoleon was right when he claimed that "a soldier will fight long and hard for a bit of colored ribbon," but the fact remains that soldiers do win such ribbons for fighting long and hard. They also receive ribbons for administrative feats such as studying the intricacies of the institution, revamping outmoded personnel systems, and redesigning force structure, yet these ribbons don't have quite the same appeal as those awarded for valor. As a result, the latter enterprises, which belong to the "institutional" rather than the "operational" force, only rarely get the kind of timely, impassioned, or sustained attention they so desperately need.

FLOAT LIKE A BUTTERFLY, STING LIKE A BEE

I took advantage of the fact that the Training and Doctrine Command conference was being held at Gettysburg to offer up a Civil War example of the kind of inflexibility I fear: the disagreement between Lee and Longstreet over the Confederate battle plan. The enduring reverence for Lee's tactical superiority—for his unparalleled ability, as I heard yet another enthusiast exclaim not so long ago, "to do more with less"—is an apologist's end run around causes and contexts, but Gettysburg also offers an example of Lee's fallibility.

As James McPherson recounts in his history of the Civil War, *Battle Cry of Freedom*, Lee hoped that Gettysburg would prove the decisive battle that would destroy the Union army. Resisting Longstreet's repeated pleas that he maneuver around the enemy to get between it and Washington, Lee pointed to Cemetery Hill and declared to his subordinate, "The enemy is there, and I am going to attack him there." On the second day of the battle, when Longstreet tried again, Lee's reply was substantially the same, and it evinced the inflexibility that culminated in Pickett's Charge: "The enemy is there, and I am going to strike him." Longstreet later wrote of his commander, "In defensive warfare he was perfect. When the hunt was up, his combativeness was overruling." In a revealing analogy, Shelby Foote likens Lee at Gettysburg to a boxer. Lee resisted Longstreet's plans and dismissed the objections of Jubal Early because they would have necessitated, in Foote's words, "a change in his preferred style of fighting . . . Early was suggesting what amounted to a change of stance, which was neither an easy nor a wise thing for a boxer to attempt, even in training, let alone after a match was under way, as it was now."

I shared Foote's parallel with a boxer named Mike, a former army captain who spent much of his time in uniform as a member of the army's World Class Athlete Program (WCAP), which exists to support Olympic caliber athletes in uniform. In a reflection of the times, WCAP also now supports an increasing number of wounded soldiers in their quest to become Paralympians. The athletes and their coaches in the program give back in turn to the force at large by participating in the reintegration process: organizing classes and physical training sessions for redeployed units, with a special focus on those soldiers contending with anger issues and PTSD. The reintegration program is animated by the belief that the discipline required to learn a new sport can enhance mental and physical resiliency as well as build trust within units.

I first encountered Mike at West Point, where I advised his senior thesis on boxing and violence in film. I occasionally perplex my students with the revelation that I am a boxing enthusiast and that I learned my love of the sweet science at my mother's knee. She, in turn, acquired a taste for the sport as a young girl watching *Friday*

Night Fights at her father's knee. There's nothing quite like chancing on a string of *Superbouts* reruns on ESPN on a weekend afternoon and devoting a few hours to some classics, preferably called by the peerless Don Dunphy: Rocky Marciano against Joe Walcott, perhaps the brief 1965 title fight between Muhammad Ali and Sonny Liston, or the elegant Sugar Ray Robinson against anyone.

Mike had come to New York City in the summer of 2011 because the team was scheduled to work out for a few weeks at Gleason's Gym in Brooklyn. One day—the hottest day of the year, as it happened—I went over to Front Street to watch them spar. With its antediluvian miasma of sweat, peeling paint, and walls covered with pictures of Golden Gloves champs and celebrities, Gleason's, one scruffy flight of stairs above street level, is the ne plus ultra of old-school boxing gyms. The only signs of changing times, scattered in and among the boxers, are a few well-heeled residents of the neighborhood's new condos, who obviously prefer Gleason's retro aesthetic to the local Equinox. In the dusty storeroom at the back you can buy a ball cap emblazoned with Muhammad Ali's immortal "Float like a butterfly, sting like a bee" or, irresistible to me, a T-shirt with a quotation from Virgil's *Aeneid* stenciled on the back:

> Now, whoever has courage and a strong
> and collected spirit in his breast,
> let him come forward, lace on the
> gloves and put up his hands.

This is Aeneas's challenge to the assembled Trojans during the funeral games held in memory of his father in book 5. The super-bout that follows is the competition's culminating event. Its story line, which has been reprised with various permutations in countless rings ever since, pits a young braggart, Darès, against an old champion, Entellus, who by his own admission is "slowed" and "spent."

Entellus initially appears in the ring with ox-hide gloves reinforced with iron and splattered with the blood and brains of past adversaries. This was an age in which the analogies between sport and war we so cavalierly throw around today actually had some teeth. Seeing his opponent quail, the old champion generously exchanges his battle-tested "gauntlets" for less lethal equipment. At first, Darës punches "like one assaulting a tall city / Or laying siege to a stronghold on a height," while Entellus holds his ground. When the latter, seeing an opening, lets loose with a monstrous punch and misses, his momentum causes him to fall "mightily to earth" like an "uprooted pine." The old veteran is so embarrassed by this miscue that he goes on the attack and in his rage would have killed the bewildered Darës had not Aeneas stepped in to end the fight and declare the winner. Victorious, Entellus marks his retirement from the ring by killing the unlucky bull that was to have been his prize with a single punch between the horns. "Here is a better life in place of Darës," he announces, "here I lay down my gauntlets and my art."

Thus Virgil describes a battle of heavyweights. Mike, a light flyweight, fights near the other end of the classification scale. In fact, you can't get much lighter. "He's a chihuahua," one of his hulking teammates joked with me at the gym, "small but vicious." Mike has always had a sophisticated understanding, further refined by the process of researching and writing his undergraduate thesis, of the ways in which (all the platitudes notwithstanding) sport, even a blood sport like boxing, is not at all like war. Mike has also acquired through his endeavors the kind of discipline and poise that served him well as an officer who had to reckon at the outset with what it meant to train for the Olympics while his classmates were fighting in Iraq and Afghanistan. As we sat in a diner one evening during his visit to New York, Mike discussed his Olympic dreams, which subsequently went unfulfilled, and his ambition to go back to school, which he has since realized; his devotion to boxing and simultaneous ambivalence about the anomalous arc of his career during a time of war; and his efforts, as the lone officer on the WCAP boxing team, to be a leader as well as a teammate.

Part of the reason the team had come to Brooklyn was to prepare for nationals by sparring against fighters with styles different from those they had grown accustomed to in Colorado, where they train year-round. The New York style, as Mike describes it, is "more aggressive" than the southern and western varieties. New York fighters "walk their opponents down. This is considered more of the professional style of boxing, where they don't throw a lot of punches, but when they do punch, they make the punches count." When I asked Mike about Shelby Foote's boxing analogy, he immediately agreed that it is a tall order to expect a boxer to change his style: "it is difficult to alter habit in the ring" after "hundreds of hours" spent perfecting a particular style that works. To reach the most elite levels of competition, however, a boxer "must always be ready to adjust" to such a significant degree that even if the "basic foundation of the style" stays the same, "the boxer will change small things about it to almost transform it into a new style altogether."

In other words, a boxer needs to be able to make so many minor adjustments to his own style that he can effectively impersonate another kind of boxer. Mike offered the following example: When an aggressive "brawler" meets a "slick, elusive boxer" who effectively sticks and moves against him, the brawler must "quickly and decisively" change his approach. "Unless you do tape study," Mike explains, "you don't know what type of style your opponent is going to have, and elite boxers know to assess the style of an opponent in a split second (right after the opening bell), employ a certain strategy, but be ready and willing to adapt and adjust strategies in an instant if the initial one is not working successfully." A solid plan A that plays to one's strengths is great, Mike concedes, but a boxer had better have "plan B, plan C, plan D, and plan E in his back pocket if the first plan proves unsuccessful." So while a boxer can't make the unnatural natural, he can embrace a new style and the discomfort that comes along with it in order to meet an unanticipated challenge. In other words, he can learn how to become a chameleon when the situation requires.

FATE, CHANCE, KINGS, AND DESPERATE MEN

It is difficult to preserve such flexibility within the context of the military's strict training regimen. Soldiers prepare by learning how to execute certain fundamental tasks: firing a weapon, for example; writing an operations order; performing a pre-combat inspection; running a firing range. They become well versed in what the army calls Tactics, Techniques, and Procedures, or TTPs. The military excels at training competencies, at inculcating a specific set of moral values that guide practice, at instilling a particular kind of emotional and physical discipline. Yet as an institution preoccupied with habits of body and spirit, its culture can seem less interested in—perhaps even ill designed for—the project of developing habits of mind or intellect. For unlike a perfect score on a physical fitness or marksmanship test, success in this domain doesn't have a uniformly predictable end, a discrete measure of success or victory. In fact, it might lead only to more questions and doubts or to conclusions that unsettle established narratives. Yet the early encouragement of such habits is absolutely necessary for a military that is in the process of having to reinvent itself (and for a nation whose governing institutions sometimes seem paralyzed).

The sense that the study of literature can create atmospheres of productive discomfort in which such traits might be fostered animates my belief in it as a teacher of strategy as well as tactics: a cadet might refine analytic skills and observation through practice at close reading, and she may also thereby acquire a sophisticated sense of narrative, in particular of the inadequacy of many of the stories we tell ourselves or of the possibility of imagining new endings. As the war comes to an end and resources continue to dwindle, one way to think of the problem faced by the U.S. military, but perhaps especially by the army—the service most strained over the last decade—is one of telling a story sufficiently convincing that the nation will undertand the force's role and that the most promising soldiers and officers will decide to stay in. How, in other words, amid the vertigo of a postwar no man's land, will the army write its next chapter?

The literature I read with cadets is replete with examples of soldiers and statesmen who fail to craft their own stories. Indeed, they remain unprepared for their futures even after they are revealed by various sources: oracles, dreams, ghosts, divine visitations. Think of Macbeth contemplating the prophesied yet logically impossible approach of Birnam Wood to Dunsinane and then finding himself incensed by news of the arrival of the enemy force resourcefully disguised in leaf camouflage. Greek literature is likewise littered with misreaders driven to commit often irreversible acts of violence because they surrender too quickly to false assumptions. Oedipus, perhaps antiquity's most celebrated misreader, assumes that by leaving what he thinks to be his natural family in Corinth, he can defy the prophecy that he will kill his father and marry his mother. Oedipus's tragedy hinges in part on the fact that his skill in deciphering riddles is simultaneously the "curse" that brings him, all unwitting, home again to Thebes: it is Oedipus's early success in solving the riddle of the Sphinx that leads the Thebans to accept this stranger as their king in the first place.

"The tragedy of preparedness," the British novelist E. M. Forster suggests, was understood much more thoroughly by the Greeks than by his own age, which assumed "that preparation against danger is in itself a good, and that men, like nations, are the better for staggering through life fully armed." In his *Histories*, Herodotus gives us a prime example of a man who built an entire career on preparing for the wrong things in the story of Croesus, the stubborn king of Lydia. After a dream reveals to him that his favorite son will one day die by a wound from an iron spearhead, the king takes a series of precautions to preserve the boy from this fate. He arranges for his marriage and a domestic haven, withdraws him from military service, and keeps him close always. He even goes so far as to order the weapons hanging on the palace walls removed lest one accidently fall on the boy. One day, denied permission to join a boar hunt, Croesus's son finally demands an explanation for this relentless paternal campaign of overprotectiveness. After being told about the dream, the boy tries to allay Croesus's fears by telling him that because the oracle specifically indicated death by iron, there is no risk in going up against the tusks of a boar. Croesus relents before this argument even though its logic is as specious as his own. In the ensuing confusion of the chase in the forest his son is killed by the errant spear of a fellow hunter, the very man assigned to be his bodyguard.

Learning next to nothing from this experience, however, Croesus goes on to misread another prophecy issued at Delphi, which states that if he invades Persia, a great empire will fall. Croesus quickly concludes that the empire referred to is that of the Persians—oracles have a way of seeming to answer our deepest desires—but he fails to request further interpretation and thus doesn't realize that it is his own empire that is meant. Herodotus has little sympathy for this king of misreading: "Croesus had no grounds for complaint as regards the oracle. Loxias predicted that if he invaded Persia, he would destroy a great empire. Faced with this, if he had thought about it he would have sent men to enquire whether Loxias meant Cyrus' empire or his own. Because he misunderstood the statement and failed to follow it up with another enquiry, he should blame no one but himself for what happened."

One of the things I've learned by reading texts such as this with cadets is that the most important difference between the student I was and the students I teach is that my students think they know exactly what it is they are preparing for. They crave this particular guarantee in a world in which most assurances are far more elusive. Whatever else they might be in life, the cadets who sit in my English class will almost certainly be second lieutenants, receiving their commissions in the U.S. Army on the very day of their graduation from West Point, bachelor's degrees in hand. They cannot know exactly what this passage entails, but they know their title, rank, and duty position. And a few still imagine themselves in Afghanistan one day, even as this fate becomes less and less likely.

As an undergraduate, I had aspirations and expectations, I envisioned possible paths and scenarios, but I couldn't have drawn the map from there to here. I had none of the certainty that can limit an educational experience in ways large and small. After abandoning sometime during my freshman year in college a long-standing plan to become a physician, I no longer had a blueprint to consult. As I reflect on my own undergraduate experience, I realize the degree to which I depended on a criterion of engagement rather than one of utility. My attitude no doubt stemmed in part from my ignorance about what the future held, and it was only when I did not find a given subject particularly compelling that I started to complain of its irrelevance. My students might protest—or might be conditioned to feel they ought to protest—that they don't have the luxury of adopting such an attitude because they know unequivocally what is and is not relevant to their future profession. But that kind of vocational sureness is illusory. Even when we know exactly what the future holds, its manner of materializing can nonetheless surprise and betray our most meticulous preparation. That's why preparing people for the future remains, even in an age so heavily indebted to calibration, assessment, technical precision, and utility—an era in which economic distress naturally prompts the minutest calculations—such a delicate and mysterious business.

We often prepare for things without knowing it. Even the piece of knowledge we will in fact never need again might be setting us up for something else entirely. We just don't know what. The very memory of having learned it—of struggling to grasp it, of wondering why on earth someone else could possibly think it so important—

may recur to us one day. And what we have forgotten is at least as important in shaping us as what we remember. When we acquire knowledge for its own sake—the very purpose of a university education, according to John Henry Newman, the nineteenth-century English cardinal and founder of what became University College Dublin—we sift it far more finely than we do when we approach it with an eye to a specific use. And while my students may think they know exactly what they are preparing for, they may in fact be preparing for something else entirely. We all thought we were preparing for war, for example, when we were really about to plunge into no man's land.

THE PERFORMER's PARADOX

When I mentioned the paradox of military preparation to one of my colleagues, Karin, who in addition to being an English professor is a trained violinist, she recognized it immediately. The musician, she explains, needs "to have prepared well enough to know that most preparation will not help in many important situations. The need to prepare to be unprepared so you can draw on what you really need when you need it. It is a performer's paradox. That on the stage, at least, no preparation can prepare you for what you need to do to really make it good, but if you aren't unbelievably prepared, you aren't prepared enough for making the most of being unprepared." Like the boxer in the ring, the musician must know the music so well that she is able to do in performance what she has never quite done in rehearsal, to adjust when something goes wrong. Precisely what might go wrong is difficult to predict, but the very act of imagining error becomes an elastic, translatable skill. "You never know what you will need to draw on," Karin elaborated. "Being really prepared means imagining possible outcomes and preparing for those, so even if you haven't imagined a particular circumstance you encounter, you've practiced the practice of imagining and adapting . . . That is a process you can use, and it can come in handy even if it is all new and you know nothing."

Although in important ways an isolated subculture, the U.S. military—to say nothing of the nation's foreign policy—is nevertheless infused with certain American cultural attributes that work against the kind of supple and expansive preparation useful to boxers and musicians alike and, it would appear, demanded by long wars. Among those characteristics are a tendency to master and standardize processes so thoroughly that they can eclipse a consideration of desired outcomes, a mistrust of any idea that cannot be readily quantified, an obsession with the short-term assessment of trends whose full significance might not be visible for decades, an impatient desire for immediate gratification, a traditional "can-do" rhetoric that discourages the necessary contemplation of potential failure. On this last point, with regard to Afghanistan, Leon Wieseltier wrote a few years ago in *The New Republic*, "I am tired of hearing that failure is not an option and that we are in this to win. Failure is *always* an option and war is not a football game." And because by many measures—military, political, economic—the century's opening has been a failure, the belated attempt to look it all in the eye leads only to more confusion.

ACCIDENTAL TOURISTS

Because history and literature offer up so many diligent failures, I find myself drawn increasingly to stories of individuals whose successful preparation for the future was in some fundamental sense unexpected and unintentional. One to which I often return in class is that of Ulysses S. Grant. As a West Point cadet, when he wasn't reading novels, Grant prepared for his military career by spending much of his time riding horses. And he became the best rider around. Sure enough, in one of his first major engagements during the Mexican-American War, Grant's impeccable horsemanship saved his life and possibly the lives of his comrades.

Forward with a small detachment, running low on ammunition, Grant volunteered to ride through the town of Monterrey, Mexico, to get a message back to the main force. His route took him through the city's open streets. Here's how he describes the scene: "My ride back was an exposed one. Before starting I adjusted myself on the side of my horse furthest from the enemy, and with only one foot holding to the cantle of the saddle, and an arm over the neck of the horse exposed, I started at full run. It was only at street crossings that my horse was under fire, but these I crossed at such a flying rate that generally I was past and under cover of the next block of houses before the enemy fired. I got out safely without a scratch."

It's a great yarn, but it is really only a minor part of the story. In Mexico, Grant fought with many of the people he had trained with at West Point, and he assumed at the time that he would always be fighting with them against a common enemy. Perhaps like many others he anticipated a coming conflict, but he could not have easily imagined fighting on the opposite side from many old friends in the Civil War. Nothing had prepared him for that. Or had it? Grant's book is replete with phrases such as "I had known so-and-so at West Point" or "I had served with so-and-so in Mexico." This is his way of suggesting that he knew how a fellow's mind worked, his capacities and limitations, what he was likely to do in a tight spot. People liked to say Grant was the only Union general who wasn't afraid of Robert E. Lee: he had served with Lee in Mexico. Always a sharp observer of human nature under pressure, Grant had all along been preparing to fight his friends. He just didn't know it. And he was better prepared than most.

One of my favorite modern-day examples of the vicissitudes of preparation is a major named Dave, who was a plebe in the very first literature class I taught at West Point. Dave was an important member of a terrific group full of strong personalities. That year we read *Henry V*, and Dave manifested an uncomplicated, boyish delight in Shakespeare's electric warrior-king. Dave ended up majoring in operations research—he was in those days, as he'll tell you, a "math guy"—but whenever we encountered each other on post, Dave was ready with a quotation from the play: "Once more unto the breach, ma'am!" "The game's afoot!" What Dave read stuck, and his experience with literature continued to percolate in his mind as he became a cavalry officer learning to navigate the shoals of army life, especially the art of communicating up and down the chain of command and, when deployed, with potential allies and adversaries.

As a scout platoon leader, Dave continued to be drawn to Henry V's powers of inspiration. Whenever he got ready to brief his soldiers before a patrol, he assumed what he refers to as his "Henry V face." Yet Shakespeare gradually became more than just a rallying cry for Dave. On his second deployment, in command of a scout troop at a series of remote outposts, he read more Shakespeare, and as he read, he began to consider more closely and thoughtfully Shakespeare's nuanced treatment of language, leadership, and war. The insights about responsibility and heroism that Dave had acquired through practice over the years now discovered echoes and parallels in the tragedies and history plays he was reading.

One day Dave surprised both of us, I think, by telling me he wanted to come back to West Point to teach English. In the e-mails that went back and forth between my office on the Hudson and Dave's combat outpost in the desert, we carried on a correspondence rich in a shared history and a curiosity about the ways in which literature can influence a life. Dave recently finished a three-year tour at West Point, having completed a master's thesis on the language of Shakespeare's military heroes, and he taught plebe English with the same gusto and inventiveness he once brought to its study as a cadet. He relished the opportunity to share with the sixty or so plebes he taught his passion for learning, for literature, and for soldiering; and the story of a rather unexpected career whose next chapter would unfold in Afghanistan.

A NIGHT AT THE IMPROV

Nothing exposes the heaviness of the burdens of military preparation on professional soldiers more clearly than a tale of amateurs. When I first saw *Army of Shadows*, Jean-Pierre Melville's 1969 film about the French Resistance, at its belated U.S. release in 2006, it was a revelation: the quietest example I knew of cinema's noisiest genre and another vision of war that would become a part of my teaching. Later, watching Melville's film in the company of cadets, I began to see much more. *Army of Shadows* depicts a network of civilian fighters poorly equipped, largely untrained, unable fully to trust even their closest comrades. One member of the cell is a veteran of the French Foreign Legion, another two served together on the crew of a bomber, but the leader of the cell, the film's protagonist, Philippe Gerbier, worked as a civil engineer before the war. And the chief of the organization is a cloistered philosopher — a man who knows that his value lies precisely in the fact that he knows "nothing about weapons."

The cadets, some of whom spend long weeks at airborne school over the summer, are typically amazed by Gerbier's sangfroid as he parachutes into occupied France without any training whatsoever. "Be careful when you hit the ground," an RAF major helpfully advises when he learns that Gerbier has never jumped before. Such improvisation tends to unsettle my students even as it awakens their admiration. "I am an expert," the U.S. Army's Soldier's Creed proclaims, "and I am a professional." Indeed, it is almost impossible to go through a day at West Point without hearing the words "professional" and "professionalism," the phrase "profession of arms," or a reference to "professional development." Amateurs don't carry many of the burdens that professionals acquire. For Gerbier and his resistance cell there are no surprises because everything is a surprise. They have no choice but to anticipate, adapt, and imagine the impossible even as they embody the soldierly virtues of knowing "how to command and how to take orders." There is a natural tension between professional discipline and making it up as you go along. In *Army of Shadows*, improvisation is all the amateur has.

One of the challenges facing my students will be to embody the discipline, expertise, and ethical standards of a highly professionalized organization while preserving the spontaneity and creativity that exigent circumstances so often demand and inspire. The longer one spends within a professional system, the less comfortable one can grow with the fluidity, surprise, and risk that are the amateur's daily diet. The army's imagination of itself as a profession is by no means a new phenomenon. It gathered considerable momentum after World War II, with the institution of a sizable peacetime standing army. The 1957 publication of Samuel Huntington's *The Soldier and the State* occasioned a new degree of self-awareness among soldiers. Huntington insisted that "the modern officer corps is a professional body and the modern military officer is a professional." He defines a profession as an entity that adheres to a codified set of institutional values; preserves the trust of those it serves; and employs practitioners with expert knowledge and skills, a sense of specialized vocation, and a commitment to a career of education and self-development.

The nation has had at least a small regular army of career soldiers for much of its history, but popular culture (especially as purveyed by Hollywood) has perpetuated the rival, often more compelling mythology of the citizen-soldier: Gary Cooper as Sergeant York, the reluctant yet resourceful infantryman who draws on his experience hunting turkeys to outfox the Germans on the western front; and, more recently, Tom Hanks as Captain John Miller, the high-school English teacher turned ranger in *Saving Private Ryan*. In these scenarios instinct and practical know-how tend to trump years of professional training; old-fashioned common sense is more highly prized than professional expertise. In addition, citizen-soldiers, because they never fully shed their role within society, have a potentially easier time returning to it. Professionals, whose identity derives from their transformation and corresponding difference, may do their job more proficiently, but their separation from society is all the more complete. It was this unfortunate circumstance of isolation that Admiral Mullen perceived—although he didn't link it explicitly to the military's embrace of professionalism—when he urged West Point cadets to remember their identities as citizen-soldiers.

The complexity of modern warfare demands expertise from its practitioners, and one reason for today's emphasis on professionalism is the lingering association of the "citizen" with the "amateur." Yet the most robust expressions of the citizen-soldier mythology assert that it is precisely the temporary warrior's stubborn connection to a civilian self that at once enriches practice and enlightens service. Perhaps that's why the term "all-volunteer force" became so important to the restructuring of the military after Vietnam: volunteering is the act of a free citizen. Yet what does it mean to call career soldiers volunteers? Presumably, they volunteer in the same way that doctors or lawyers do: they elect their profession rather than having it chosen for them.

One hears frequent references to professionals in contemporary American culture, but here again the rhetoric is tricky. There are "consummate professionals" and "quiet professionals"; in baseball there are "professional hitters." Then there's the professional gunfighter, that legendary figure of the frontier popularized by ballads, novels, television, and films. All of these uses of the term suggest an aura of businesslike cool and efficiency; they imply expertise but not necessarily an animating ethos; these professionals may have a code, but it is personal and idiosyncratic. Engaging as they do in what the philosopher Simone Weil calls "the business of killing and dying," the gunslinger of the Old West offers a most provocative case. This figure, like today's military contractor, is a mercenary, not a professional in Huntington's—or the contemporary army's—sense of the word. The Western acquires its tragic dimension whenever the professional killer grows weary of outlawry and begins to long for the social system outside of which he has lived for so long and within which he can no longer find respite: Shane, for example, or the reluctantly resurrected gunfighter of Clint Eastwood's *Unforgiven*.

Especially in the case of a professional who deals in violence, the coexistence of skill and guiding moral principle is essential. Moderation in the use of force, Weil suggests, requires "superhuman virtue," for "excess" often proves "an irresistible temptation." Doctors have trouble enough decoding the apparently straightforward injunction "above all, do no harm." How much more complicated, then, is a profession, like the military, that *demands* the infliction of harm in certain circumstances? One of my former colleagues, Robert Underwood, whose work as a philosopher centers on military ethics, proposed that the army's "professional ethic could resolve itself to a similar sentence: 'above all, do no unnecessary harm,' or 'above all, do only necessary harm.' Of course, the conceptual weight of 'necessary' in each is considerable."

As they watch the amateurs in *Army of Shadows* reckoning with violence—with their willingness to apply it as well as their capacity to endure it—the aspiring professionals in my class reflect on what it means to exercise force. Unbound by doctrine or a clear code of conduct, or by the kinds of professional expectations that pervade the military culture to which my students belong, Melville's characters freely confess their lack of preparation for, and ambivalence about, the violent nature of their missions. They even meditate on their own occasional cowardice. Cadets don't have that luxury.

Early in the film, a new recruit who wants to prove himself is asked to assist in the assassination of a traitor who has betrayed members of the organization to the Germans. When he demurs, insisting to his more experienced comrades that it is his "first time," Gerbier responds, "It's our first time too. Isn't that obvious?" A resident fresh from medical school isn't asked to perform unsupervised brain surgeries; a first-year law associate doesn't argue before the Supreme Court. Yet a lieutenant, in charge of a platoon in a remote Afghan valley, has of necessity become a full-fledged, largely independent, professional practitioner of war.

Huntington suggests that one of the factors differentiating a profession from a trade is the breadth of a professional's learning and an "awareness" of the broader societal contexts and traditions of which the profession forms a part: "professional education consists of two phases: the first imparting a broad, liberal, cultural background, and the second imparting the specialized skills and knowledge of the profession." Yet connecting practice to context is especially difficult in the case of the soldier, whose theater of practice—the battlefield—is so radically removed from all societal context. This dynamic is further complicated by the fact that undergoing in many ways the most intense and extreme military experience—combat— at the beginning of one's career can substantially distort what follows. In some sense, military careers work in reverse.

There remains a persistent strain of romance in contemporary doctrinal literature centering on the nobility of the warrior ethos— a soldier is "the guardian of freedom," for example. But the dominant rhetoric is that of professionalism, its cultivation an attempt to shape the all-volunteer force and to give it standing in a nation increasingly inattentive to its role. It had the unintended consequence of widening the gap between the technical accomplishments of soldiering and the underlying causes and contexts those accomplishments serve. The Pew Research Center studies that place the military at the top of the list of institutions Americans trust arguably show that they trust the military to do something they no longer see fit to do themselves.

The army recently finished a comprehensive yearlong study of the profession of arms. When they initiated the campaign in the late fall of 2010, army leaders emphasized the need to examine the impact of a decade of war on the force, to understand the ways in which the profession had evolved under stress, and to adapt to future challenges. Professions change over time in response to a variety of factors: to the discovery of new knowledge, perhaps, or to developments in culture, law, or social policy. But professional reformation or melioration is usually an organic, incremental process. Few professionals, perhaps, are as dramatically transformed by practice as the military professional can be by war.

A LEAN AND HUNGRY LOOK

All wars seem long to those who fight them. Yet even a fifteen-month deployment, if this century's war commuter was lucky enough to survive it, will stand as one searing episode in a much longer narrative. It is difficult, especially in wartime, for young officers to recognize the value of the diverse attributes and capacities that longer careers of service require. The warrior's timeline is short, sometimes cruelly abbreviated. There are occasions when being a guardian of freedom involves pushing a pen rather than pulling a trigger, studying a trend rather than scouting an enemy position. There's little romance in such work, and it requires the citizen's broad view as much as the warrior's immediate grasp. But that's the life of a true professional. In today's army an officer might have a career as long as thirty or forty years, but the average length of service is in fact closer to ten.

I suspect that it is the rare lieutenant who has never once, if only fleetingly, imagined himself the chief of staff, even if he doesn't know precisely what that job entails. In 1839, General Winfield Scott, who would become the army's general in chief a few years later, visited West Point and attended a cadet parade. Among the cadets was Ulysses Grant, who confessed that Scott's "commanding figure, his quite colossal size and showy uniform" seemed to him "the finest specimen of manhood my eyes had ever beheld, and the most to be envied. I could never resemble him in appearance," playfully noted the diminutive Grant, who was always self-deprecating and often ambivalent on the subject of his own military ambitions, "but I believe I did have a presentiment for a moment that some day I should occupy his place on review—although I had no intention then of remaining in the army."

In his landmark treatise *On War*, Clausewitz asks "whether history has ever known a great general who was not ambitious; whether, indeed, such a figure is conceivable." Clausewitz knew that ambition had gotten a bum rap. "Other emotions," he explains, "may be more common and more venerated—patriotism, idealism, vengeance, enthusiasm of every kind—but they are no substitute for a thirst for fame and honor." According to Clausewitz, those other motivations could never produce the comprehensive investment required of a commander in chief: "They cannot give him, as can ambition, a personal, almost proprietary interest in every aspect of fighting, so that he turns each opportunity to best advantage." Clausewitz argues, "It is primarily this spirit of endeavor," at "all levels" of command, that could foster the "inventiveness, energy, and competitive enthusiasm, which vitalizes an army and makes it victorious." In war, he explains, ambitions "are the essential breath of life that animates the inert mass."

Today, honor is enshrined, along with duty, integrity, loyalty, personal courage, respect, and selfless service, as one of the seven U.S. Army values. It is defined as the capacity for "living up to" the other six, and it has also been decoupled from the now suspect desire for fame. "Ambition," meanwhile, has become a dirty word. Promotion and retirement ceremonies celebrate honorable military careers, but there is only vitriol for perceived careerists and a collective unease at the proposition that the success of military enterprise might in fact hinge as much on the presence of sufficiently ambitious individuals as on an army's enthusiastic acceptance of a self-abnegating ethos of sacrifice and cooperation.

Ambition and martial distinction have long been linked in the Western imagination. What Clausewitz called "fame and honor" the ancient Greeks termed *kleos*, and they regarded hunger for it as the warrior's chief motivation. The promise of spoils certainly helped—an enemy's armor, perhaps, or a captured concubine— and the desire to avenge one's comrades galvanized soldiers in the midst of a fight. But, in the end, what was the point of risking one's life if not for the possibility of doing something worthy of the longevity secured by means of poetic remembrance? Ancient historians depict Alexander the Great brooding before Achilles's tomb, envious of his predecessor's good fortune in having a Homer to immortalize his exploits in epic song.

Like courage, ambition has a kind of moral neutrality; nevertheless, it is more readily associated than is courage with a lack of scruples. Remember Lady Macbeth's complaint that her husband is "not without ambition, but without / The illness should attend it." Shakespeare understood that a plot cannot do without ambition. The statesman and philosopher Francis Bacon, Shakespeare's contemporary, proposed that, like drama, history itself could not advance in the absence of the ambitious. It is ambition, Bacon wrote, that drives men "forward," but once their progress is "checked," the ambitious become "secretly discontent . . . and are best pleased when things go backward."

Plutarch, whose work influenced both Shakespeare and Bacon, also understood ambition as a necessary catalyst, but he had a Stoic's mistrust of its inherent volatility and ambiguity. The ambitious are always chasing after "glory," which is but a poor copy of virtue, and the results are uniformly "misshapen and unnatural." Yet this chase is the very essence of public life—the motor of history. Plutarch proposed that ambition at once explains the past and enables the future because those possessed of it are always chafing against the present. They collide with all the force of planets in intercepting orbits, their energy proving at once an organizing principle and an entropic force, capable, as in the case of Alexander, of moving men and matériel from Macedonia all the way to the banks of the Ganges, where the forward march of conquest degenerated into the desultory retreat of thwarted desire.

In his life of Lucullus, consul during the late Roman Republic, Plutarch offers a potential cure for the runaway passion of ambition. Lucullus devoted himself to the habitual study of "the liberal arts," a project requiring the dedication of his "contemplative faculties." This pursuit instituted a "timely check" to his unsettling "feelings of emulation and ambition." But most of the careers Plutarch considers show us ambition run amok. And his fundamental suspicion of ambition was echoed by many of his most devoted eighteenth-century readers, including John Adams, who regarded this incendiary passion with the deepest suspicion because he believed that "emulation next to self-preservation will forever be the great spring of human actions." For Adams, ambition—the catalyst driving an individual to outdo everyone else—was a fundamentally undemocratic force. Only "the balance of a well-ordered government," he insisted, could prevent "emulation from degenerating into dangerous ambition," the defender of liberty from turning tyrant.

In today's military culture, ambition is regarded no longer as a vexing catalyst but rather as a distraction from corporate success. As a result, it has been forced underground—precisely, Bacon reminds us, where it is most "malign and venomous." Personal ambition is fundamentally at odds with perhaps the thorniest army value: selfless service. Doctrine exhorts soldiers: "Put the welfare of the nation, the Army, and your subordinates before your own." If the only alternative is selfishness, I'm all for selfless service, but I think this is a false dichotomy. The army notionally encourages the project of self-development, but a thorough indoctrination in the value of selflessness makes ordinary acts of self-cultivation—especially intellectual pursuits without manifest, near-term military application—look like self-aggrandizement. To have certain career targets—to command a battalion, for example—is acceptable, but activities that reveal a desire for achievement and distinction as well as service, that suggest a more particular investment in the self with a strategic eye to the distant future, garner suspicion in certain quarters. How dare you think of tomorrow when there is so much to be done today? Yet the totality, the all-or-nothing gambit, of selflessness—the denial of self as opposed to its development—lacks the momentum necessary to propel the soldier forward over the long haul. It cannot promote the sense of personal responsibility, accountability, or "proprietary interest" that Clausewitz celebrates in his chapter "On Military Genius" and that today's army leaders deem elemental to a professional force.

Stuck in what Robert Gates called in his speech to West Point cadets "institutional concrete" and a "bureaucratic rigidity in its assignments and promotion processes," the army hews to antiquated career models. It theoretically accommodates, all the while retaining a deep cultural bias against, those experiences that are not primarily physical: graduate school, teaching and training others, policy work, fellowships in government or industry. Such endeavors, of course, might actually help officers to acquire the capacity for strategic thinking the army itself admits to lacking in its senior ranks and that it will need if it is to maintain its readiness and relevance in an era of dwindling resources and technological transformation. The romance of muddy boots does little to defend us against, for example, a cyber attack on the power grid or the banking industry.

The case of one of the last decade's most visible soldiers, David Petraeus, illustrates the contemporary unease with ambition. The unfortunate closing chapter of his career of public service, involving as it did an extramarital relationship with his biographer Paula Broadwell, will for a time skew assessments of his contributions to the country. Admirers attribute to Petraeus the very inventiveness, energy, competitiveness, and capacity for investment Clausewitz attributes to a "thirst for fame and honor," while critics have dismissed him as a careerist. Fred Kaplan suggests in *The Insurgents* that Petraeus had, even as a cadet at West Point, "an odd streak of drive and ambition. It wasn't dark or scheming, but rather bright, even sunny, bursting with outsized enthusiasm." At least some of Petreaus's "peers," Thomas Ricks observes in *The Gamble*, considered him "ferociously ambitious." Ricks adds, "Even among his admirers, there churns an ambivalence about him, often provoked by his overwhelming drive." Kaplan reports that when the time came to consider Petraeus for the position of Chairman of the Joint Chiefs of Staff, Rahm Emanuel, President Obama's chief of staff, "openly worried that the most famous general of his generation might possess a white-knight complex, an urge of destiny to run for president." Yet the qualities that provoked discomfort among politicians and Petraeus's peers were arguably the very ones that gave hope to his subordinates in crucial moments, such as the surge in Iraq. Ultimately, the unease he caused notwithstanding, Petraeus twice proved the clear and best choice for command during two of the most critical moments in the post-9/11 campaigns: first, when he took command of the surge in Iraq in 2007, and then when he replaced Stanley McChrystal in Afghanistan in 2010.

It is easy to accuse others of ambition, less easy perhaps to understand the link between manifest ambition and particular ends. What do the ambitious really want? Do they always know it themselves? Awards, medals, badges, advancement, victories—these are the certifications of a soldier's desire for recognition. Nevertheless, military ambition—like that of the scientist, activist, or political leader—might also motivate an unselfish quest in which personal accomplishment furthers a more encompassing goal: to minimize suffering, maximize the potential of others, galvanize or transform an institution. That kind of ambition, which doesn't rest purely on achieving the next rank, prize, or honor, has in a military context the additional advantage of fostering a kind of maturity that envisions meaning after armed conflict, contribution beyond the battlefield, and the cultivation of a postwar identity that does not depend exclusively on killing and dying under arms.

This kind of ambition tends not to dwell on past failures but also not to romanticize early successes. The sentimental celebration of the battlefield exploits of the last dozen years often stultifies rather than encourages such ambition because it insists that the highest glory is past and that the future can only ever be a less dramatic second act. An exclusive cultural focus on the battlefield excludes a serious consideration of all that follows, especially the vital but unglamorous labors of coming home, reintegrating, and imagining a narrative in the absence of immediate mortal danger. By contrast, a robust ambition refuses to wallow in a sense of belatedness, missed opportunity, and nostalgia because it is too busy dreaming up the future and, with it, all those personal and institutional transformations necessary for productivity and success.

The word "ambition" derives from the Latin *ambitio*, denoting lawful campaigning for public office—literally "going round" to garner support. The modern sense of striving for recognition, popularity, or fame was also alive to the Romans, and they never pretended they could do without it. For Bacon, later, a sort of open and free market of ambition was essential to the public weal: "He that seeketh to be eminent amongst able men hath a great task, but that is ever good for the public. But he that plots to be the only figure amongst ciphers is the decay of an whole age."

Montesquieu optimistically proposed that a "love of equality in a democracy limits ambition to the sole desire, to the sole happiness, of doing greater services to our country than the rest of our fellow-citizens." An ambition to serve prompts many to a military career, yet over the course of that career superior service may periodically require pursuits that focus exclusively on the self: individual experiences—conducted outside the context of conventional military operational, training, and educational environments—that deepen competence, broaden perspective, or unsettle preconceptions and biases. The army prizes uniformity, which it sometimes confuses with equity, and shared experience, which if unleavened encourages a debilitating groupthink rather than a productive esprit de corps. Yet given sufficient (and sufficiently capacious) avenues for exercise, personal ambition might still be harnessed for good. A commander without ambition, Bacon reminds us, is about as useful as a cavalryman stripped of his spurs. Don't expect to win a war, he admonishes, with a general like that.

"Whether I shall turn out to be the hero of my own life, or whether that station will be held by anybody else," proposes David Copperfield, the eponymous hero of Charles Dickens's deeply autobiographical novel, "these pages must show." Another way to define ambition might be the ability to tell a story: the ambitious must be able to imagine what comes next, to dictate the narrative of their lives before they happen and whether or not they conform to preestablished familial, institutional, or cultural plots. The ambitious must know how to weave a narrative out of the unseen and the out-of-bounds. Sometimes that narrative becomes tragic; John Adams suggested that tragedy was in fact the inevitable end of military ambition. A necessary evil in war, soldiers became threats to democratic society in peace, he argued. Not only were their wounds evidence of a communal willingness to indulge in violence, but they themselves proved a constant source of inspiration to a people looking for heroes rather than doing the much harder work of looking to themselves as "the fountain of power" and of learning how to manage that power.

Julius Caesar and Napoleon were the bogeyman of Adams and other civilian founders, but not even George Washington escaped their criticism. In Washington, however, the young republic had in fact an exquisite example of a soldier whose ambitions, while never unalloyed or uniformly lofty—he was preoccupied with his material fortune, jealous of his honor, obsessed with his reputation—nevertheless remained subordinated to a commitment to principles and a larger vision for the United States. As Washington explained to his protégé Lafayette, he returned to public life and assumed the presidency, after having surrendered his sword and retired to Mount Vernon, because he feared the rise of "some aspiring demagogue who will not consult the interest of his Country so much as his own ambitious views." Thus in the figure of this general who became a president we find one parable of ambition worth remembering. Washington's investment in the Republic depended as much on his enduring identity as a citizen—on his refusal ever to lay aside that citizenship—as it did on his temporary role as a soldier.

3

"ON THE VERGE OF THE TRUE FOREST"
Trusting the Imaginary Forces

The Wart was on the verge of the true forest . . . further from the castle than the boy had ever been . . .

Wart would not have been frightened of an English forest nowadays, but the great jungle of Old England was a different matter. It was not only that there were wild boars in it . . . nor that . . . surviving wolves might be slinking behind any tree, with pale eyes and slavering chops . . .

There were magicians in the forest . . . as well as strange animals not known to modern works of natural history. There were regular bands of Saxon outlaws . . . who lived together and wore green and shot with arrows which never missed. There were even a few dragons . . .

Added to this, there was the fact that it was getting dark.

—T. H. White, *The Once and Future King* (1958)

WIZARDRY

Not all that long ago, during a casual conversation after work one day with my friend Suzanne, I discovered something important about myself, something I probably should have known before, when she informed me that I am a Muggle. It sounded like a slur, but I couldn't be sure. "What," I demanded, "is a Muggle?" All those who have devotedly followed the adventures of J. K. Rowling's Harry Potter for the last decade will no doubt wonder where, precisely, I've been hiding. Here I had been thoroughly persuaded of my own formidable, albeit eccentric and esoteric, brand of English-professor magic only to discover that I had no witchcraft at all. At one efficient stroke, the last vestige of my long-preserved childhood fantasies—soothsaying, sorcery, superpowers—had been destroyed. Sometimes it's good to be disabused of one's delusions. It's what one does with such revelations that matters.

That weekend I marched myself over to the children's department of my local bookstore. After a revelatory detour through the robust teen paranormal romance section—teeming with defanged, domesticated high-school vampires who wear letter sweaters, have cowlicks and orthodontist appointments, and wouldn't last a New York minute in a room with toothy old Transylvanian Count Orlok—and a fruitless visit to the fantasy section, I finally located *Harry Potter and the Sorcerer's Stone* on a large display table (so big that I had sailed right by it) devoted to the retailing of all things Potter. I don't think I had read a Scholastic book since the eighth grade, but the pages had an instantly recognizable feel and (I sniffed earnestly) a familiar smell.

Of course I had long known of the phenomenon that is Harry: the midnight lines, the movies, and the personal struggles and triumphs of Rowling herself, all of which added to the appeal of the series. But I hadn't really begun to appreciate the profound effect the books had on so many eighteen-year-olds of my acquaintance until the spring of 2011, when in my capacity as director of West Point's freshman literature course I asked more than a thousand future lieutenants to create something called a literary autobiography: an audio recording of those cultural artifacts—books, music, and films—that had shaped their sense of who they were and who they might become. A majority of the cadets in my own class spoke eloquently and feelingly of the pivotal experience of having encountered Harry Potter; many of my colleagues found the same thing in their classes. He so clearly mattered to our students.

It turns out that West Point, while performing a good deal of magic in its forty-seven-month experience, does little to diminish

Harry's importance for many cadets. As the seniors in my seminar loved to remind me—in the midst of a spirited campaign in the fall of 2011 to get me to read the entire series—they were eleven in 1998, when the eleven-year-old Harry first appeared in the United States. And they described themselves as having grown up along with him. Judging from the ecstatic audience reaction to Rowling's Harvard University commencement address in 2008, her novels hold considerable sway over that student body as well.

In the September 12, 2011, *New Yorker* issue commemorating the tenth anniversary of the attacks on the World Trade Center, Lorrie Moore wrote a Talk of the Town piece about Rowling's books and the generation that grew up on them. The magazine's memorial issue, with its illuminated reflection of absent twin towers in the river, was yet another attempt to provide a punctuation mark to the story of a decade dragging its slow and bloody length along. I shared Moore's essay with my seniors on the day I revealed that I had finally finished the first book. Moore's students, like so many of mine, selected one of the Harry Potter novels as their "desert-island book." To be steeped in Harry's universe, Moore argues, is to absorb "a magical, Manichaean, neo-Biblical view of the world" that "may be less possible for those belonging to an older generation." Nevertheless, it seems to me that what Moore calls "the good-versus-evil wizardry of J. K. Rowling" is entirely of a piece with a narrative that pits freedom lovers against an "axis of evil," devised by an older generation steeped in its own Cold War Manichaeism and sufficiently persuasive to so many members of Congress and private citizens in the wake of September 11, 2001.

Moore seems at once protective and dismissive of the naive optimism and "idealism" that sees the world as the kind of struggle the books present. Ian Parker, in a profile of Rowling written soon after the publication of her first novel for adults, *The Casual Vacancy*, in 2012, proposed that part of the appeal of the Harry Potter series is that "Rowling's respect for a youthful world view never wavers, and her characters do not learn their way out of it." I encounter that worldview and its resilient idealism all the time in the many Potter aficionados of my acquaintance. There are moments, I suppose, when I wish I could share it, but to teach—to invite students out into the world of only occasionally congenial and frequently contradictory ideas—is inevitably, sometimes even unwittingly, to disabuse them of certain idealistic notions. The goal is somehow to preserve their resiliency, ambition, and imagination in the process of educating them for a world that is rarely as Manichaean under the sensational surface as they might like to think.

By the time I took over the direction of the plebe course in 2010, the limitations of my own worldview had become undeniable: it was during this time that the arc from peace to war began to reveal its fault lines and fissures. Reading A. J. Liebling's *Mollie and Other War Pieces*, a collection of World War II journalism that has become increasingly important to me because of its clearsightedness in the midst of chaos and its scrupulous honesty about the charged relationship of reason and sentiment in wartime, I encountered the following passage, appended by Liebling years later: "I have been advised to write an epilogue to this book to 'give it unity' and 'put it in perspective,' but I find this difficult, because war, unlike drama, has no unities, classical or otherwise. It is discursive, centrifugal, both repetitive and disparate." Liebling's meditation on the virtual impossibility of finding coherence in the middle of no man's land gave me courage by reinforcing for me the value of equipping my students to live lives that may lack unity, symmetry, and sufficient perspective. It was no longer simply a matter of somehow preparing these young men and women to go to war. Mine had become by this time a far more complex charge, one that took into account the need to contemplate obscure and distant ends from the very beginning. That's a tall order for a Muggle.

MAMA BEARS AND PAPA BEARS

I decided to air a public confession of my circumscribed powers to the very people for whom I most wanted to be superhuman. In 2012, for a second time, I was addressing the parents of all those plebes whose education I was responsible for in Eisenhower Hall ("Ike," as it's called), which happens to be the second-largest theater in the United States east of the Mississippi. Only Radio City exceeds its capacity. "That's a big stage," Karin—she of the performer's paradox—said when she learned I would be speaking there, "really big. You can't fill that stage all by yourself. You'll need something, a few pictures at least. Maybe the Rockettes." Performing my one-woman show in this vast expanse was at once easy and impossible. The speech was a cinch because the plebes are, and have been for a long time now, my favorite people: I love to talk about them to anyone who'll listen. Just on the verge of indoctrination, they manage to combine a passion for their chosen vocation with a healthy perspective on the vagaries of the system. But it was difficult all the same because I was talking about them to their parents, who had assumed to my admittedly overactive imagination the appearance of a formidable sleuth of Mother and Father Bears.

Preparing for that first speech in 2011, a year with such resonances, I knew I had to communicate to them the ways in which I believed the course I had designed helped to ready their children for whatever lies ahead: that in addition to the obvious goal of refining their daughters' and sons' ability to communicate clearly and persuasively, it aimed at cultivating self-awareness, patience and deep attention, analytic judgment, and the synthetic faculty of imagination. I knew I had to articulate for the parents both the paradox of preparation and the ways in which we tried to escape it through a combination of readings that have included, over the years, everything from Ovid's *Metamorphoses* to *Hamlet* to Chang-rae Lee's *Native Speaker* and events that have ranged from the literary autobiography to performance workshops with professional actors from the Hudson Valley Shakespeare Festival, a company headquartered just across the river from West Point. In figuring out what to say to all those mothers and fathers, I also came to understand that this freshman literature course—which I have taught every single year since coming to West Point in 1997 and through which more than four thousand future officers passed during the four years I directed it—is the most important trust I have been given in my professional life.

I felt very small behind my lectern. I had intended the images flashing on the screen behind me to be familiar and reassuring (primarily to me, but also, I hoped, to the bears), but their giant size turned them alien and intimidating: a first edition of Grant's *Memoirs* bound in deluxe morocco; the facade of the nineteenth-century cadet library where Grant checked out his books; Antoine de Saint-Exupéry's Little Prince perched atop his asteroid, gazing at the galaxy; the one-volume Shakespeare my friend Scott, now the head of our department, was issued as a plebe and that is now held together with "hundred-mile-an-hour tape" after jumping with him from at least one airplane, surviving a war, and being hungrily read in all manner of places. "I liked having it," Scott tells me, borrowing a line from Wordsworth's *The Prelude*, "it was a . . . talisman to me, a promise of 'something evermore about to be.'"

There's a wonderful passage in Marisha Pessl's 2006 novel, *Special Topics in Calamity Physics*, in which a professor in the act of contemplating a course catalog explains to his daughter that the work of college—or, more precisely, of the college professor—is to make order from chaos:

> "Is there anything more glorious than a professor? Forget about his molding the minds, the future of a nation—a dubious asser-tion; there's little you can do when they tend to emerge from the womb predestined for Grand Theft Auto Vice City. No. What I

mean is, a professor is the only person on earth with the power to put a veritable frame around life—not the whole thing, *God* no—simply a fragment of it, a small *wedge*. He organizes the unorganizable. Nimbly partitions it into modern and postmodern, renaissance, baroque, primitivism, imperialism and so on. Splice that up with Research Papers, Vacations, Midterms. All that order—simply divine . . . And so it is with the curriculum. That celestial, sweet set of instructions, culminating in the scary wonder of the Final Exam. And what *is* the Final Exam? A test of one's deepest understanding of giant concepts. No wonder so many adults long to return to university, to all those deadlines—ahhh, that structure! Scaffolding to which we may cling! Even if it *is* arbitrary, without it, we're lost, wholly incapable of separating the Romantic from the Victorian in our sad, bewildering lives."

On hearing this disquisition on the divine art of professorial order, the narrator promptly tells her father he has "lost his mind." It's a seductive vision, and there's no professor who hasn't at least momentarily indulged in such mock-heroic visions. Yet the classroom has for a long time now felt to me less like a place of Swiftian "order from confusion sprung" than like a universe in constant flux, akin to that described by the ancient philosopher Heraclitus, where we can never step into the same river twice. I know from their e-mails and letters that some of my former students cling to the memory of their classroom experience as to a kind of life raft when they find themselves confused or numbed in places of true peril. But in the process of learning how to imagine those places—of embracing my own war vertigo—I've come to feel that the classroom is rather like Marianne Moore's baseball game: I can never be sure exactly "how it will go," nor, frankly, do I want to any longer. Standing in the middle of the diamond or the middle of the river or the middle of the classroom can open the door to surprise, serendipity, or happy accident, on the road toward knowledge of self and world. During wartime almost everything can be made to seem a luxury, but there must be a vigorously defended space for aspiring lieutenants as well as established generals to practice taking the long view. It takes patience and courage to carve out space for self-examination and to pause in the midst of wartime's onrushing momentum to think about things seemingly unconnected to the moment: that's the kind of intellectual ambition I would like my students to indulge. That capacity is one of the most important factors in determining a soldier's and an army's postwar fate. If you've waited until you are a general to develop it, it will be too late.

On my giant stage, peering out into the dim auditorium and beholding the eyes of all those vigilant bears staring back, I began to articulate a new philosophy for them and for myself. It had to do with ambition and imagination and the ways in which these attributes could be cultivated even in the newest members of an organization who were still trying to learn its languages, rhythms, and customs. Fostering even in its most junior members whatever it takes to endure beyond the end of the battle—helping them to cultivate the art of long-term survival—is one of the chief responsibilities that a professional army owes to those who serve in it. Far-thinking soldiers have always honed this capacity even in the most exigent circumstances. I have come to think of this attribute as a "desert-island state of mind," but it transcends geography: the desert island, like no man's land, is an apt image for the age. It's Wilfred Thesiger's state of mind: the ability to determine whatever is most essential to one's survival, not just physically but intellectually and emotionally. It's the kind of armature Adam learned to forge during three tours in Afghanistan, where he found a great deal of congeniality in Saint-Exupéry's *Wind, Sand, and Stars*, a memoir about the author's days flying the mails over deserts and mountains and surviving more than one crash. "I was amazed," Adam wrote to me from Afghanistan, by the similarities between flying in his era and our current operations over here. My favorite passage is one in which the author experiences IIMC (inadvertent instrument meteorological conditions). IIMC occurs when you suddenly lose visual contact with the ground because of weather, clouds, etc. It's a heart-pounding experience, especially when the aircraft you are flying is not properly equipped for instrument-only flight (neither Saint-Exupéry's aircraft nor mine contains the proper instrumentation). I've experienced it once and don't care to do it again.

Adam had prepared as diligently as anyone could for his deployment, but his arrival in country still proved "something of a shock." Losing sight of the ground is a vertiginous experience, the symbolism of which we both appreciated: "We flew our helicopters in through some of the most unforgiving terrain I've ever seen. It looked like the surface of some alien planet." It is the unexpected—the "shock"—for which military professionals must always be prepared, if one can ever be sufficiently prepared for that. For Adam, it was the combat death of a fellow pilot and mentor, an experienced warrant officer who taught him a great deal. This event changed Adam. Loss will do that, and perhaps never being quite the same again is the very thing, as Shawn suggested while we sat outside Walter Reed after our visit, for which we must try hardest to prepare in this life.

That's no easy revelation to share with the parents of the eighteen-year-olds in your care. The cultivation of a desert-island state of mind is a difficult endeavor, a lifelong process that grows no less complicated with each success, each promotion, each year of the experience that enlightens yet also tends to blind us to the flaws, alternatives, and potential tyrannies of the system. As I've suggested, I fear the army works, often inadvertently, to curtail the time horizons of young officers by telling the lieutenant and the captain that command is everything and failing to persuade them of the value of what follows or to encourage them to take a more comprehensive view of things. Indeed, one of the most forceful discoveries I have made in my conversations with former students is the degree to which giving up their platoons or companies seems to cast them adrift. It is extremely difficult for many to accommodate themselves to life in uniform after command. Staff work, necessary though it is, isn't something they can easily assimilate into their view of a heroic military life: it isn't one of their ambitions but a "dreaded" if necessary way station en route to something more glamorous. And so amid all the other confusions that attend freshman year in college, I add this wrinkle to the plebes' lives: they are wondering whether they have what it takes to be lieutenants while I'm thinking about what kinds of generals they might make and whether they have what it takes to survive in no man's land.

ESSENTIAL EQUIPMENT

It is to cultivate the state of mind I've been describing that I instituted the literary autobiography exercise, modeled on *Desert Island Discs*, the BBC Radio 4 program I fell in love with years ago while living in Scotland, which felt a little like a desert island to me, a stranger in a strange land really for the first time. The premise of the show, which first aired during wartime in 1942, is that a celebrity guest selects the eight records, together with a book and a luxury item, that he or she would most wish to have if marooned on a desert island. Shakespeare's complete works and the Bible are always thrown into the bargain. There's little by way of apology, much by way of surprise: General Sir Charles Guthrie, then chief of the British Defence Staff, selected Liza Minnelli's "Cabaret" and a surfboard, while Blondie's Debbie Harry opted for Mahler's Symphony no. 5 and Tolstoy's *War and Peace*.

Often the plebes, each and every one a budding MacGyver, take this conceit quite literally. They ask a lot of technical questions about the size of the island; its latitude and longitude; the climate, flora, and fauna. Ease up, I'll say in response to their initial lists of water-filtration systems, meals ready-to-eat, and inflatable rafts, this is about the needs of the mind, not the body. Let's face it, with sufficient training and preparation even *I* might be able to learn what my body most needs to survive in an emergency. Indeed, in preparation for foreign travel I have at the army's insistence successfully completed an elementary version of the military's Survival, Evasion, Resistance, Escape training. Watch out.

Predicting whatever it is the *mind* might need to survive in such terrain—anticipating what it might need for survival in the long term—is a far more complicated proposition. And perched behind my lectern at Ike, I told the assembled parents that trying to figure it out is one of the chief responsibilities that military academies owe to those who attend them—to those whose profession might in some sense be described as that of periodic castaway, deposited in unfamiliar places and on sometimes hostile shores, scanning the horizon for the ship that will carry them home. That's the kind of survival Saint-Exupéry tells us something about. And his meditations on solitude, courage, craft, and responsibility—rather than any practical advice about surviving aviation mishaps—are the reason he remains a potential touchstone for a twenty-first-century aviator.

Few of us have been castaways, but we've all spun variations on the exercise of figuring out whatever is essential to the life of our minds. On graduating from West Point or sometimes just before they deploy, former students frequently ask me if I have on hand, or could create, a list of indispensable books they can buy or download to their e-readers. Whitney, now a captain home from her first tour in Afghanistan, dubbed it the "House-on-Fire List." If I smelled smoke, she demanded, which books would I grab first? I like Whitney's sense of urgency. Choosing books for courses can prove tricky, but such selections always have a particular context. Assembling a House-on-Fire List is a bit trickier. First, I like to clarify the rules: Are these books I would take with me or books I think you ought to take with you? Are these books I read when I was about your age or books I've read since? Are these books about war, peace, or somewhere in between? In other words, whose desert island is this supposed to be? Depending on the answers to these questions, the list varies, but it often includes the following: Virgil's *Aeneid*, Montaigne's *Essays*, Stefan Zweig's *Beware of Pity*, Virginia Woolf's *Orlando*, Evelyn Waugh's *Sword of Honour* trilogy, and David Mitchell's *Black Swan Green*.

I think new lieutenants are perhaps more likely than their civilian peers to ask for a House-on-Fire List because they can more readily imagine themselves stranded on war's desert island. It is also true that lists and checklists are ubiquitous in military culture. The "professional reading list," usually dominated by military history, biography, and memoir, is a staple of army culture. Some lists, like that of the chief of staff, are published in an official pamphlet (Center of Military History Publication 105-5-1). But individual commanders often make their own recommendations, which they discuss with subordinates in venues of greater or lesser formality. They may build "officer professional development" sessions around an assigned book. West Point commandants, for example, run a book club for cadets; Jim Frederick's *Black Hearts: One Platoon's Descent into Madness in Iraq's Triangle of Death* and Vanessa Gezari's *The Tender Soldier: A True Story of War and Sacrifice* have been among the selections.

The model for this kind of literary mentorship is Fox Conner, who served in the army during the first decades of the twentieth century and retired as a major general in 1938. Conner was a guide to the likes of Eisenhower, George Patton, and George Marshall. Stationed in Panama early in his career, Eisenhower worked for Conner and had free run of his commander's personal library, where he found, according to a book by Eisenhower's granddaughter Susan, works of Plato, Shakespeare, Nietzsche, and Clausewitz. The two men evidently discussed this reading on horseback while out on maneuvers. In the military—to say nothing of formal education systems in general—book lists generally come from the top down. I'm a little stubborn, so I inverted the dynamic by inviting the plebes to curate their own lists of books, music, and movies that shaped their sense of who they were and who they thought they might become. I imagined that I could learn something from a list that was generated from the bottom up, one that wasn't designed explicitly to professionalize cadets—to work their metamorphosis into someone else—but rather to reveal (to them as well as to me) who they imagined themselves to be in the first place. Without such an investment in the necessarily slow and patient cultivation of a knowledge of self, I worry that all of the army's subsequent attempts at transformation—and professionalization—can never wholly succeed. In other words, I think we need to make time to hear what a plebe has to tell us. In doing that, and responding thoughtfully, we initiate the kinds of conversations about ambition, imagination, conformity, and dissent that might enable them to carry on in the no man's land that awaits.

In listening to my students talk about the books that had shaped them—how they acquired them, when and where they read them, what they understood at the time and what only later—I discover far more about the mental terrains in which they operate than I would had I asked them in a more direct way just to tell me a little bit about themselves. When I first assign the autobiography, several plebes invariably tell me they haven't even read (or can't remember having read) ten books. Yet, in the end, all of them are able to unearth the requisite number of artifacts. A few more confess that they didn't really understand the project until it was over, when they realized all the things they had forgotten, all the hidden influences that explained them to themselves. It brought them, said one, into a new relation with what they were being asked to read now as undergraduates. One of the most important things I was able to tell their mothers and fathers was the role they had all played in this process. Almost without exception, the autobiographies recount experiences of reading books introduced by parents and siblings and reveal the ways in which family life has been textured by a discussion of books, music, and film. I hope this revelation of an enduring connection proves something of a salve to parents who fear that they have surrendered their children to an institution that, whatever else it might do, will somehow turn them into strangers.

I discovered hidden depths and designs to my students' intellectual and emotional lives. I learned, for example, the enduring importance of *Oliver Twist*, Charles Dickens's novel about a much-abused orphan, to a plebe who had been homeless for a time as a child without a guardian and about the influence of a book of chess moves on the way another cadet approaches both people and problems. I learned about a student who had as a young boy found his father's old Marvel comics and an 1868 edition of the Arthurian legends in family attics. The experience of devouring the former and struggling through the latter, its language as yet only half understood, catalyzed his enduring fascination with heroic legends. Another student's recording, infused with his usual combination of humor and earnestness, revealed his musical priorities: "Beethoven, Bach, no." Michael chose Led Zeppelin, first introduced to him by his older brother, because they had written the best music "in the history of forever." That's my kind of island. Michael also deemed *Animal Farm* the book that had the greatest influence on him. Forced to read Orwell's novel in high school, he read it again a year later because it changed the way he saw the world. "You think these pigs are going to run a beautiful farm, better than Farmer Jones could," he explained, but then everything falls apart. Michael saw in the pigs' transformation the ease with which "you can end up becoming . . . what you set out to destroy." That's useful information for a castaway confronted with the problem of building a new society; maybe it will come in handy for Michael one day, too.

WARTIME READING

The seeds of the literary autobiography project had been sown a few years earlier, during the visits my classes customarily made to the library archives. Susan, one of the archivists, and I organized mini-exhibits each spring. When I took over the course, we expanded the exhibit for the entire class. My original motivation for this activity had been to show the plebes issues of *Harper's Weekly* in which Charles Dickens's novel *Great Expectations*, a staple of my course for several years, was first serialized in 1860–61. To this, Susan added some wonderful treasures, including Edgar Allan Poe's court-martial records, a sketch made by Ulysses S. Grant, and the handwritten borrowing records from previous generations of cadets. Armed with protective white gloves several sizes too small for them, the cadets turned the pages of *Harper's*, far less interested in Dickens's novel than in the illustrated magazine's strange little poems, humor pieces, and advertisements for everything from Eureka Clothes Squeezers to Allen's Cocaine Tablets.

Throughout much of the nineteenth century West Point cadets were permitted to check books out of the library only once a week. "On Saturday afternoon," the 1857 regulations state, "any book that a Cadet may have been reading during the week, may be taken to his quarters, on the approval of the Librarian, and shall be returned on the succeeding Monday. If not then returned, he shall be reported by the Librarian." Decades of weekly borrowing activity are recorded in handwritten ledgers now preserved in the archives. I've spent a fair bit of time looking through them, following the charge record of a given title or tracking the reading habits of an individual cadet. There are storied names in the ledgers: Lee, Sherman, and Grant, who refers in his memoirs to the "fine library connected with the Academy from which cadets can get books to read in their quarters." But usually I end up trailing an unknown.

A few years ago, hunting for a wartime reader who might have something to say to my classes of wartime readers, I discovered John T. Pitman Jr., who graduated in 1867. Pitman was an unpredictable borrower, his name absent from the records for weeks at a time before it reappeared next to Bossut's *General History of Mathematics*, the second volume of Goethe's *Werke* (in German), or a

Dickens novel (*David Copperfield, Dombey and Son, Barnaby Rudge*). The first book he took back to his quarters, just a few weeks after arriving in 1863, was *Great Expectations*. I don't know why he chose it. Perhaps, beginning a new phase of his life, he found something of moment in the story of a young man reckoning with the attendant confusions of "great expectations."

Dickens didn't conceive of *Great Expectations* as a wartime novel, but when a reader encounters it in *Harper's*, where it ran from November 24, 1860, to August 3, 1861, it inevitably becomes one. To follow Pip's adventures in that context is to follow the United States into war: Lincoln's election and inauguration; the secession of the southern states starting with South Carolina; the fortification and fall of Fort Sumter; the First Battle of Bull Run. As the war went on, the long-standing advertisements for beauty soap and patent-medicine cures for stammering and catarrh become interspersed with those designed expressly for a wartime audience. In addition to guns and bulletproof vests, there was Rawson's U.S. Army Patent Elastic Self-Adjusting Suspensory Bandage. The Universal Joint and Artificial Limb Company offered its four-pound, self-adjusting prosthetic at a sixteen-dollar discount for soldiers. An express company offered "half rates" for "Friends of Soldiers" sending articles to Union troops. Meanwhile, London's S. W. H. Ward flogged made-to-measure French flannel army shirts by the dozen.

Companies seemed eager to profit from the crisis. S. C. Rickards & Co., in a representative example, informed soldiers who found themselves with spare time in camp that they could "make easily $15 per day" selling "GREAT NEW and WONDERFUL UNION PRIZE AND STATIONERY PACKAGES, NOVEL AND UNEQUALED, and unlike all the old styles; containing all New Articles, and of fine quality. Writing Materials, Games, Useful and Fancy Articles, Likenesses of Heroes, Camp Companions (for the Army), rich gifts of Jewelry, &c., &c., altogether worth over $1, for ONLY 25c." Rickards promised, "They are just the thing for a present to your friend in the Army. No family should be without one. Profits immense, sales quick. Soldiers in camp can act as Agents, and make money fast." In similarly dubious fashion, the Philadelphia publisher G. G. Evans touted *The Soldier's Guide to Health* as "an invaluable companion" to every officer and soldier at ten or twenty-five cents, with free shipping: "THE RULES FOR PRESERVING HEALTH and INSTRUCTIONS FOR OBTAINING FURLOUGHS AND DISCHARGES are worth one hundred-fold its cost."

Perhaps John Pitman had had his first introduction to *Great Expectations* in a copy of *Harper's Weekly* in an army camp. He served in the Union army before coming to West Point. In July 1861, only three days after enlisting as a private in the 1st Rhode Island Volunteer Infantry, he joined the rest of the innocents at the chaotic Battle of Bull Run, the first major engagement of the Civil War. "Nearly all of us," William Tecumseh Sherman, in command of a brigade there, wrote of the inexperienced troops, "for the first time then heard the sound of cannon and muskets in anger, and saw the bloody scenes common to all battles, with which we were soon to be familiar." Two years later, having been promoted to second lieutenant—the rank at which West Point graduates are commissioned—Pitman became the oldest member of the academy's newest class. President Lincoln personally appointed him to fill a slot left vacant because it was assigned to one of the southern states.

I introduced John Pitman to the plebes at the beginning of the semester, and he became so much a part of us that whenever I neglected to mention him, Michael demanded, "Hey, ma'am, what's up with Mr. Pitman?" Pitman's ghostly presence in class led us down a path of inquiry we might not otherwise have followed: How would future generations know who these plebes were, how their minds worked, what moved them, where their passions led? When I put all these questions to them, they agreed that the clues about their lives and interests probably wouldn't be found in library records. Indeed, they marveled that checking out a book was such a rare treat for their predecessors. As privileges go, this one didn't seem especially decadent. "But aren't books a good thing?" Eli asked. "An educational thing?" Today's plebes are more likely to download recreational books or buy them online than to check them out of the library. And they have so many more sources of diversion than Pitman had. If it survives at all, the record of the plebes' curiosities, of the subjects that excite them, will probably be virtual: Michael's online purchases, Trip's Netflix queue, Eli's iTunes library, R.J.'s Mustang forum posts. Mary and Alex predicted with some disappointment that maybe their traces would consist largely of emoticon-filled Facebook status updates.

E-mails, too, might reveal something about the life of their minds. I get that type of e-mail all the time. At around the time I was getting to know John Pitman and the plebes, I received such a message from Liz, a lieutenant running a battalion aid station in Afghanistan at the time. She wrote about the reading habits of her soldiers, to whom she is clearly devoted and whose abilities she greatly admires: "I am amazed at the amount of books some of my soldiers plow through. Some read biographies, other[s] historical fiction, others lighthearted 'beach reads' (as I call them); it is fun to see their personalities matched alongside their reading choices." Liz has long been interested in the nexus of war and writing. At West Point she wrote a prizewinning thesis on American soldier-poets of World War II, whose voices have been neglected in favor of their novel-writing contemporaries. She argued that the poetic traces of these soldiers—visceral, frank, irreverent—can enrich our understanding of the Greatest Generation. In Afghanistan, Liz, a soldier-poet herself, read and wrote constantly. "I have been keeping a written record of the books I have been reading over here," she reported in a letter that arrived at the beginning of the semester, "and have been considering writing an article about [how] reading . . . affects our wartime experience. It may not go anywhere except my journal, but it is a concept that keeps grabbing my attention."

That's how I thought of the literary autobiography—part commonplace book, part playlist; a little old school and a little new—in which plebes could discuss the novels, poems, stories, and other texts that have had the greatest impact on them. And one day, maybe, some twenty-third-century English professor hunting around in a virtual West Point archive will light on these serendipitously preserved artifacts and transmit them by whatever undreamt-of technology is then at her disposal to a new class of plebes, who will try to penetrate the inner lives of their predecessors in their own search to imagine the future.

FULL-SPECTRUM THINKING

The last book Pitman checked out—the final trace I could find of him in the ledgers—was the first volume of Thackeray's *Virginians*, a historical novel that opens with the narrator expressing the desire to re-create "bygone times and people" by "poring over the documents" they have left behind. "They are hints rather than descriptions," he admits, "indications and outlines chiefly," yet from such traces one might still try "to imagine the situation of the writer, where he was, and by what persons surrounded." I don't know if Pitman ever finished Thackeray's novel, nor do I know what books he read after graduation. But I like to imagine that he remained an eclectic reader throughout his career in the Ordnance Corps, which was long and successful—he retired as a brigadier general in 1906—yet largely uncelebrated outside of friends, family, and weapons experts.

Early in his career Pitman returned to West Point as assistant professor of chemistry, mineralogy, and geology and assistant instructor of ordnance and gunnery. Photography was one of his hobbies, and his photographs offer a pictorial history of the period during which he served on the faculty. Pitman eventually became a "powder specialist" who, as his nomination to the Ordnance Corps Hall of Fame explains, made "invaluable contributions to the development of small arms, explosives, and propellants." Among those contributions were a series of volumes on weaponry, *The Pitman Notes*, and the production of a variety of "smokeless powder"— ammunition that replaced the black powder that for centuries fouled weapons and obscured battlefields with clouds of smoke. The propellant grain he developed is still in use today.

Pitman spent a great deal of time experimenting with metals for bullet jackets, pressure gauges, and primers. There is also a sense in which his life serves as a kind of practical primer for cadets today. He is the model of a soldier, not a legend or larger-than-life hero—How many of us become those?—but a thoughtful, curious, devoted professional, who throughout a life of action found it essential to exercise a life of the mind and made invaluable contributions to the army by doing so. In exploring John Pitman's inner life, I thought, perhaps the plebes would discover a path of their own. But the traces I followed have nothing to do with munitions: they are entirely literary. I found John Pitman, and introduced him to the plebes, because he happened to enjoy a good novel. Battle-tested in his youth at Bull Run in 1861, Pitman, able to imagine something beyond survival, found new challenges to keep him in the service through the beginning of the twentieth century. He was defiantly a specialist, with a superior technical competence, but his spirit of experimentation and his broad range of interests and avocations suggest that he was precisely the kind of model that Gates recommended in his speech to cadets, in which he expressed the fear that the army would lose those junior officers who have had such intense tactical experience over the last decade precisely because it would fail to foster their entrepreneurial spirit and to promote the kind of "full-spectrum" thinking that the force would require. "The consequences," Gates confessed, of failing to encourage and to challenge "battle-tested" junior officers but instead funneling them into predictable, well-trod career paths and warehousing them in rigid assignment and promotion patterns "terrify me."

Pitman's story and our acquaintance with it—with his eclecticism, lifelong passions, and ambitions—became essential to our undertaking and to the ways in which I conceived of the course I was directing. It was unified by the deliberately broad theme of knowledge: its shapes and modes, its evolution over time, its uses and abuses. A battle rages within cadets between a certain bravado meant to signal there's nothing they don't know and a looming suspicion there's nothing they do. It's the same battle that rages in the rest of us; it's simply the case that with age we grow more adept at concealing it. The struggle is intensified in my students by the fact that they are also cadets at a military academy, where initial training impresses upon them their radically diminished authority and where the predestination of their first job understandably tempts them to probe the immediate application of whatever knowledge comes their way. The tension is especially acute in the plebes, who reside at the bottom of the institutional hierarchy and who are bombarded on arrival with new facts, terms, and concepts that can eclipse whatever it is they thought they knew about the way the world works.

I therefore began the custom early in the semester of asking the plebes, enrolled as they were in a course advertising itself to be about knowledge, what they knew best. I emphasize that this knowledge need not be academic in nature. In fact, I almost prefer that it not be, because part of what I want the cadets to understand is the fundamental connection between what they already know and what they might learn in class, between the knowledge hard won from experience and that retrieved from books and thoughtful conversation. After a semester working with literary texts—learning their history, thinking and writing about them, performing, creating their own original work—my students will, I hope, have learned not only something about language and culture but also a great deal about themselves and their intellectual and professional potential.

Often what plebes think they know best is physical—a particular sport or craft—but the responses have ranged from Roman history to the high jump, from fly-fishing to the Beatles. Many students do not rate their knowledge very highly; they divorce their private or extracurricular expertise from the knowledge they acquire in a formal academic context. They don't yet know how to value either what they know or what they don't know, and they can't imagine that what they know has anything to do with what I know or with what they might discover while reading Shakespeare or Nella Larsen or Thomas Hardy or Dashiell Hammett or any of the authors we might encounter in class. Moreover, divorcing mind and body, they sometimes doubt the possibility of mastering both pen and sword.

I realized that a problem like this one demands some special assistance, and with all the earnest discretion of a Victorian lady in distress, I appealed to none other than Mr. Sherlock Holmes. Although it involved no blackmail, missing persons, or stolen jewels, my case posed little difficulty for him: Holmes is nothing if not adaptable. Indeed, he is one of fiction's most versatile figures. I'm referring not simply to his penchant for disguise but also to his remarkable afterlife in literature, television, and especially the movies: fighting Nazis in a series of films from the 1940s and, much more recently, foiling a nineteenth-century plot involving a rather twenty-first-century weapon of mass destruction in Guy Ritchie's *Sherlock Holmes*. In his review of Ritchie's movie, the *New York Times* critic A. O. Scott called Holmes "a proto-superhero, amenable to all kinds of elaboration and variation." Arthur Conan Doyle's mastermind endures because, as he informs an astonished thief in "The Adventure of the Blue Carbuncle," "It is my business to know what other people don't know."

I've taken to visiting 221B Baker Street on the first day of class because I can't think of anyone who leverages what he knows more effectively. I typically ask my students to read a passage near the beginning of A *Study in Scarlet* (the detective's first appearance), in which Dr. Watson vainly attempts to itemize precisely what it is Holmes knows: next to nothing about literature, philosophy, astronomy, and politics; idiosyncratic facts of botany, geology, anatomy, and British law; the most minute details of chemistry and "sensational literature." After concluding his list by noting that Holmes not only "plays the violin well" but also "is an expert singlestick player, boxer, and swordsman," Watson throws "it into the fire in despair" of ever figuring out what kind of profession could possibly require this eclectic catalog of "accomplishments."

Holmes himself professes a ruthlessly utilitarian attitude toward knowledge in A *Study in Scarlet*. He tells Watson that "a man's brain originally is like a little empty attic" into which only a limited stock of furniture can be made to fit. For this reason, he insists that he wants to know exclusively what is "useful" to his work but that he endeavors to "forget" everything else. Is Holmes, after all, but a tyrant of relevance? It soon becomes apparent that almost nothing is irrelevant to the consulting detective, as he styles himself: Latin, French, rare books, the plays of Shakespeare and the works of Carlyle, world politics, history, zoology, geography, psychology, Buddhism, pottery, warships, and wine. Holmes reveals a familiarity with all of these subjects and more over the course of his adventures. (What he doesn't already know he studies intently.) In the end, determining exactly what Holmes knows turns out to be beside the point, for it is not the amount of knowledge he stores in his prodigious "brain-attic" but the way in which he *uses* it that distinguishes him. Holmes reveals the underlying principle to a skeptical Watson after surprising his friend with an allusion to Darwin on their very first case together: "One's ideas must be as broad as Nature if they are to interpret Nature."

It is to channel Holmes's mode of engaging with knowledge, even of the most surprising kinds, that I set the idea of him before the plebes. I call up the detective's example—that of a man who fully realizes his innate gifts, but only through rigorous discipline—to convince my students that they can learn to distinguish information from noise, differentiate the red herring from the important clue, and synthesize seemingly unrelated spheres of knowledge. I hope to help them see that they are capable of reading the evidence all around them, just as Holmes encourages Watson to decipher a man's identity from his hat:

> "I can see nothing," said I, handing it back to my friend.
> "On the contrary, Watson, you can see everything. You fail, however, to reason from what you see. You are too timid in drawing your inferences."

This was no easy task for a Victorian, but my students belong to a generation deluged from the very start by enormous quantities of unfiltered information swirling in a virtual world. Yet, as Holmes reveals again and again, even in the absence of perfect knowledge, one can learn what to look for, where to find it, and how to make sense of one's discoveries in order to arrive at an informed decision. Think of the police inspector in "The Adventure of the Dancing Men," who marvels that Holmes has located a bullet hole in a window sash:

> "By George!" cried the inspector. "How ever did you see that?"
> "Because I looked for it."

Both men have access to the same field of evidence, but only one knows how to coax a story from it. That is the point of foils like the inspectors Lestrade and Gregson, who can assemble the basic facts of a case yet who lack Holmes's powers of analysis and synthesis.

What Holmes—not Doyle's original character, but this creation that almost from its birth seemed to outstrip the imagination of its creator—seems to have mastered is a certain mental agility. A similar attribute, "operational adaptability," has become one of the keynotes of U.S. Army doctrine in recent years. As General Martin E. Dempsey, at the time the leader of Training and Doctrine Command, explains in his foreword to *The Army Capstone Concept*, developing leaders who possess "operational adaptability," and are "comfortable operating under conditions of ambiguity and uncertainty," requires the cultivation of "a *mindset* based on flexibility of thought." One can see the same philosophy at work in "mission command," a concept of command and control that has become a crucial part of U.S. military doctrine in recent years. Mission command builds on the experience of decentralized operations that have characterized our twenty-first-century wars. Here it is defined in *Command and Control for Joint Land Operations* (2010):

> Mission command is the conduct of military operations through decentralized execution based upon mission-type orders. Successful mission command demands that subordinate leaders at all echelons exercise disciplined initiative, acting aggressively and independently to accomplish the mission. Essential to mission command is the thorough knowledge and understanding of the commander's intent at every level of command. Under mission command, commanders issue mission-type orders, use implicit communications, and delegate most decisions to subordinates wherever possible.

Perhaps "flexibility of thought" is not an aptitude conventionally associated with the military mind—tenacity, maybe, but not a Holmesian suppleness. Yet this ability to use what one knows in order to see what others cannot is precisely the power that future military officers need. There is, after all, almost nothing that is not useful to such work.

In a 2012 white paper on mission command, Dempsey, who had by then become the Chairman of the Joint Chiefs, invoked a capacity Clausewitz calls "the inward eye." In war, Clausewitz notes, "the commander continually finds that things are not as he expected." He goes on to say, "If the mind is to emerge unscathed from this relentless struggle with the unforeseen, two qualities are indispensable: *first, an intellect that, even in the darkest hour, retains some glimmerings of the inner light which leads to truth; and second, the courage to follow this faint light wherever it may lead.* The first of these qualities is described by the French term, *coup d'oeil*; the second is *determination*."

Moltke the Elder, whose writings strongly reflect the influence of Clausewitz, regarded the art of supreme command as a "free, practical, artistic activity, schooled obviously by military training and guided by experience, either from military history or from life itself." Moltke's own training, as it happened, was rather unconventional. At Germany's General War School, taking the minimum number of required courses in military reading, he focused instead on geography, literature, and languages. The historian Hajo Holborn describes Moltke's unorthodox life as a young officer:

> As a lieutenant he never had an extra penny to spend. Dire need compelled him to write short novels, which appeared in installments in a popular journal. In order to purchase mounts, without which he could not serve on the general staff, he translated six volumes of Gibbon's *Decline and Fall*. It is impressive to see the young Moltke wrestle with the problems of genteel poverty and yet acquire an Attic education in the Spartan setting of Berlin.

Perhaps all this literary moonlighting gave Moltke, who is generally regarded as one of the nineteenth century's preeminent military strategists, a more supple understanding of the elusiveness of narrative—of the ways in which a historical train of events doesn't advance in a straight line but more often takes a circuitous and surprising path full of the disorder, gaps, and reversals familiar to adept readers—and writers—of fiction. "Everything depends," Moltke wrote in an essay on strategy, "on penetrating the uncertainty of veiled situations to evaluate the facts, to clarify the unknown, to make decisions rapidly, and then to carry them out with strength and constancy." It takes many hours of study, training, and experience, however, before one is capable of making rapid but also wise decisions.

In Arthur Conan Doyle's stories, Holmes accomplishes his feats of mental agility through avenues that sometimes befuddle a literal-minded observer like Dr. Watson, who reports that his friend's intellectual motor often requires the lubrication of music. Playing the violin helps Holmes to think clearly and to work out complex puzzles. As I discover frequently with my students, you never know what someone's violin is —what secret, out-of-the-way, seemingly irrelevant knowledge or skill animates the whole.

When I told one cadet that Holmes was my superhero of the moment, he gently suggested that those who make a careful study of such things actually regard the detective as more akin to an "action hero" because his powers, while astounding, are not superhuman. At the time, Cody was in the process of schooling me in the subtleties of superheroes and superpowers while he wrote a senior thesis on comic books. He didn't always want to write about comic books; more precisely, he didn't always *know* he *could* write about them. When we began to discuss the project, he told me he wanted to research heroism in American literature, a dizzyingly broad topic. During an early conversation, as we attempted to define cultural heroes and antiheroes, I had occasion to mention Batman (and thereby nearly to exhaust my knowledge of comic books). But I had inadvertently opened an encyclopedia, and I soon realized that Cody had been unintentionally concealing a wealth of information in fact directly related to his interest in American heroes. He had not sufficiently valued this private storehouse of information or imagined the ways in which it intersected with what he thought of as a discrete academic pursuit. He subsequently needed little coaxing. Throughout the months of collaboration that followed, Cody taught me the difference between the golden age and the contemporary comic-book industry, between powers accidently acquired and powers with which one is born, between *Sgt. Fury* and *The 'Nam*. And a young man who seemed initially a bit reluctant to disclose this arcane knowledge discovered, as I hope all my students one day might, that his "brain-attic," as Holmes would put it, is rather smartly furnished.

At a loss to know "how he finds things out," characters in Doyle's stories frequently attribute Holmes's feats to some magical ability. They haven't witnessed the years of training, study, and experimentation that inform the detective's career. And if, like Watson, they mistakenly regard his pursuits as "desultory," "eccentric," or "out-of-the-way," they will never understand that such pursuits in fact constitute the very foundation of his practice of the science of deduction: the professional secret behind those expertly tuned habits of mind; those powers of observation, skills of analysis, and situational awareness that make him seem superhuman. Sherlock Holmes is constantly expanding our sense of what is practical, useful, and important. "To a great mind," he admonishes Watson, "nothing is little."

All of this I tried in one way or another to communicate to the plebes' parents assembled each spring in Ike. In spending time with this particular audience—so invested in the same people with whom I spend my days, so interested in a world about which they know only as much as their teenagers will tell them—I have begun to see a way clear of my war vertigo. Perhaps it is more accurate to say that I grew more comfortable with that vertigo and started to find ways to turn it to my advantage and to create the conditions that would help my students to understand that they were headed, one way or another, whatever the individualized geography, into no man's land.

PATIENCE AND TIME

My increasing dissatisfaction with old blueprints for a landscape so difficult to decode has only stoked my long-standing attraction to the figure of the detective and the processes of detection. As a result, in the fall of 2011, on the tenth anniversary of 9/11, with all those seniors who had grown up alongside Harry Potter, I explored the archetype of the investigator. We studied everything from the historian Jonathan Spence's *Treason by the Book*, an account of a Chinese emperor's attempt to ascertain the seriousness of a rebellion in a distance province, to *The Earrings of Madame de . . .* , a film by Max Ophüls in which so much depends on the repeated loss and recovery of a piece of jewelry, to Colson Whitehead's *The Intuitionist*, a novel that pits "empiricist" and "intuitionist" elevator inspectors against one another in order to solve the mystery of a fallen car. A lawyer introduced us to the rules of evidence; a physician demonstrated the arts of taking histories, interpreting symptoms, and diagnosing disease; and the cadets investigated various aspects of institutional culture and their own acculturation.

The course forced us to ask ourselves how we know what we know and to question our own assumptions and preconceptions. It also counseled deep attention, a quality that sometimes seems so rare today as to be almost extinct. Military organization is uncomfortable with "white space," those unstructured moments on the calendar that afford scope for imaginative and reflective work; that permit wandering, error, and failure as well as epiphany. Moreover, like the larger society it serves, military culture has grown increasingly enslaved to technology, caught up in the rage for multitasking despite the warnings of cognitive scientists such as Stanford University's Clifford Nass and his colleagues about the powerful delusion that multitasking is synonymous with omnicompetence. The "hyper-attention" cultivated by multitasking has contributed to the erosion of the faculty of "deep attention." We speak so often today about generational differences and various kinds of learners. Yet I worry that in playing to the apparent strengths of today's college students—their habitual multitasking, their facility with visual culture, their craving for constant stimulation—we allow certain underutilized faculties to remain unexercised. In other words, we encourage particular weaknesses to stay weaknesses.

We have persuaded ourselves that we live in a world of unprecedented change and uncertainty. But we are by no means the first people to think of themselves and their world in this way. Every age likes to flatter itself that its challenges are unprecedented. Technology accelerates the speed of that change, alters the appearance of things and sometimes their natures, and taxes some faculties while allowing others to atrophy. But none of that is exactly new. Think of Plato's warning that the technology of writing would erode memory. Think of the printing press. In her novel *Wolf Hall*, Hilary Mantel crawls into the head of Thomas Cromwell, the man who engineered Henry VIII's break with Rome in the 1530s, as he wrestles with the contributions of the printing press to a volatile world. Having just interrogated a woman accused of treasonous prophecies, Cromwell thinks about how much the world has changed since the machine's invention in 1450: "When the last treason act was made, no one could circulate their words in a printed book or bill, because printed books were not thought of. He feels a moment of jealousy toward the dead, to those who served kings in slower times than these; nowadays the products of some bought or poisoned brain can be disseminated through Europe in a month."

Or consider the advent of mechanized transportation in the nineteenth and early twentieth centuries, the way the unprecedented speed of such conveyances altered not merely the experience of human movement but also that of human perception. In a speeding automobile, Virginia Woolf writes in *Orlando*, "what was seen begun . . . was never seen ended. After twenty minutes the body and mind were like scraps of torn paper tumbling from a sack." She concludes, "the process of motoring fast out of London . . . resembles the chopping up small of identity." And this is to say nothing of the radical shift in perception that accompanied the invention of flight, here described by Saint-Exupéry:

> The airplane has unveiled for us the true face of the earth. For centuries, highways had been deceiving us . . .
>
> Roads avoid the barren lands, the rocks, the sands. They shape themselves to man's needs and run from stream to stream . . . join village to village . . .
>
> Thus, led astray by . . . roads, as by other indulgent fictions, . . . we . . . have elected to believe that our planet was merciful and fruitful.
>
> But a cruel light has blazed, and our sight has been sharpened. The plane has taught us to travel as the crow flies . . . Freed henceforth from . . . happy servitude . . . we set our course for distant destinations. And then, only, from the height of our rectilinear trajectories, do we discover the essential foundation, the fundament of rock and sand and salt in which here and there and from time to time life like a little moss in the crevices of ruins has risked its precarious existence.

The same sorts of things can be said for space travel and satellite imaging, for digital communication and the Internet. My point is that it is easy to forget that paradigm shifts are by no means new. Change is old, and so is our amazed response to it and our feeling that no one has lived through such turbulence before.

And the particular change that seems so radical to one generation turns into the norm for the next. Because they have grown up immersed in enormous amounts of unfiltered information—have never known anything else—my students are not always its savviest consumers or the most discriminating readers of evidence. They are impatient readers, and they are so persuaded of the omniscience and infallibility of the Internet—so habituated to think that all information resides in the ether—that they will put down the book they are reading and Google information that is actually contained within because they haven't thought to look there. It isn't natural to them.

Students, and in this respect they are no different from anyone else, often labor under the impression that because so many things can be measured with scientific precision, the act of interpretation is some quaint skill that belongs only to the study of poetry perhaps. They fail to recognize that the skill of interpretation—of a text or of any other kind of knowledge or evidence—is more important than ever in a world glutted by information. It isn't enough to know something; one must be able to use that knowledge. There are times when surrendering ourselves to a problem—losing ourselves in its intricacies—is the only thing that will enable us to solve it. The deep attention required for interpretation is the faculty we seem to be most in need of these days. On January 5, 2010, after the attempted Christmas Day airline bombing, President Obama noted, in what has become a frequently quoted speech, "The U.S. government had sufficient information to have uncovered this plot and potentially disrupt the Christmas Day attack. But our intelligence community failed to connect those dots." Connecting dots is an act of interpretation and synthesis; it requires sustained attention to find significance in an indiscriminate welter of information.

That is the ability Sherlock Holmes so clearly possesses, the disciplined process behind his seemingly miraculous solutions. He is able to weave a narrative from facts: to turn the data before him into a plausible story. While some of his discoveries are impressive because of their efficiency—his ability to identify a type of cigar ash, for example—his solutions impress largely because of the stamina of his intellect. Holmes's tenacity allows him to ponder a puzzle even at the neglect of eating and sleeping.

I would like to think that such deep attention is a venerable, if unfashionable, military virtue. It is, as I told the plebes' parents, a capacity I hoped their children could acquire at West Point. Grant did. Horace Porter, a member of his staff, describes the general's single-minded focus on campaign:

> He wrote nearly all his documents with his own hand, and seldom dictated to any one even the most unimportant despatch. His work was performed swiftly and uninterruptedly, but without any marked display of nervous energy. His thoughts flowed as freely from his mind as the ink from his pen; he was never at a loss for an expression, and seldom interlined a word or made a material correction. He sat with his head bent low over the table, and when he had occasion to step to another table or desk to get a paper he wanted, he would glide rapidly across the room without straightening himself, and return to his seat with his body still bent over at about the same angle at which he had been sitting when he left his chair . . .
>
> I cannot dwell too forcibly on the deep impression made upon those who had come in contact for the first time with the new commander, by the exhibition they witnessed of his singular mental powers and his rare military qualities . . . [H]ardly anybody was prepared to find one who had the grasp, the promptness of decision, and the general administrative capacity which he displayed at the very start as commander of an extensive military division, in which many complicated problems were presented for immediate solution . . .
>
> His powers of concentration of thought were often shown by the circumstances under which he wrote. Nothing that went on around him, upon the field or in his quarters, could distract his attention or interrupt him . . . [N]othing short of a general attack

along the whole line could divert his thoughts from the subject upon which his mind was concentrated.

Tolstoy's General Kutuzov, who waits out Napoleon with the watchwords "patience and time," to the frequent consternation of his more aggressive generals, had this ability, too. His mantra expresses a philosophy of history and causality that refuses the primacy of great men. Generals, whatever their grandiose delusions, are not, according to Tolstoy, the motors of historical change. Instead, they are subject to myriad forces they can't even see. One of the great revelations of *War and Peace* is its representation of man's ignorance, at best his nascent realization, that he is subjugated to invisible laws of necessity—to his place in a long historical chain of cause and effect. Only in surrendering the fiction of control over the direction of affairs can a general gain any actual control in the novel. Tolstoy provides an example of this capacity in the command style of Prince Bagration, here described by Prince Andrei, whose faith in Napoleon's greatness has heretofore influenced his understanding of battles:

> Prince Andrei listened carefully to Prince Bagration's exchanges with the commanders and to the orders he gave, and noticed, to his surprise, that no orders were given, and that Prince Bagration only tried to pretend that all that was done by necessity, chance, or the will of a particular commander, that it was all done, if not on his orders, then in accord with his intentions. Owing to the tact shown by Prince Bagration, Prince Andrei noticed that, in spite of the chance character of events and their independence of the commander's will, his presence accomplished a very great deal. Commanders who rode up to Prince Bagration with troubled faces became calm, soldiers and officers greeted him merrily and became more animated in his presence, and obviously showed off their courage before him.

The control exerted in this passage, translated by Richard Pevear and Larissa Volokhonsky, is passive: it rests primarily on the recognition of timeliness. One might compare it to the mature Hamlet's understanding, after his time-bending sojourn with the pirates, that "the readiness is all." Gone are Hamlet's former anxieties about action: "If it be now, 'tis not to come. If it be not to come, it will be now. If it be not now, yet it will come." Hamlet embraces a kind of fatalism here, but there's something arresting and wholly antithetical to the way most Americans tend to look at the world now in his comprehension of the complex web of causes that shape the present moment: about his place in a network rather than his defiance of all. Such patience about the unfolding of events is markedly absent from contemporary culture and perhaps especially from military culture. *Restrepo*, a film by Sebastian Junger and the late Tim Hetherington about a company on a fifteen-month deployment to a remote outpost in the Korengal Valley of Afghanistan, offers up a most illuminating example of modern impatience in its elegant articulation of the difference between American and Afghan time.

At a weekly *shura* with the elders from a nearby village, the company commander, Captain Kearney, repeatedly insists that his arrival in the valley marks a new beginning: he wants the elders to forget everything that happened during his predecessor's command, to put the previous captain's policies, as he says, "behind us" and wipe "the slate clean." For the young Kearney, time effectively starts over with this proclamation. Then, describing what for him, on his fifteen month deployment, is a future almost geologically distant, he announces to the assemblage of old men that in "five to ten years" there will be a paved road through the valley, commerce, health care, and many other marks of progress. This vision makes no impression on the elders, their traditional dress— the shalwar kameez—accessorized with new wristwatches, one of them attempting to figure out how to punch a straw through a juice box the Americans have given him. The Afghans clearly regard the alternate assurances and bullying on the part of the captain just as their predecessors did the promises and threats of the Taliban, the Soviets, the British, Babur, Alexander the Great, and every other invader who has come before him: as ephemeral gestures that are as nothing in the face of the endurance belonging to the survivor.

AN ABSENCE OF METHOD

With examples before me of well-intentioned officers nonetheless trained to impatience, culturally and constitutionally ill equipped for the fight in which they find themselves, I have been casting about in recent years for models, such as Holmes, of the patient, inquiring, disciplined mind the times require. This quest accounts for my latest obsession: Georges Simenon's Inspector Maigret, whom Julian Symons calls "the archetypal official detective of the 20th century." Simenon wrote about seventy-five Maigret novels. They were Hemingway's tonic "for that empty time of the day or night." Symons admires Simenon's books for their psychological insights, and he is not alone in this. Simenon's detective evidently impressed at least one professional policeman: Jean-Pierre Sanguy, once the director of the Paris police, thought of Inspector Maigret, as "a lesson of classic discipline in his investigations and humanity in his contacts."

Unlike Holmes, however, Maigret is often seen at a disadvantage. Many of the novels take place in Paris, where Maigret rises to the rank of chief superintendent, but just as many unfold in small villages where the rhythms and personalities involved are wholly unfamiliar to Maigret. Even in Paris, there are milieus in which he is ill at ease. Simenon's detective spends much of his time just wandering around searching for the often atmospheric key to a case. In *The Hotel Majestic*, for example, which opens with a murder in the elaborate basement kitchen of a large Paris hotel, Maigret appears to be "making an amateurish study of how a grand hotel functions." In *Lock 14*, he tries to make sense of riverboat life: "During the hour that he had been there, the chief inspector had thought of nothing but of how to familiarize himself with a world that he had suddenly discovered and about which, on his arrival, he had only vague, mistaken ideas . . . People wondered what his theory was, but in fact he had none. He was not even trying to find a clue properly speaking, but rather to steep himself in the atmosphere, to familiarize himself with this canal life that was so different from all that he knew."

The novels themselves are quite short; reading them is the work of an evening or two. But Maigret himself refuses to be hurried along. He recognizes that difficult problems—and human motive is the most difficult problem of all—often require a great deal of time to solve. Part anthropologist, part psychologist, part method actor, Maigret likes to ease himself into a new world slowly. "They give me a few weeks," he complains in *Maigret in Court*, "sometimes only a few days, to steep myself in a new atmosphere, to question ten, twenty, fifty people I knew nothing at all about till then, and, if possible, to sift out the true from the false." In *The Bar on the Seine*, the policeman divides his process of detection into two parts:

> Firstly, coming into contact with a new environment, with people he had never even heard of the day before, with a little world which some event had shaken up. He would enter this world as a stranger, an enemy; the people he encountered would be hostile, cunning or would give nothing away. This, for Maigret, was the most exciting part. He would sniff around for clues, feel his way in the dark with nothing to go on. He would observe people's reactions—any one of them could be guilty, or complicit in the crime.
>
> Suddenly he would get a lead, and then the second period would begin. The inquiry would be underway. The gears would

start to turn. Each step in the inquiry would bring a fresh revelation, and nearly always the pace would quicken, so the final revelation, when it came, would feel sudden.

The inspector didn't work alone. The events worked for him, almost independently of him. He had to keep up, not be overtaken by them.

Outpacing events is no simple matter, and far from being in control, Maigret often seems completely at a loss, lacking self-confidence, frustrated, and "bad-tempered." The habits and social world of the people he must investigate remain stubbornly opaque to him. Sometimes in his misery he is said to resemble a "huge sick animal." The magistrates to whom he answers criticize him for going "off on his own like a retriever. How could he explain," he broods, "that he had to see things, sniff around, and get the feel of a place?" And he dreads that moment in any investigation when an unexpected turn of events will force his hand. But whenever that moment does come, Maigret responds honestly, if sometimes with ill humor. He works to assimilate himself to the new rather than attempting to fit the unexpected in with his preconceived notions of a case. There is often a point in the novels at which Maigret must start over completely, surrendering a theory that the evidence no longer supports. In one especially difficult case (*Maigret Loses His Temper*) this happens repeatedly.

Maigret, like Holmes, puts a great deal of weight on small things, things that others might think irrelevant. "One can never be sure," Simenon writes in *Maigret and the Ghost*, "that some quite trivial detail may not turn out to be important." Yet in contrast to Holmes's vaunted method, Maigret readily confesses to having no method at all. When he has no "ideas," "no definite plan," no leads, he usually goes back to the neighborhood of the crime to soak up whatever information he can. The wonder lies not so much in his capacity for dazzling us as in the spectacle of his ornery perseverance. When Inspector Pyke of Scotland Yard, having heard of Maigret's success, comes to observe his French colleague in action, Maigret becomes thoroughly embarrassed by Pyke's expectation that he will follow some specific protocol instead of doing what he is inclined to do: simply wander around the Mediterranean island on which the crime has taken place. "It was just as well that the journalists who praised his methods didn't know how he sometimes went about things," Simenon writes in *Maigret and the Millionaires,* "for his prestige would undoubtedly have suffered."

We see the detective at perhaps his greatest disadvantage in this novel and in *Maigret Loses His Temper,* where his integrity is called into question in the middle of a difficult case. Maigret meditates on his own mental processes and on the temptations of pursuing the wrong course:

> And all of a sudden, just when you least expect it, the case slips out of your grasp. You cease to be in control of it. It is events that are in command and that force you to take measures you had not foreseen, and for which you were not prepared . . .
>
> You ask yourself whether you were headed in the wrong direction from the start, and whether you are not going to find yourself faced with a blank wall or, worse still, with a reality different from what you had imagined . . .
>
> If a single one of these hypotheses—or, rather, of these convictions—was incorrect, the whole of his case fell to the ground.
>
> Perhaps that was why he kept his bad-tempered look and moved ahead only with a certain repugnance.

Yet Maigret does move ahead in Simenon's novels, even when the next step proves him entirely wrong. His vanity always bows before the facts of a case. Despite the considerable deference paid to him by his subordinates, he rarely allows his reputation to eclipse his better judgment. As the novels progress and Maigret rises in the ranks of the police force, the temptation to appear omniscient and to be praised for it grows. It is the same temptation that attends any climb up the hierarchy—to chief of police or general-in-chief of an army. But being efficient or preserving a reputation of infallibility is never more important to Maigret than ferreting out the truth.

And so creating an experience in which those attributes—patience, deep attention, the capacity to admit error—can be allowed to grow in cadets, especially plebes, became the goal of my course design. And I like to think, having now finished *Harry Potter and the Sorcerer's Stone*, that it is the kind of educational program my students can understand. The book might have failed to transport me the way the works of Roald Dahl or T. H. White once did, but the school Rowling imagines has elements I admire, and her book gave me a new vocabulary with which to describe to my students, her avid readers, the enterprise on which we were together embarked.

First, I was greatly impressed by both the specificity and the utility of the Hogwarts School's standard set of gear (what plebes are taught to call a TA-50, which is short for Table of Allowances 50: Clothing and Individual Equipment): a winter cloak with silver fastenings, dragon-hide protective gloves, a customized wand, and "an owl OR a cat OR a toad." The school's comprehensive list of course books also reassured me, especially one title in particular, *The Dark Forces: A Guide to Self-Protection*. That, I suspect, is something each of us wants. Moreover, among Harry's virtues are several I hope to encounter in my own students: "daring, nerve," and a wonderful capacity "for spotting things other people didn't." Harry likewise possesses an admirable willingness to call things by their right names. He is unafraid, for instance, to use the name Voldemort, the very incarnation of evil, even though almost everyone else prefers the euphemistic You-Know-Who.

What I found most attractive about the book was Hogwarts, a

school that was also a kind of no man's land, full of trolls and three-headed dogs lying in wait around the corner. Because its doors and passageways move, it takes Harry some time to get his bearings, to decode the predictably unpredictable landscape. What I liked above all was that Hogwarts seemed to be a school animated by the spirit of risk. As headmasters go, Dumbledore is rather elusive. We could describe his leadership style as emphatically hands-off. He lets Harry be, even though, as Harry eventually figures out, the headmaster knows everything that goes on. Harry's loyal friends are upset by the "terrible" possibility that Dumbledore has failed to intervene—that he has allowed Harry to walk into danger, maybe even intended that the boy confront the dreaded Voldemort.

Harry has a decidedly different take on things. This kind of leadership isn't terrible at all, he counters: "He's a funny man, Dumbledore. I think he sort of wanted to give me a chance. I think he knows more or less everything that goes on here, you know. I reckon he had a pretty good idea we were going to try, and instead of stopping us, he just taught us enough to help . . . It's almost like he thought I had the right to face Voldemort if I could." This kind of trust, this willingness to give just enough to those you teach or lead and to let them figure out the rest for themselves, this investment in the kind of autonomy that allows us to imagine many sequels to the first battle, seems to me as valuable a principle for a military academy as it is for a school of witchcraft and wizardry.

SHAKESPEARE AND THE FORCES OF IMAGINATION

To some of the plebes, perhaps one of the strangest rites of spring is the acting workshop through which we put them as part of their introduction to literature. We commandeer classrooms, auditoriums, even the gymnasium, for an afternoon of improvisation and trust exercises. Shouting, whispering, leaping about, freezing in tableaux, hamming it up, or wishing (like Henry V's soldiers before the Battle of Agincourt) that they could be anywhere but where they were, the cadets all must reckon with what Shakespeare's words made them do with their minds and their bodies. Shakespeare is the figure with whom I associate the most meaningful transactions with my students because there is no writer who more thoroughly intuits and celebrates the force of imagination or more rigorously challenges readers to exercise it.

For the past several years, every plebe at West Point has been issued a one-volume collected Shakespeare. "It's a really big book," my student Kyle helpfully informed me one day. This really big book connects cadets—in some unexpected ways—to their profession and to their predecessors. A collected Shakespeare was once standard-issue at West Point. It's a tradition I revived not simply for the sake of tradition but because so many graduates have told me how important Shakespeare has been to them in war and in peace, of the places he has traveled with them, of the hardships he has endured alongside them. The plebes today read various plays and sonnets, memorize and perform a speech of their choosing, and participate in a semester-long competition we've taken to calling "Academy Idol."

Theatrical endeavor has an interesting history at West Point. In 1936, the superintendent approved the organization of a dramatic club called the Cadet Players. There were some restrictions imposed: no "farces based upon humorous criticisms of local affairs," no unapproved scripts, and no plays written by a "local amateur." But the photographs in the old West Point yearbooks reveal the richness and variety of the performances the cadets staged. The sets—far more elaborate than anything we can manage today—clearly required extensive carpentry, and the costumes appear similarly labor-intensive. The fact that some members of the all-male casts perform in drag reflects the nature of the student body at the time but also suggests a lack of self-consciousness I see only infrequently today: I did have one male senior volunteer to play Titania from *A Midsummer Night's Dream*, and he made quite a nice job of it.

As I learned on a visit to Maryland's Fort Meade, the army's history with Shakespeare goes at least as far back as World War II. Fort Meade is known for being the home of the clandestine National Security Agency. I went there to see a neglected repository of old newspapers and photographs housed in an ice-cold warehouse with a corrugated roof behind a locked gate and a barbed-wire fence. Inside the archives, friendly librarians helpfully piled boxes of artifacts before me and left me to my research. During lunch, I paced back and forth behind the fence thinking about theater and the prisoners of war in Jean Renoir's *Grand Illusion* awaiting a shipment of costumes from Paris to use in their stage revue.

The U.S. Army of the 1940s was a massive organization mobilized to confront an immediate threat. But its leaders, especially Chief of Staff George C. Marshall, adopted and preserved a strategic view even in the middle of a desperate fight: victory, Marshall understood, would require the successful imagination of peace. Major General Frederick Osborn, who in his capacity as the head of the army's Information and Education Division was responsible for morale, among other things, manifested a kindred spirit in his description of his duties as giving soldiers an understanding of not only "the causes of the war" but also "what it will mean if we can bring them back . . . resolved that as citizens they will see to it that those things are done that will make for a permanent peace."

Osborn's division included something called the Special Service units, whose members were trained "to provide athletic, recreational, informational and exchange services to troops on duty overseas." During World War I, morale had been outsourced to civilian organizations, but their efforts proved to be so uneven the army decided it had to incorporate their functions into the force itself. In the next war, the result was the Special Services, which provided the perfect place for the professional wrestlers, boxers, vaudeville comedians, musicians, theatrical producers, and occasional Broadway actors who happened to find themselves in uniform.

Among the Broadway stars was Captain Maurice Evans, a British actor who became a naturalized U.S. citizen before the war. The headline of the *Fort Meade Post* on Friday, October 30, 1942, read, "Meade May Have Big Theatrical Season." One of the lead stories was titled "Maurice Evans Soliloquizes in Coveralls on School Hike." Evans was about to graduate—along with classmates Glenn Miller, the bandleader, and John Shubert, the theatrical producer—from the School for Special Service, initially housed at Meade before being moved to the campus of Washington and Lee University. Its curriculum was designed to train athletic, theatrical, and other "technicians" so that they could deploy their skills overseas. The main subjects of instruction were "morale, recreation and theatrical functions, as prescribed in laws and regulations." Recreation officers were to be proficient in "devising, planning, and supervising practicable recreation and welfare activities for combat troops in Theaters of Operations, domestic and overseas."

In the spring of 1942, at his own expense, Evans had staged an exceptionally well-received performance of *Macbeth* with Judith Anderson and other professional actors at Meade. In order "to prove his contention that soldiers could and would enjoy the highest type of entertainment," Evans, the newspaper article explained, "went to the War Department in Washington with his results and those he conferred with acquiesced that entertainment standards could well afford to be raised." Evans believed that there was "too much spoon-feeding of the men on movies." Although he conceded that films "serve a valuable purpose here," he also argued that "there will be little opportunity to go to the movies in the combat areas. Those men will miss their former diversions and will look to live entertainment. Unless they get that live entertainment it is possible there might be a serious breach in morale." Evans's vision was to field "a troop of soldier players organized under Army Specialist Corps direction to go overseas and present plays to the men in the field." He subsequently went to Hawaii, where he coordinated performances by professional entertainers from Jack Benny to Yehudi Menuhin (two rather different violinists) and also directed mixed casts comprising GIs and stars (including Anderson and Boris Karloff) in performances of *Arsenic and Old Lace, The Mikado*, and an abridged version of *Hamlet*, in which he starred along with soldiers and which played on Broadway after the war.

Thousands of GIs had been in attendance at the original performance of *Macbeth* at Fort Meade. As an Army Ground Forces Replacement Depot, this army post saw millions of troops pass through during the war years: not only units headed out but also wounded soldiers returning from overseas. As a result, Meade became a center of entertainment for military personnel, and stars took great delight in visiting: everyone from Marlene Dietrich to Private First Class Dastagir, otherwise known as Sabu, Hollywood's elephant boy, who served in the Pacific as a tail gunner on a B-24 Liberator. Meade became a kind of out-of-town tryout for Broadway plays: the Fort Meade paper boasted that *Theatre Arts* magazine had lauded it "as an outpost of Broadway and a theatrical proving ground for legitimate plays before soldier audiences." There were six theaters at Meade, and the Post Field House had a capacity of four thousand. The *Fort Meade Post* reads more like *Variety* in those years than like a typical post newspaper. Helen Hayes told a reporter in June 1943, "Ever since I knew I was going to do 'Harriet' I have wanted to play it at Fort Meade." Bela Lugosi, on tour with his Broadway play *Dracula*, made a stop at Meade to play Theatre 4: admission was twenty-five cents.

When Evans graduated from it, the curriculum of the School for Special Service was hardly ideal. Theatrical training was a new concept for the army, and by all accounts the first several iterations of the course were not especially inspiring. Evans observed, "It was typical of the Army that we who had been teaching in the field were then brought together at Fort Meade to be taught how to teach." But that the army had created such a school at all is remarkable, and its graduates, presumably armed with the theater manual that Captain Jerome B. Coray, an actor and director at the Hollywood Playhouse before the war, had drafted when he became the head of its theater department in the fall of 1942, brought their craft to military personnel all over the world. Also included in the equipment Special Service units carried was a standard-issue theatrical kit containing "everything from false hair to stage money." With it, the theatrical technicians of the Special Service—I like to think of them as *commandos of the imagination*—could stage a show, as the *Fort Meade Post* quipped, "at the drop of one of the funny hats in the same kit."

The comedian Don Knotts, a member of the Special Service Branch, describes in his autobiography how he was chosen to be part of a company formed to entertain troops overseas because he listed his occupation as "ventriloquist" on his entrance papers. When the company reached the Pacific, a general reportedly told them, "We will be following your progress. Be assured that we will know where you are at every moment." Yet for weeks, in a comedy of errors, the unit sailed around the Pacific with no orders. Their theatrical campaign was full of snafus, including the assignment of four accordion players to the same unit. Sometimes the troupe landed in camps so muddy the tap dancers had no place to practice. But they worked whenever and wherever they could, eventually playing a show, under orders from Douglas MacArthur, for survivors of the Bataan Death March.

Meanwhile, the Special Services produced a robust program of shows for U.S. forces in Europe in 1945 and 1946. At the archives I read announcements for Special Service "theatre workshop productions" of *Volpone, Here Comes Mr. Jordan*, Noël Coward's *Hay Fever*, and several other shows at the Wiesbaden Opera House, their casts composed of U.S. military personnel and civilian actress technicians (or CATs). To see these handbills or one of the millions of paperback Armed Services Editions distributed to military personnel across the globe is to understand how tightly connected American political and cultural imaginations once were. The idea of exporting democracy during World War II was a robust one that retained a respect for the citizen-soldier as someone who needed intellectual sustainment as well as technical proficiency. It's the same idea that animated Admiral Mullen's exhortation that West Point's newest lieutenants "go beyond the technical knowledge" they had acquired and "broaden" their "views." Yet it is quite clear that not everyone shares this understanding of the modern soldier. The prospect of unleashing the forces of the imagination seems more intimidating to some military minds than unleashing massive firepower. You can aim a weapon with scientific precision these days, but you never know quite where the imagination will take you.

UNDISCOVERED COUNTRIES

Perhaps the most celebrated stage direction in all of Shakespeare, it is also one of the most bizarre: "Exit, pursued by a bear," It comes from *The Winter's Tale*, a moody, often brutal play that twenty cadets and I had the opportunity to see a few years ago at the Brooklyn Academy of Music. It is also the mantra with which I sang myself to sleep one June night in a tent on the North Slope of Alaska while imagining the consequences of meeting up with a grizzly. Antigonus, the character who exits pursued by that bear in *The Winter's Tale*, does not, I should make clear, return.

Many readers associate Shakespeare with royal courts and dynastic struggles, but some of the most provocative moments in his work occur in mysterious forests, on rugged heaths or haunted islands, and in mythical wildernesses where, together with savage creatures, the imagination itself runs wild. The "imagination bodies forth / The forms of things unknown," Shakespeare writes in *A Midsummer Night's Dream*. A "strong imagination" plays such extraordinary "tricks . . . / That if it would but apprehend some joy / It comprehends some bringer of that joy; / Or in the night, imagining some fear, / How easy is a bush supposed a bear!"

No wonder I turned to Shakespeare when I found myself with nothing but a tent flap between me and the entire bear population of the North Slope. Over the last few years Alaska has become for me a land of "things unknown," a destination that liberates and strengthens my imagination. On my first visit—made a few months before my trek to the North Slope—as I waited in the Anchorage airport for a flight to Fairbanks, I had been struck by one name that kept popping up on the departure board: "Deadhorse, AK." No other objective seemed at once so ominous, so intriguing, so thoroughly, seductive.

When I reached Fairbanks, I met up with several young officers, including Joel, whom I knew from their time as cadets. In anticipation of their upcoming deployment, they had devised a long list of expeditions to be undertaken over the summer, when the lingering sun makes it possible to live two days in every one. It seemed as if they wanted to touch as much of the state as they could before leaving. What they were doing, a friend suggested to me later, no doubt recalling his own rituals before heading out for Vietnam, was "saying goodbye" to a place they had learned to think of as home. Among the catalog of strange and unfamiliar places they recited was one that I recognized: Deadhorse. Serendipity.

"What is it?" I asked.

"Come back in June," Joel replied, "and you'll see for yourself."

And that's how I found myself with two lieutenants, Joel and Tom, and Laura, Tom's sister, in a Subaru wagon making my way up the Dalton Highway, a.k.a. the Haul Road, which connects Fairbanks with the oil fields of Prudhoe Bay: about 440 miles of gravel and dust. Rolling into Deadhorse in the morning mist and fog after a night on the tundra, I felt as if I had reached the top of the world or the end of the earth. I didn't know quite which.

We gazed out on an expanse of trailers, trucks, and drilling equipment. Standing beneath a Halliburton sign in the midst of the muddy expanse, Joel declared, "You would not believe how much this place reminds me of a FOB." The official oil-company-sponsored tour ends on the beach, where we had the enticing opportunity, which I was the only member of our party successfully to resist, of plunging into the Arctic Ocean (thirty-four degrees Fahrenheit). Someone had to stand guard, after all. Before we exited the bus, our guide had given us some vital instructions: "If you hear the horn honking, it means there is a polar bear in the vicinity. You should all gather together on the beach, hold your jackets over your heads, and look big." Seriously?

Back in Fairbanks, Joel had taken me on a tour of Fort Wainwright. On the eve of a major deployment, an army post wears a sad, abandoned look. In June 2008, Wainwright seemed a ghost town. The post is home to the 1st Stryker Brigade Combat Team, 25th Infantry Division ("Arctic Wolves"), but there were no signature Stryker vehicles in sight. They were already on a train headed south on the first leg of the long journey to Iraq. But we finally found an up-armored M1151 HMMWV stranded in a parking lot. "This is something you need to do," Joel said as I climbed into the driver's seat. Then he unexpectedly closed the door, walked away, and left me there alone. It was the only moment in the vast space of Alaska when I felt confined. It was tough to see; the armor restricted so much of my view. Sitting behind the wheel with my feet comfortably touching the pedals, I felt as if I had entered one of those historical exhibits that compel visitors to exclaim idiotically, "People were so much smaller in those days!" I'm five four on a good day. What must it be like for someone like Joel, who is over six feet, to ride around in it with body armor, Kevlar, a weapon, and three other soldiers? He left me there long enough for my imagination to perform its work.

The imaginative faculty is central to my understanding of cadets. Because I have never known many of the circumstances in which they might find themselves, the imagination—the sympathetic imagination—is where I meet them. It is also where, as individuals wrestling with their own private transformations, they learn how to meet one another in the fundamentally cooperative endeavor of soldiering. And it is what will allow them one day to take up the citizen again, as Washington put it. By means of the imagination we reach destinations as yet unvisited, anticipate experiences we've not undergone, encounter solutions to problems we didn't know we had. We must imagine courage as well as cowardice; victory but also disaster; home and what Hamlet calls the "undiscovered country." Then, at some later date—maybe in a HMMWV in Iraq or a Kiowa in Afghanistan or in the comfort of home—those imaginative labors become actual for the men and women who were studying *Othello* or *King Lear* in English class not so long ago.

So many of the moments that have defined for me what it means to teach at West Point have some connection with Shakespeare's work: watching Joel hold his own with a group of professional actors in a performance at West Point; witnessing a brilliant cadet named John pace up and down my office wrestling with Hamlet's figures of thought and his own; listening with a class of rapt plebes to one of their classmates, Matt, speak eloquently of *Macbeth*, violence, and his own prior service in Iraq; rehearsing a scene from *Twelfth Night* late one Friday afternoon in the parking lot because we had been kicked out of an auditorium so someone could rehearse a PowerPoint briefing; having the president of the West Point alumni association, a retired colonel who once worked as a Pentagon planner, materialize in my class one morning brandishing the edition of Shakespeare he had been issued while a cadet; beholding Chris Goeke movingly bring to life the role of Jaques, the melancholy philosopher of *As You Like It*, who wanders the forest meditating on mortality.

In these moments cadets took intellectual, emotional, and, sometimes, physical risks—risks encouraged by Shakespeare's themes and by the language in which he couches them. Serving as a stage manager for my friend Scott's production of *As You Like It* in 2008, and subsequently adapting and directing two shows, *Seduced by Shakespeare* and *This Can't Be Love: A Shakespearean Revue*, I discovered a new and different kind of engagement with cadets. Moreover, I came to understand that many of the elements of successful theater—absolute trust, teamwork, superior listening skills, and the courage to take risks—are also attributes of successful military organizations. I knew the cadets had figured this out when they all showed up early for rehearsal one day, in costume, and began running through their scenes unprompted. I floated my new theory to a captain named Dan, who had as a senior discovered untapped inner resources while mastering the part of Orlando in *As You Like It*. And Dan enriched the idea by adding another element: faith in the mission, be it dramatic or military. The actor and former marine Adam Driver drew a similar parallel on NPR's *Studio 360* when he characterized the military and the theater as endeavors demanding cooperation in a mission greater than any one person, accelerated intimacy with a particular group, the cultivation of trust, and the practice of "discipline" and "self-maintenance."

My trip up the Dalton forged a kind of solidarity. As travelers we shared certain unspoken expectations about this adventure. Alaska remains a realm of unanswered questions and undiscovered truths. It is a place where the lieutenants had been able to measure and define themselves, to reflect on their training and education, and to test their imaginations. John McPhee, an extraordinary observer of Alaska, rightly notes that the Arctic sun "strikes" rather than shines. That far north, of course, it doesn't even set in June. It just seems to slide a bit to the east to indicate that night has turned to morning. Self-exposure and self-discovery are unavoidable under such unrelenting illumination. Alaska is defiantly a no man's land. Traveling through it in such company, I came to understand the many ways in which experiencing such a landscape had become a necessity for me.

Before my journeys to the Last Frontier, the closest I had ever come to Alaska was memorizing Robert W. Service's "The Shooting of Dan McGrew" in the sixth grade. The Malamute saloon, where McGrew meets his end, had always been for me a place in which wonderful or terrible things might happen. On the North Slope the great grizzly bear became the embodiment of such possibilities. On my first visit to Alaska, bears had been in hibernation; when I returned, the enormous stuffed grizzly I had seen in the university museum in Fairbanks, terrifying though it was, no longer seemed enough. We encountered Dall sheep clinging to steep rock faces, caribou and musk oxen dotting the tundra, moose in parking lots and in the wild, but the bear eluded me. Emerging from the tent unscathed in the morning, I realized that seeing a bear was the thing I most feared and in fearing it exactly what I most desired. It's a difficult paradox, but one I think lieutenants can understand.

REWRITING THE STORY

The weekend during which the plebes' parents visit takes place just before the spring leave period. Sometimes their children will make the trip home with them for the week, but just as often my students inform me that they are off to one of those destinations that college students typically find appealing, while the intercollegiate athletes among them are often traveling with their teams. Going home continues to be important, but come spring it has already become less expected. It is over the winter holidays, back with their families really for the first extended period since arriving at West Point the previous June, that plebes are confronted by the fact that no matter how familiar home may feel, they are nevertheless in some ways newly estranged, reshaped by their experiences. They may have an uneasy sense that some of the things they had long assumed to be straightforward truths turn out to be stories that no longer fully persuade. Similarly, some of the West Point truths they report to their families create parts of a new mythology, which they, eager apprentices in the art of the "war story," do not yet fully recognize as such. After all, to attend West Point is to enter the misty world of legend: everyone from Edgar Allan Poe, briefly a recalcitrant cadet, to Robert E. Lee, who graduated without a single demerit—he waited a few years to break some rules—plays a part in the romantic mythology of the Long Gray Line.

Yet these are only some of the tales with which plebes must reckon. The engagements of the last decade have presented all cadets with many more: stories without the clarity imposed by time's passing, stories that confuse because they lack definition, stories of irrevocable loss. Having only recently begun a military career, plebes tend to depend heavily on others' stories. They eagerly play the roles that someone else constructs for them. Momentous career choice once made, they come to believe that they have effectively ceded control over their own narratives. How easy it can become to let a uniform, with all its signs and signals, tell one's story.

I am reminded of Lieutenant Carl Joseph von Trotta, the hapless protagonist of Joseph Roth's *The Radetzky March*, a book some of the plebes I read it with a few years ago found inordinately depressing. Trotta is the grandson of Captain Joseph Trotta von Sipolje, the "Hero of Solferino," a soldier knighted for saving the emperor's life. By the time the novel opens, however, the Hero of Solferino has been forgotten. Chancing on a wildly inflated, almost unrecognizable account of his deeds in the official imperial schoolbook his son brings home, an outraged Captain Trotta complains to the government. The minister of culture responds to him with the following explanation: "It was the intention of the . . . educational authorities . . . to introduce the pupils in the Monarchy to the heroic deeds performed by members of the Armed Forces and to depict them in accordance with the juvenile character,

imagination, and patriotic sentiments of the developing generation without altering the veracity of the events portrayed." But
Trotta refuses to let the matter be, as he is instructed to do, and
takes his case all the way to the emperor. As a result, the entire
episode quietly disappears from subsequent editions of the text-
book, the Hero of Solferino from the public consciousness.

The hero's grandson nevertheless grows up under the intimidating shadow of his grandfather's portrait: "The dead man revealed nothing; the boy learned nothing. From year to year, the
portrait seemed to be growing paler and more otherworldly, as if
the Hero of Solferino were dying once again and a time would
come when an empty canvas would stare down upon the descen-
dant even more mutely than the portrait." With his life scripted
for him by this weighty yet elusive legacy, the hero's grandson
never has the opportunity to figure out for himself what kind of
life he will lead, what kind of man he ought to be. The novel ends
with his death in a forgotten skirmish on the northeast frontier of
the Austro-Hungarian Empire. "This was the end of Lieutenant
Carl Joseph, Baron von Trotta," Roth writes, after his protagonist,
armed only with a delusionary sense of his own invincibility, is
shot while getting water for his platoon: "The end of the grandson
of the Hero of Solferino was a commonplace end, not suitable for
the textbooks in the elementary schools and high schools of Imperial and Royal Austria. Lieutenant Trotta died holding not a
weapon but two pails."

Among those authors who have the most to teach the plebes about
creating their own story is the Roman poet Ovid, who sets out in
his poem *Metamorphoses* to narrate the history of change since
the origins of the world: chaos into cosmos, human beings into
beasts and (sometimes) back again. The plebes are themselves
poised to enter a world rife with Ovidian volatility, uncertainty,
and surprise; the transformations they are undergoing—and will

continue to undergo—only seem less radical than the fantastic metamorphoses Ovid recounts. Wrestling with the poem's exuberance offers them a chance to begin accommodating themselves to the strange new world they have joined and to the intricate network of stories informing it.

It is my hope that their introduction to writers such as Ovid will save them from the fate of unthinkingly living someone else's life—a father's, a grandmother's, or some more distant hero's; that this kind of literature might equip them with the ability to interpret the stories they have (often unwittingly) inherited as well as with the ingenuity to create new ones. Ovid is one of literature's wiliest fabulists; his is no systematic chronicle. The structure of *Metamorphoses* mirrors the shape-shifting instability of the world it depicts, one in which chaos always threatens to rend the universal order to which it gave birth. The poem itself often misbehaves right along with its protagonists. Perhaps a story refuses to end or is interrupted by another tale only to resume later; sometimes one story—maybe naturally but often quite arbitrarily—becomes another one altogether; tragic and comic elements often intermingle.

Ovid's world is one in which even form and matter threaten to dissolve before our eyes: A boy who happens to be the son of the Sun King borrows his father's chariot and nearly incinerates all creation before plunging like a comet headlong from the sky. A girl, pursued by lustful Jupiter, is transformed by his jealous wife, Juno, into a cow terrified by the sound of her own incomprehensible lowing and left to scratch in the dirt with a hoof the story of her terrifying abduction and imprisonment in the body of a beast. A man who founded a kingdom by killing a venomous serpent and sowing the fields with its teeth cries out in despair at the litany of misfortunes that have since befallen him; in his grief, he becomes a serpent himself, destined to dwell, in the company of his similarly transformed wife, in an Illyrian grove—a pair of genial snakes living in peace with human beings because they remember what they used to be.

After reading these myths, I sometimes ask the plebes to invent one of their own: to unleash their unpredictable, insufficiently exercised creativity in the modern reimagining of an ancient metamorphosis. By setting a shape-changing episode within the known worlds of home, high school, or West Point, they learn to make the familiar strange and the strange familiar and thus to recognize more clearly the lineaments of the stories that envelop them. In transplanting Ovid to new soil and exerting some measure of control over a narrative—complex, contradictory, and alien though it may seem—they begin their own transformation from consumers into authors of myth. Such an act of imagination seems especially appropriate at this critical phase in the plebes' journeys as soldiers and storytellers. Because sooner or later they will arrive at a moment we all experience—the moment Didion captures in "The White Album," when the old stories on which we have relied stop working.

Maybe, like Harold Crick, the hero of *Stranger Than Fiction*, a film I often watch with cadets, we discover that we are "somehow involved in some sort of story" that is in fact being dictated by someone else. And maybe we're not sure whether it will turn out to be a comedy or a tragedy or whether we'll even have a say in the matter. Maybe it happens when we finally escape from home, go to college, join the army, go to war, watch someone die unnaturally and too soon. Or maybe it happens again when we return home, years later, from whatever new world we've joined and in the guise of whatever new self we've fabricated to live in it. But one day we awaken to the realization that the plot of our life wasn't quite what we thought it would be, that its very genre has transformed before our eyes—perhaps comedy has become tragedy, tragedy comedy, or romance satire. That's the moment when we have to improvise, when we must determine how hard to fight for the rights to our own story. We must identify who wrote the myths by which we have been living and decide which ones are ultimately worth keeping.

What will my students do when they awaken one day to discover that the narratives they've woven in order to get up in the morning have lost the power to contain experience? This crisis often arrives at the time when we can least afford it: in a hostile place where we are responsible for others as well as for ourselves and where there is little luxury to think about anything but survival, or, more disorienting still, at home in a familiar place that has suddenly lost its aura of safety and ability to comfort. What alternatives will my students construct to replace the old dichotomies between war and peace, between home and distant lands? How will they handle the restlessness that comes with learning that one persists in a kind of limbo, over here and over there?

But maybe my students will be better equipped than I was when I realized that the old story was no longer good enough and I had to imagine a new one. Whenever it happens, perhaps they will remember what it was like once, as plebes in the throes of their own disconcerting metamorphoses, to grapple with the ungovernable in Ovid, to behold the liberation and pains of becoming something new, to chase down the stories whose ends insist on eluding us. Maybe they will have the resourcefulness and endurance to write an end to the war story for both the army and themselves, the sense of risk to carve out a new and constructive space where the dangers of no man's land turn to opportunity and where ambition and imagination are not only acknowledged but prized as the means to winning the decisive battles of their futures, wherever and however they happen to be fought.

In my own ongoing quest to rewrite the story, I returned to the first volume of T. H. White's *The Once and Future King*, *The Sword in the Stone*, the memories of its long-ago enchantment sparked by my foray into the world of Harry Potter. It rewarded me with the same pleasures I had experienced as a younger reader, but it had also become in the interim a quite different book, a wartime book whose depiction of a totalitarian ant farm—something I had not remembered from my initial reading—reflected the European milieu in which it was created: the book was originally published in 1938. Arthur, or the Wart, as he is called, was the same as I remembered, a boy of courage and heart, ignorant of his royal parentage and thus another example of someone unwittingly preparing for a momentous destiny.

Near the beginning of the book, the Wart finds himself lost, having followed a hawk, "on the verge of the true forest." He is initially afraid to find himself so far from home; nevertheless, after a time, he surprises himself with the realization that he is "no longer frightened." Arthur adapts, calming his wilder fancies about what lurks in the dark by trusting the animals "to be themselves," and showing the first glimmerings of that self-reliance that his tutor, the magician Merlyn, will try to encourage in him along with the gift of perspective that comes from being metamorphosed into a fish, an ant, a bird, or a badger.

In Merlyn, the Wart has a teacher armed with magic yet burdened with the many complications that arise from existing in backward time. "If you know what is *going* to happen to people, and not what *has* happened to them," Merlyn tells his pupil, "it makes it difficult to prevent it happening, if you don't want it to have happened, if you see what I mean? Like drawing in a mirror." Lacking Merlyn's gift of foresight, I could not know when I came to West Point that I was standing on the verge of the true forest. There's nothing I could have prevented from happening, yet there are certain aspects of that story that I now desperately wish to rewrite. The power of revision, it turns out, is the superpower I most desire.

CODA
The Accident of Elegies

All comedy, is tragedy, if you only look deep enough into it.
—Thomas Hardy to John Addington Symonds, April 14, 1889

I initially read Joseph Heller's *Catch-22* while squirreled away in a Toronto hotel room during the 1997 Modern Language Association convention. It was December, and I had just finished my first semester teaching at West Point. Heller's novel was a revelation—an outrageous fiction opening a window onto the various paradoxes and pathologies that characterize not just armies but institutional cultures everywhere: universities, hospitals, government agencies, corporations. More important, it helped me to make sense of my own recent delivery into military culture. Heller's glorious caricatures—ex-P.F.C. Wintergreen, the clerk to whom even generals defer; Major Major, the squadron commander who is never in his office except when he's out; Colonel Cathcart, the group commander at once "dashing and dejected, poised and chagrined . . . complacent and insecure"—became bywords for their real-life avatars, whose often interdependent virtues and foibles daily presented me with new puzzles.

Catch-22 was the extreme case, a system gone wild, that illuminated the quotidian and thus made suddenly intelligible to me a new world's unfamiliar vocabularies, rituals, preoccupations, and assumptions. It showed me what was different about this culture from those that had shaped me. How, for example, authority operates in an organization in which the participants actually wear their status on their shoulders. "That *was* clever," a naked general exclaims appreciatively on being informed that his uniform has been thrown out a hotel-room window by Yossarian, Heller's stubborn protagonist, and his pals. "We'll never be able to convince anyone we're superior without our uniforms . . . That was a splendid tactic."

Alone in my own hotel room, grinning like Orr, the pilot whose "deranged and galvanic giggle" so infuriates Yossarian, I thought *Catch-22* was just about the funniest, most outrageous thing I'd ever read. Until recently, however, I hadn't been able to bring myself to read it again. Over the course of the intervening years I would return to favorite passages. I continued to refer to people who were never in their offices when I went looking for them as "Major Major." Yet whenever I tried to reread the novel through to the end, I was stopped short by the appearance of Snowden, the gunner who dies in Yossarian's arms from a shrapnel wound. The story of Snowden's death recurs throughout the novel, each iteration revealing a bit more detail until we are confronted in the book's penultimate chapter with the whole abject mess of it.

Snowden's death is arguably one of the only nonparodic episodes in the book; it was the motif to which I had paid so little attention the first time through. Somehow, in the meantime, it had become its insistent core, and that recognition confused my relationship with the rest of Heller's novel. Perhaps I was too slow to realize the degree to which internal and external events had combined to remake me as a reader. I was no longer a stranger to the culture the book satirized and no longer a peacetime but a wartime consumer of the "hilarity and horror" that Robert Brustein praised in an early review. Heller's book, explained Brustein, expertly navigates "the borderline" between those two extremes, yet, as I kept trying to reread it, it seemed as if someone had moved the border in the intervening years right into the middle of the horror, just as Yossarian surreptitiously moves the bomb line—that red ribbon of demarcation on the map indicating the area beyond which targets can be safely attacked without endangering friendly ground troops—to circumvent a dreaded mission to Bologna.

As it rains day after day at their air base on the fictitious island of Pianosa, Yossarian and the rest of the men begin a "macabre vigil" around the bomb line map as if to will its movement.

"I really can't believe it," Clevinger exclaimed to Yossarian in a voice rising and falling in protest and wonder. "It's a complete reversion to primitive superstition. They're confusing cause and effect. It makes as much sense as knocking on wood or crossing your fingers. They really believe that we wouldn't have to fly that mission tomorrow if someone would only tiptoe up to the map in the middle of the night and move the bomb line over Bologna. Can you imagine? You and I must be the only rational ones left."

In the middle of the night Yossarian knocked on wood, crossed his fingers, and tiptoed out of his tent to move the bomb line up over Bologna.

Yossarian postpones but cannot finally avert the mission. Once embarked, however, he induces Kid Sampson, the pilot of his plane, to turn back. Later Yossarian awakens from a nap on the beach to behold a perfect formation of bombers coming home to their island base: "Bologna was a milk run. There had been no flak there at all."

But there's another cruel twist to the tale of Kid Sampson, who survives Bologna only to be killed, in a bizarre accident, by a fellow member of the squadron. Sampson is standing on a raft in the water enjoying himself when McWatt, the pilot "who loved flying too much" and "never missed an opportunity to buzz" Yossarian's tent or the beach where the men swim, decides to zoom in low over the water. Yossarian feels himself "prepared for any morbid shock" but the one McWatt delivers that day when an "arbitrary gust of wind or minor miscalculation of McWatt's senses dropped the speeding plane down just low enough for a propeller to slice" Kid Sampson, who is at the same time playfully reaching up to touch the plane, "half away."

And so, I put the book away until, after a decade of war and the deaths of a few Sampsons and Snowdens of my own, I decided in 2011, the fiftieth anniversary of its publication and the tenth anniversary of 9/11, to try again.

Recalling that *Catch-22* is a great favorite of my friend Nick, who flew a Chinook helicopter in Iraq, I thought he might be able to help me make a new kind of sense out of Heller's novel, especially of those elements that no longer seemed so outlandish. Take, for instance, Yossarian's incessant complaint, "They're trying to kill me," introduced at the same moment we learn of Snowden's death. "That's what you come to understand," Nick explained, "they *are* trying to kill you, and not haphazardly or sporadically. There are people who are devoted every day to the business of killing you, and they're good at it. You can do absolutely everything right, and they can still kill you." The "immoral logic" that confounds Yossarian's friend Chaplain Tappman, as he tries to get the men who've reached their quota of missions sent home as originally promised, is the immoral logic of war itself.

There were other things that didn't seem quite so fantastic anymore: the mess officer Milo Minderbinder's grand plan to contract war out to "private industry"; the civilian discomfort with the "obligation of continuous sympathy" for the bereaved; or that warped brand of patriotism that reads anything less than total agreement as disloyalty and rationalizes almost any action on the grounds that it is "for the good of the country." "Morale was deteriorating," Heller writes, "and it was all Yossarian's fault. The country was in peril; he was jeopardizing his traditional rights of freedom and independence by daring to exercise them." That's Nick's favorite passage in the book, which he made sure to read just before deploying. "I think," he told me, "more than anything else I'd read at the time, the novel prompted me to ask about a particular assignment or mission, why are we doing this? It's not really a question anyone prepares you to reckon with, but it is one that is critical for commanders to ask . . . Soldiers know when a leader knows why he or she is doing something as opposed to just relaying a command."

When I closed the book—this time on the final page—what stayed with me above all else was the impotence of Yossarian in the face of the "grim secret" disclosed by the dying Snowden: "It was easy to read the message in his entrails. Man was matter."

"I'm cold," Snowden said. "I'm cold."
"There, there," said Yossarian. "There, there."

Snowden dies, and there's nothing Yossarian can do about it. That is the source of the outrage, the extremity, the thing against which the spectator is powerless—against which I'm powerless. That—not the naked generals, crazed colonels, and invisible majors—is the wartime heart of Heller's book. And that is what I could not see the first time around.

As it happens, there was a great deal I didn't understand in that Toronto hotel room. How could I have done? No man's land was just a relic of history then, its contours the stuff of poetry and its hazards academic, silted over with the years. I had not yet become one of its denizens, all unwitting; lacking appropriate preparation, adequate maps, or means of escape; keeping company with ghosts. I didn't know then that it sometimes happens this way.

They sit in your class poring over Dante's *Inferno* or grousing good-naturedly about the silent film you've insisted they admire. They graduate to crawling through the mud at Ranger School or learning how to fly a Chinook in Alabama. They write to let you know about the milestones and about the weirdness, ask what's new on your end, and tell you not to work "too hard." They stop by the office whenever they're back in town for a wedding or a class reunion. They become, for reasons you think you understand, more active correspondents the farther away they find themselves.

Messages—sometimes old-fashioned letters—roll in from Mosul or Herat, from places you can't even find on a map but the names of which give you a sense of the general atmosphere—COP Crazy, FOB Warhorse—or from one of those encampments named for the dead: Bostick, Caldwell, Fenty, Herrera, Keating, Sweeney. You do your best to respond to the mood they set, and you somehow grow closer at an impossible distance in what you imagine must be a distinctly wartime way. It isn't the complex intimacy of a family member, nor is it the transitory connection of strangers on a plane. It survives its long silences and permits—on both sides—frankness and a lack of self-consciousness about exhilaration or despair. It is free from an impulse to censor or a need to shield the recipient. It is occasionally urgent, often wry, and (whatever the register) always authentic. Perhaps it is best described as the intimacy of having known how another's mind works and of having watched it grow in response to unprecedented stimuli and responsibilities, to the confusion that attends even the most carefully orchestrated operation, and to the challenges of improvisation. In such correspondence, one finds, to paraphrase Wordsworth, the epic growth of the soldier's mind when it is engaged in a dangerous, unusual, sometimes downright bizarre enterprise: teaching an Afghan unit to fire old Soviet artillery with a manual written in Russian, serving in the military police at a detention facility in the wake of Abu Ghraib, or leading a company of paratroopers on missions through Zabul Province.

Then one day, maybe, even though you have known somewhere deep inside from the start that this is one of the possible endings to the story, you find yourself unable to comprehend the fact that the last message you sent will go forever unanswered. Days later you sit in a pew staring at a flag-draped coffin that holds the remains of a man not yet thirty. A coffin surrounded by a wife and a mother and a father, by a sister who also wears the uniform, and by a lot of other young men who aren't yet thirty. Men who call him—repeatedly and forcefully—their best friend. Friends permitted to grieve unabashedly in this place as they struggle through their eulogies but who suffer invisibly terrible things elsewhere. And then you discover that distance is no insulation, that Zabul Province is unendurably close. You realize that your ritual of scanning the casualty notices on the DOD website and *The Washington Post*'s Faces of the Fallen page hasn't really conditioned you at all.

Department of Defense News Release No. 093-10, dated February 3, 2010, announced that two soldiers, Captain Daniel P. Whitten, twenty-eight, of Grimes, Iowa, and Private First Class Zachary G. Lovejoy, twenty, of Albuquerque, New Mexico, "died of wounds suffered when enemy forces attacked their vehicle with an improvised explosive device Feb. 2 in Zabul province, Afghanistan. They were assigned to the 1st Battalion, 508th Parachute Infantry Regiment, 4th Brigade Combat Team, 82nd Airborne Division, Fort Bragg, N.C." Captain Whitten commanded C Company; Private First Class Lovejoy was one of the paratroopers in his company.

Dan Whitten graduated from West Point in 2004. He was my student. Together we read everything from Montaigne to *The Maltese Falcon*; we watched *His Girl Friday, Citizen Kane, Grand Illusion,* and *Night and Fog.* Dan was a kind of student I always hope to find in class: one who keeps the rest of us honest. He was direct and impatient with muddled thinking, yet he delivered his arguments with such wit and humor and from a place of such scrupulousness that no one could justly resent a correction. He wrote a thesis with one of my colleagues on beauty and elegance in scientific theory, but he could be equally engaging on the subject of *Braveheart* (a film about which we disagreed) or *Billy Madison* (about which we were in absolute accord). And he made me laugh. He was buried Friday, February 12, 2010, in the West Point cemetery.

In the years since his graduation, Dan had become a correspondent—someone whose messages I welcomed, whose insights I valued. When I asked what he needed, he would say he needed nothing: "No specific needs or desires right now, but I'll let you know if I lose/break anything." When I asked him how he was, he would say, "Life is good. Except the whole Afghanistan thing."

In one of those strange coincidences that make the army seem small, another former student was one of Dan's lieutenants in Afghanistan. After Dan died, the lieutenant told me he had come to understand more about leadership in a few months with Dan than at any passage in his life. Knowing about the connection, Dan had shared with me his own observations on the lieutenant's progress, and I could see the care he took with him. The specificity and humanity of his reflections suggested the kind of attention he paid all the men he commanded. From past experience, I knew, too, the equanimity with which Dan greeted setbacks as well as successes. That quality must have helped prepare his men for even this eventuality.

Dan balanced what all thoughtful officers must learn how to balance: in his words, "day-to-day business and improving the lives of [his] paratroopers," on the one hand, and, on the other hand, reflecting, in moments that allowed, "on the purpose, conduct, and end state of this conflict." In his last e-mail to me he wrote of becoming "a little more restless," as a man with an active, conscientious mind is apt to become when he finds himself in a foreign, hostile place—in what the marine I met at Walter Reed called, while staring at what was left of his leg, "a sea of variability"—in the middle of a story whose end he cannot readily discern.

Many soldiers—from Alexander the Great to Babur, the sixteenth-century Mughal emperor, from the British general Frederick Sleigh Roberts to those Soviet artillerymen who left their guns behind—have gone to war in the punishing terrain of Afghanistan. I returned recently to Babur's memoir, the *Baburnama*, which I have read with cadets alongside Rory Stewart's account of his walk across Afghanistan, *The Places in Between*. Idiosyncratic and capable of great cruelty, Babur was also a keen observer of the landscapes, customs, and peoples of Afghanistan, including the region in which Dan served.

Babur lived in an age of contradictions. Perhaps in some sense its amalgam of sensitivity and cruelty is not so unlike our own. Salman Rushdie suggests that like Machiavelli, the Western thinker he "most resembles," Babur was "blessed, or perhaps cursed, with a clear-sightedness that looks amoral; as truth so often does." Babur fills his memoir with the detailed observations of a dedicated naturalist. Overwhelmed by the diversity of tulips covering some foothills, he ordered men to count the different kinds: "There turned out to be thirty-two or thirty three unique varieties." In the *Baburnama* there are notes on climate, long catalogs of indigenous crops, loving attention to newly transplanted species such as a sour cherry tree, whose health Babur monitors with great interest. And then, just as naturally, he plants a crop of an entirely different kind:

> When the assault was made from all sides, the Afghans were not able to put up a fight. In a flash a hundred, 150 embattled Afghans were seized. Some were captured alive, but mostly only heads were brought. If Afghans are unable to fight they come before their enemies with grass in their teeth, as if to say, "I am your cow." We witnessed that custom there: the defeated Afghans held grass in their teeth. Those who were brought in alive were ordered beheaded, after which a tower of skulls was erected in the camp.

Despite the largely unsentimental tone of Babur's book, the legend of his death suggests a man of powerful affections: with his son Humayun dying of fever, Babur, as Rushdie tells it, "after consulting a mystic, walked three times round Humayun's bed and offered himself to God in his son's place. Whereupon Humayun strengthened and recovered, and Babur weakened and—on December 21, 1530—died."

On his journey through Afghanistan, Babur had also revealed a remarkable capacity for endurance. Toward the end of 1506, he began a winter trek from Herat to Kabul. Following the advice of one of his counselors to take the northern route, Babur at one point found the snowy roads virtually impassable: "During those few days we endured much hardship and misery, more than I had experienced in my whole life," he reports, here in Wheeler M. Thackston's translation. Babur commemorated the journey in a couplet: "Is there any cruelty or misery the spheres can inflict I have not suffered? / Is there any pain or torment my wounded heart has not suffered?"

Stopping for a night at a cave too small to accommodate all his men, Babur found a shovel and dug himself a chest-deep shelter by its mouth: "There I sat down. Several people asked me to come inside, but I refused. I figured that to leave my people out in the snow and the storm, with me comfortable in a warm place, or to abandon all the people to hardship and misery, with me here asleep without a care, was neither manly nor comradely. Whatever hardship and difficulty there was, I would suffer it too." And there Babur remained, "all huddled up" with frostbitten ears, until further inspection revealed that the cave was larger than it had seemed. There, too, Dan would have remained; he just wouldn't have felt the need to tell you about it afterward.

In Dan's West Point yearbook entry, where most cadets include a paragraph, customarily penned by their friends, full of inside jokes and allusions to various struggles or triumphs, Dan offered only one cryptic line: "I will show you fear in a handful of dust." It comes, of course, from T. S. Eliot's *The Waste Land*—from the poem's first section, "The Burial of the Dead." Heavily indebted to Jessie L. Weston's exploration of the myth of the Holy Grail in *From Ritual to Romance* (1920), Eliot's poem, published in 1922, is also rooted in the spiritual and physical devastation of his age, symbolized by the western front's no man's land. According to versions of the legend, a questing knight must restore the Waste Land, a once fruitful but now blasted kingdom ruled over by an impotent, dying Fisher King. The hero's mission is vague, his destination mysterious: he is challenged to ride into the heart of the land, to the aptly named Perilous Chapel, where he must ask a series of questions in a particular way to heal the king and redeem the earth. Eliot found Weston's mythology useful in evoking the complex postwar chaos of modern Europe. Dan, sufficiently imaginative and sophisticated to understand that he was about to enter a no man's land himself, seems likewise to have found in the poem's landscape an allegory for his own historical moment, one that seems intent on reviving an antiquated heroism while preserving the ironic, knowing, disillusioned sensibility of the modern age. I see a kind of prescience in his choice: how right Eliot's imagery has become for evoking the confusions of our own era.

Dan's eventual mission into the heart of a land laid waste by a series of conquerors stretching back to Alexander ended up being as murky as that of the old questing knight. Dan fought there, with the 82nd Airborne, a division steeped in its own paratrooper mythology, on behalf of a nation that still clings hungrily to the image (shown to us in, for example, HBO's *Band of Brothers*) of the World War II paratrooper giving a chocolate bar to a grateful European child. It is a nation that also registers—intermittently, at least, at some primal level—a certain discomfort with the belated and unsettling invocation of the image of the World War II liberator in the context of our recent military expeditions.

One of the films Dan and I watched together in class, Jean Renoir's *Grand Illusion*, dramatizes this fault line between chivalry and modern warfare, the no man's land between the Old World and the New. The film also includes what could be called, were it not for the gravity of the consequences, a running joke. It involves the battle for the fortress of Douaumont, near Verdun. We first learn of its capture by the Germans while reading, along with a group of French prisoners, twin notices printed in French and German, on a prison camp bulletin board: "Douaumont est pris!" reads the French version. In spite of the news that Douaumont has been taken, the prisoners decide to go ahead with a planned musical revue. In the middle of the show news that the Allies have retaken Douaumont prompts the prisoners to stop the production and sing "La Marseillaise" triumphantly. The celebration is short-lived. Its ringleader, Lieutenant Maréchal, played by Jean Gabin, ends up in solitary confinement. Moreover, a new bulletin is posted shortly thereafter announcing that the fortress has changed hands yet again: "Douaumont est repris par les troupes allemandes." On reading this bulletin, one of the prisoners wryly remarks, "Can't be much left of it." Going over the same ground again was the definitive action of the entrenched warfare of the western front, but it could be said to express at least to some degree the movement of all wars, not least our war in Afghanistan, itself a reliquary of past conflicts, the layered complexity of which is so well documented in Stewart's *The Places in Between*.

This motif of retreading the ground has a rich literary tradition. One of its earliest contributors was the Roman poet Virgil. At the end of the first book of his *Georgics*, Virgil introduces the theme of Rome's recently ended civil wars by predicting that farmers working the fields of Philippi or Pharsalus will one day dig up the relics of Roman soldiers killed in the internecine conflict:

> Then, after length of time, the labouring swains,
> Who turn the turfs of those unhappy plains,
> Shall rusty piles from the ploughed furrows take,
> And over empty helmets pass the rake.
> Amazed at antique titles on the stones,
> And mighty relics of gigantic bones.

The plowman turning up relics of battles past is a recurring motif that offers an image of war's persistence: it may go underground, yet it always threatens to break out again, even in the bountiful harvest of peace. In the ensuing centuries, writers continued to meditate on the traces of war because they were so suggestive of the degree to which a martial past could continue to exert its hold on even a peaceful present. Thomas Hardy invoked the same trope in his nineteenth-century meditation on history in *The Mayor of Casterbridge*, where old Rome materializes not only aboveground in the shape of the ruined amphitheater but also underground in the graves of the imperial soldiers periodically disclosed by the town's gardens and fields:

> Casterbridge announced old Rome in every street, alley, and precinct. It looked Roman, bespoke the art of Rome, concealed dead men of Rome. It was impossible to dig more than a foot or two deep about the town fields and gardens without coming upon some tall soldier or other of the Empire, who had lain there in his silent unobtrusive rest for a space of fifteen hundred years. He was mostly found lying on his side, in an oval scoop in the chalk, like a chicken in its shell; his knees drawn up to his chest; sometimes with the remains of his spear against his arm; a fibula or brooch of bronze on his breast or forehead; an urn at his knees, a jar at his throat, a bottle at his mouth; and mystified conjecture pouring down upon him from the eyes of Casterbridge street boys and men, who had turned a moment to gaze at the familiar spectacle as they passed by.
>
> Imaginative inhabitants, who would have felt an unpleasantness at the discovery of a comparatively modern skeleton in their gardens, were quite unmoved by these hoary shapes. They had lived so long ago, their time was so unlike the present, their hopes and motives were so widely removed from ours, that between them and the living there seemed to stretch a gulf too wide for even a spirit to pass.

The passage of time serves to take the emotional edge from the discovery of the Roman Empire's skeletal remains for the inhabitants of Casterbridge, but the "breaking of nations" that Hardy and the world subsequently witnessed at the beginning of the twentieth century created fresh wounds of a more urgent kind. New soldiers, like those Romans of old, would occupy, in the poet Rupert Brooke's celebrated phrase, "some corner of a foreign field." The image of the French farmer dislodging remains and unexploded ordnance from those fields became commonplace after the war, and to this day France's Département du Déminage is kept busy defusing relics of what has come to be called the "iron harvest."

In the next war, the same motif crops up in the journalism of A. J. Liebling. In *The Road Back to Paris*, Liebling, staying with American troops at a remote airstrip in North Africa, sees fit to note,

> That field had been fought over many times before in the course of history and a corner of it had been the site of a Numidian city. Bent, a pilot who talked with a British accent and had once done some digging among old ruins in England, said that every time he flew over that corner he could plainly see the gridiron pattern of the ancient streets on the ground. Horse, the bearded pilot, was irreverent about Bent's archaeological claims. "Maybe a couple of thousand years from now," he said, "people will dig around this same field and find a lot of C-ration cans that we've left and attribute them to archaeology. They'll say, 'Those Americans must surely have been a pygmy race to wear such small helmets. It scarcely seems possible they had much brains. No wonder they rode around in such funny airplanes as the P-40.'"

In the years since World War II, in the corners of Korea, Vietnam, Iraq, Afghanistan, we have sown new fields that might disclose their contents to the curious thousands of years from now. Even West Point has an iron harvest: unexploded ordnance occasionally disturbed by construction or, as was the case in the summer of 1999, by forest fires. In 2010, with excavation under way for a new building, the post newspaper warned that unexploded ordnance (UXO)—leftover munitions unceremoniously dumped or mortars (commonly World War I–era Stokes mortars) fired in practice years ago—might be found anywhere at West Point. The article gave detailed instructions for recognizing and reporting the discovery of UXOs. It didn't provide any guidance for those less literal discoveries one might make while blundering through no man's land.

It was about six months after Dan's death that I felt the full force of an iron harvest and learned the ache of being compelled to go over the same ground again. Starting out one morning in July 2010 for West Point, I stowed in the trunk a package I intended to mail. It was addressed to Lieutenant Christopher Goeke, at FOB Nawbahar, a.k.a. FOB Nowhere, Afghanistan. That afternoon I was at my desk thinking it was about time to head out to the post office when an officer called from Fort Bragg to give me the news that Chris had been killed in action two days before. I hung up and gazed out the window at the Hudson, in the very place where Chris and I had spent so many hours talking about books and ideas, the army, his future.

Whenever I encounter coincidence in one of the novels I read with my students, it gives me a jolt of pleasure, but this coincidence was all too real. In its literary manifestations—in Sophocles, for instance, or in the novels of Hardy or Dickens—coincidence tends to acquire a larger significance, carrying melodramatic and intensely satisfying overtones of fate, (mis)fortune, benevolent or malevolent design. I had recently finished reading *The Mayor of Casterbridge* with my students, and we had discussed the propensity of Hardy's superstitious protagonist Michael Henchard for interpreting a random "concatenation of events" as "the scheme of some sinister intelligence bent on punishing him," even though events had "developed naturally."

Statisticians account for seemingly chance occurrences with theories of probability, while cognitive scientists and psychologists variously explain the emotional repercussions of *apophenia*, or the mind's capacity to attribute patterns of significance to random events. Nevertheless, real-life coincidences are often interpreted as some kind of paranormal phenomenon. How irresistible it is to find false significance in chance occurrences. Jung proposed the theory of "synchronicity," or meaningful coincidence, in which an underlying principle somehow unites discrete events.

Devotees of Plutarch, and I am one, will find a tantalizing explanation for the psychological appeal of coincidence in his description of historical parallels:

> It is no greater wonder if in long process of time, while fortune takes her course hither and thither, numerous coincidences should spontaneously occur. If the number and variety of subjects to be wrought upon be infinite, it is all the more easy for fortune, with such an abundance of material, to effect this similarity of results. Or if, on the other hand, events are limited to the combinations of some finite number, then of necessity the same must often recur, and in the same sequence. There are people who take a pleasure in making collections of all such fortuitous occurrences that they have heard or read of, as look like works of a rational power and design; they observe, for example, that two eminent persons whose names were Attis, the one a Syrian, the other of Arcadia, were both slain by a wild boar; that of two whose names were Actaeon, the one was torn in pieces by his dogs, the other by his lovers; that of two famous Scipios, the one overthrew the Carthaginians in war, the other totally ruined and destroyed them; the city of Troy was the first time taken by Hercules for the horses promised him by Laomedon, the second time by Agamemnon, by means of the celebrated great wooden horse, and the third time by Charidemus, by occasion of a horse falling down at the gate, which hindered the Trojans, so that they could not shut them soon enough; and of two cities which take their names from the most agreeable odoriferous plants, Ios and

Smyrna, the one from a violet, the other from myrrh, the poet Homer is reported to have been born in the one and to have died in the other. And so to these instances let us further add, that the most warlike commanders, and most remarkable for exploits of skilful stratagem, have had but one eye: as Philip, Antigonus, Hannibal, and Sertorius, whose life and actions we describe at present; of whom, indeed, we might truly say, that he was more continent than Philip, more faithful to his friends than Antigonus, and more merciful to his enemies than Hannibal; and that for prudence and judgment he gave place to none of them, but in fortune was inferior to them all.

The spontaneous coincidences that Plutarch catalogs in this passage are essentially meaningless: two deaths of people with the same name by the attack of a wild boar, two dismemberments, three falls of Troy, four one-eyed commanders. One gets the feeling he could go on, but he turns instead to a consideration of the way in which historical narrative is constructed. If there is an "infinite" amount of raw material, fortune has a field day. If the material is "finite," however, so, too, is the number of possible combinations. Frequent repetition is inevitable. Collectors of such phenomena—epic poets, historians, biographers, anyone trying to accord meaning to life's accidents—misconstrue coincidental resemblances as "works of a rational power and design." Plutarch concludes instead that such patterns are inscrutable.

I knew only that my coincidence was unbearable; its meaning eluded me. The day the phone rang was the very day on which I had planned to mail Chris a package; that concatenation was sufficient to confuse me. Additionally, how was I to process the fact that Chris was the lieutenant to whom Dan had given so much of his care and attention? Grief, it would appear, is a condition always gathering into itself new depths and complexities, burrowing ever further into a network of correspondences and coincidences out of which we try to tell some story.

Of course Chris was the very person who might have helped me sort all of this out. He had a sense of equilibrium and self-awareness seldom found in twenty-three-year-olds. He was keenly interested in Jung, whom he was reading in Afghanistan, together with an eclectic library of writers, including Pirsig, whose *Zen and the Art of Motorcycle Maintenance* he was getting ready to read for a third time. "I suddenly had the thought," he wrote to me from his base, "that Zen has a lot to do with important mythologies/schemas that keep us from going crazy as we process the chaos of the world's events." Chris was finding more than his share of chaos to process. Events in his district started to go "a little haywire" in February 2010: there were kidnappings and beatings; Afghans who worked with the Americans suffered intimidation by the Taliban. Then, with the coming of the fighting season, things started to get "busier." "There are more bad guys around now," Chris reported, "more IEDs." In late May he announced, "I think these last few months are going to be the toughest ones yet." He was right.

Intensely spiritual in a catholic way, Chris wrote a senior thesis with me on literature's role in cultivating our emotional intelligence. Shortly before he deployed to Afghanistan, he told me, "I'm gaining a clearer understanding of my passions." It seemed to me that Chris was constantly finding new ways to harmonize reason, faith, and emotion, but he wasn't looking for a formulaic solution. He had ambitions to attend graduate school in counseling one day. In the meantime, in the middle of what was often a fierce fight, he pursued an ambitious course of study on his own. He reread *The Autobiography of Benjamin Franklin*, relishing Franklin's sly observation "So convenient a thing it is to be a *reasonable creature*, since it enables one to find or make a reason for everything one has a mind to do." He made his way through the Koran, sped through Faulkner's *As I Lay Dying*, and worked to improve his Farsi. He was also working hard at a new marriage from long distance, and he had found in Kelsey, it seemed to me, exactly the right sort of mate, confidante, and friend—someone, I sensed, with whom he could have continued to grow up.

So many of these details—the whole tone and texture of our correspondence—came back to me as I sat in my office trying to figure out what I ought to do. Knowing no other protocol, I drove the box back home, where I hid it away in a closet, tucked behind some winter coats, until I no longer remembered what was inside. For four months the box stayed there. When Pandora opened the jar, the Greek poet Hesiod tells us, she loosed trouble and sickness into a world that knew only peace, ease, and contentment. All the evils are out now; they have been for a long time. Open it, I kept telling myself, and then one day I did. It was even harder than I imagined. I needed a letter opener, scissors, and a Swiss Army knife to cut through the layers of tape I had bound it with for the journey: tossed into airplane cargo holds, bounced around on trucks, perhaps deposited at its destination by helicopter. It couldn't have been this hard for a recipient on the other end: curiosity, the anticipation of receiving anything whole and undamaged amid a landscape of destruction, must easily tear through all that tape. Inside I found the note I had written to Chris, on the obverse of a postcard featuring Charlie Chaplin's gentle Little Tramp in *City Lights*. It was a message for the living, not the dead, full of mundanity, incidental observations and updates, cheering wishes. It was a trifling installment in an ongoing conversation, the promise of which remains undelivered.

Emptying the box, I placed the postcard together with all the messages Chris and I sent back and forth across that incalculable distance. Then I flattened the cardboard and carried it down the hall to the recycling room. I have a song on my iPod that Chris wrote and recorded for a seminar on travel literature. It's called "Far from Home." In Afghanistan, he must have felt the truth of his song as never before. He sings about a callow traveler who exhausts himself trying to collect enough information about the various countries he visits to impress his friends and family back home. "What do I think?" the traveler asks, "That when I come back / They won't look at me the same? / That they will stare in awe and mystery? / That I will drink of the wisdom / Of the countries I can name / As if no one has ever traveled / There but me?"

In providing the background to the song, Chris revealed that he had tried on a trip to Germany "to hold on to everything that might impress my non-traveled friends . . . : my vanity distracted me." As Chris recognized with characteristic self-awareness, this trip did its "eye-opening" work by sharpening in him the desire for a different kind of journey, one where continued honest reflection on sensory experience might refine his ability to process, as he would later put it, "the chaos of the world's events." Chris had to process that chaos as far from home as it is possible to be. Every day, he had to open the box and look inside.

It's hard to know how to end a story about the inadequacies of stories. It's hard to salvage something from a landscape defined by emptiness, dislocation, and devastation. It's all well and good to make symbols out of no man's land, but the truth of that place is as stark, barren, and unequivocal now as it was in 1918. "I think I have never seen (or imagined there could be) such appalling desolation," J. F. Bloxham, the chaplain of the 16th Sherwood Foresters, wrote of the appearance of a ridge during the Third Battle of Ypres: "Not a single sign of vegetation, not a blade of grass. Nothing but shell holes and dry clay and pools of water and broken wreckage of all kinds, and wire and everything hideous that can be imagined." Because I've proposed that my problem also has social, cultural, and political significance, no doubt many readers will expect me to provide a solution. Because I declared that the narrative arc from peace to war that once sustained me has imploded, they will want me to offer another in its place.

Back home in Seattle after his transcontinental journey, Kevin tells me that good rides are like good stories:

Some roads seem to have their own narrative arc, if you will. The better rides start out one way and slowly change into something else, sort of taking you through a tension and release along the ride. Any mountain road is an easy example. The Yosemite ride . . . the switchbacks leading up to the Sierras helped add tension right along with the altitude climb. The release was when it leveled out, the views closed in, and then I was at the gates of the park. Which brings me to the other obvious component of a good ride: . . . the destination . . . There should be some important place you want to go, somewhere legendary that you've never been. In my opinion, the best rides can't be loops that bring you back to where you started. Even my huge motorcycle trip was much less of an adventure after New York, when I stopped getting farther from Seattle and started going back toward it. I guess it's a sense of prospect that was missing.

To teach is to be always in the middle of the next story—always to have a new prospect in view. This realization strikes me anew each autumn, as the days lose more light and my students accelerate into the end of semester scramble. Then, suddenly, it's finished. But as the old year breathes out all around me in a welter of regret, missed opportunities, and diminished returns, I already have my eye on the next class, the next group of students, the chance to do it all again—and maybe better. The most persuasive solution a teacher can offer are the students she casts into no man's land: officers capable of reflecting on where they've come from and imagining where they might be going; leaders capable of telling stories but also of recognizing when those stories have lost their power and become obsolete; men and women willing not only to rewrite their own narratives but to contribute to the reinvention of a national narrative that will bear the weight of future meaning.

RECOMMENDED BOOKS AND FILMS

Ensnared as he was in the no man's land of the western front, Lieutenant Edmund Blunden found a powerful, perhaps unlikely ally in Edward Young, a long-dead poet whose voice called to him with "a profound eighteenth-century calm" beneath the roar of a twentieth-century chaos. "At every spare moment I read in Young's *Night Thoughts on Life, Death and Immortality*," Blunden reports in *Undertones of War*, "and I felt the benefit of this grave and intellectual voice, speaking . . . often in metaphor which came home to one even in a pillbox. The mere amusement of discovering lines applicable to our crisis kept me from despair." Metaphor—whether savored in pillbox, foxhole, mud cave, or cockpit—has long kept soldiers from despair by helping them to forge and sustain the enduring human connections that war works to destroy.

It has helped me, too, as a wartime reader attempting to navigate the no man's land in which we find ourselves searching for those "undertones" that might disclose what the noise of war obscures. I discover those tones in the work of several of Blunden's contemporaries: Edith Wharton's *Fighting France*, the poems of Isaac Rosenberg (reissued recently in the 21st-Century Oxford Authors series), Henri Barbusse's *Under Fire*, Ernst Jünger's *Storm of Steel*, and several volumes of first-person accounts drawn from the archives of the Imperial War Museums and edited by Malcolm Brown: *1914: The Men Who Went to War*, *The Western Front*, *The Somme*, and *1918: Year of Victory*.

Invaluable poetic voices from other wars have been anthologized in *The Columbia Book of Civil War Poetry*, edited by Richard Marius and Keith Frome; the Library of America's *Poets of World*

War II, edited by Harvey Shapiro; and John Hollander's little gem of an anthology, *War Poems* (Everyman's Library Pocket Poets).

I have gravitated in recent years to books that have something to say about the moment when the old stories we've woven with such care give way before new realities. Stranded as I so often felt in no man's land, I could not have done without the Library of America edition of A. J. Liebling's *World War II Writings*, Joseph Heller's *Catch-22*, Joan Didion's *The White Album*, Michel de Montaigne's *Essays*, Tobias Wolff's Vietnam memoir *In Pharaoh's Army*, Annie Dillard's essay "Living Like Weasels," Georges Simenon's Maigret mysteries, Joseph Roth's novel *The Radetzky March*, Leo Tolstoy's *War and Peace*, Ulysses S. Grant's *Personal Memoirs*, Antoine de Saint-Exupéry's *Wind, Sand and Stars*, Plutarch's *Lives*, Herodotus's *Histories*, the ancient epics—Homer's *Iliad* and *Odyssey*, Virgil's *Aeneid*—Ovid's *Metamorphoses*, the odes of Horace, the plays of Shakespeare, Jonathan Spence's *Treason by the Book*, Sun Tzu's *The Art of War*, and David Hinton's marvelous translations of Chinese sages and poets (especially the anthology *Classical Chinese Poetry*).

Among the many recent and older books written about either Afghanistan and the Middle East or the consequences of our recent wars in those regions, the following offer especially enriching perspectives: the *Baburnama* (the autobiography of the emperor Babur); Robert Byron's *The Road to Oxiana*; Freya Stark's *The Valleys of the Assassins* and *The Southern Gates of Arabia*; Wilfred Thesiger's *Among the Mountains*, *Arabian Sands*, and *The Marsh Arabs*; David Finkel's *The Good Soldiers*; George Packer's *The Assassins' Gate*; Rory Stewart's *The Places in Between* and *The Prince of the Marshes*; Anthony Shadid's *Night Draws Near*; Dexter Filkins's *The Forever War*; Brian Castner's *The Long Walk*; Ben Fountain's *Billy Lynn's Long Halftime Walk*; and Kevin Powers's *The Yellow Birds*.

The spectacular war epic has been a staple of cinema since the silent era, but there is another tradition of films about war—some made in Hollywood, others abroad—that offers a more nuanced and deeply ambivalent account of the psychological and cultural dimensions of no man's land. Perhaps the most celebrated of the Hollywood films about the postwar trials of the returning veteran is William Wyler's *The Best Years of Our Lives*, but the strain runs deeply and broadly, ranging from dramas of the interwar period to noirs of the late 1940s. An especially rich treatment can be found in the Westerns that the director Anthony Mann made with James Stewart—the actor had recently returned from service as a bomber pilot in World War II—playing a series of Civil War veterans trying to survive postwar dislocation on the frontier (*Winchester '73*, *Bend of the River*, *The Man from Laramie*, *The Naked Spur*). The undertones of war can also be heard in a very different tradition in the French director Jean-Pierre Melville's cinematic meditations on World War II, *Le Silence de la Mer* (1949) and *Army of Shadows* (1969). Two films made by Melville's countryman Bertrand Tavernier, *Life and Nothing But* (1989) and *Captain Conan* (1996), provide visions of World War I and its aftermath as subtle as they are uncompromising.